Housing the People
in Victorian Bristol

Redcliffe Press/The Regional History Centre,
University of the West of England, Bristol

Housing the People
in Victorian Bristol

Redcliffe Press/The Regional History Centre,
University of the West of England, Bristol

Peter Malpass

First published in 2021 by Redcliffe Press Ltd.,
81g Pembroke Road, Bristol BS8 3EA
e: info@redcliffepress.co.uk
www.redcliffepress.co.uk

Text © Peter Malpass

ISBN 978-1-911408-79-6

 RedcliffePress

 Follow us on Twitter @RedcliffePress

British Library Cataloguing-in-Publication Data
A catalogue record for this book is available from the British Library

All rights reserved. Except for the purpose of review, no part of this book may be reproduced, stored in a retrieval system, or transmitted, in any form or by any means, electronic, mechanical, photocopying, recording or otherwise, without the prior permission of the publishers.

Design and typesetting by Stephen Morris www.stephen-morris.co.uk
Garamond 12/12
Printed and bound by Short Run Press Limited, Exeter

Cover: Jacob's Wells Buildings, built by Bristol Industrial Dwellings Company in 1875.
    (Courtesy: M Hooper)

Contents

Acknowledgements 6

Chapter One   Victorian Bristol: between the railway and the motorcar 7

Chapter Two   Understanding the Housing Problem 17

Chapter Three   The Growth of the Town 29

Chapter Four   Housing Production: the Key Actors 58

Chapter Five   The Housebuilding Process 75

Chapter Six   The Houses and their Settings 88

Chapter Seven   House and Home: the consumer experience 123

Chapter Eight   The Politics of Housing 145

Chapter Nine   Conclusion 167

Notes 181

Index 194

Acknowledgements

This book derives from a decades-long interest in housing and several years of active research on the history of Victorian Bristol but it was actually written during the period of the coronavirus pandemic, a time of severely restricted access to everything but online sources. I must therefore begin by acknowledging the enormous value of one particular website, Know Your Place (maps.bristol.gov.uk), which I have used on an almost daily basis and which readers will also find useful as they go through the book. The new and improved online catalogue of the Bristol Archives, launched in 2020, is another valuable aid to local research. Most of the research for this book relied upon the knowledge, skill and assistance provided by staff at the Bristol Archives and Central Reference Library. In addition to expressing my thanks to members of staff in these invaluable institutions I would like to acknowledge the help provided by Mike Hooper, William Evans, Ruth Hecht, Moira Martin, June Hannam, Kath Thompson, John Stevens, Bob Lawrence, Adrian Nardone, David Cheesley and Geof Tarring. Thanks also to Simon Holder who not only readily agreed to read an earlier draft but made insightful comments in quick time.

I thank Bristol Museums, Galleries and Archives, the Ordinance Survey, the University of Bath, Mike Hooper and David Cheesley for permission to reproduce materials for which they hold the copyright. In addition, thanks to Geoffrey Tarring who agreed to the reproduction of photographs from the collection of his late father, Herbert Frank Tarring. In the case of other materials, every effort has been made to trace the copyright holders; apologies are offered for any omission and the publisher will be pleased to add any necessary acknowledgement in subsequent editions.

I am also grateful to Professor Steve Poole and Clara Hudson for agreeing to include the book in the Redcliffe Press/Regional History Centre series, thereby helping to make the research available to the widest possible local and regional audience.

As ever, I thank my wife Mina for her continuing support for my work and her forbearance in the face of so many conversational gambits that begin with some new discovery or thought about Bristol in the nineteenth century.

Peter Malpass, July 2021

CHAPTER ONE

Victorian Bristol:
between the railway and the motorcar

Queen Victoria reigned from 1837 to 1901, dates which in themselves have no urban historical significance, although they do conveniently cover the period between the arrival of the railways and the coming of the motorcar, two events that certainly were of great importance for the development of Bristol and all British cities.[1] This was the 'age of great cities',[2] the result of sustained population growth and migration from rural areas. By the middle of the century towns and cities accounted for more than half of the people in England and Wales; by the end of the century the proportion was closer to eighty per cent. No other country approached this level of urbanisation until after 1900. The Victorian period, then, was a time when Bristol, and other established centres of population, experienced unprecedented and transformational change. The population of Bristol doubled in the first forty years of the century, and then more than doubled again. Providing houses for all these extra people proved to be one of the most intractable problems of the period. The response to the problem had consequences, in terms of who lived where, in what kinds of houses and at what cost, not only for the people of that time but also for those who came later. Houses accounted for most of the growth of the built up area, creating many new neighbourhoods (including the appropriately named Newtown to the east of Old Market) and enveloping established but previously separate settlements (notably Clifton and Bedminster). Although a great many of the oldest, smallest and least suitable Victorian houses have disappeared, in the twenty-first century, for better or worse, we still live with a substantial legacy of houses and neighbourhoods built at that time. In that sense, then, Victorian Bristol is very much a part of our everyday experience of the city.

This book aims to explore and explain how the people were housed in Victorian Bristol, but first this opening chapter looks at the wider context of the development of the city at that time. In the previous century, before the industrial revolution really got going, Bristol had prospered from trade through the port, which, for a time at least, was considered the second most important port in England after London. Bristol had been the 'metropolis of the west'[3] and its merchants had grown rich on the profits of slavery and sugar. Whereas earlier generations of historians tended to see this as a 'golden age' it is now recognised as a shameful stain on the city's history, still etched into the physical and social fabric of the city. In a memorable, if anonymous, observation, 'There is not a brick in the city but what is cemented with the blood of a slave'.[4]

By the 1830s Bristol merchants no-longer trafficked people across the Atlantic, but a number of honoured citizens continued to own enslaved people on their Caribbean estates and benefited handsomely from the government's compensation fund when slavery was abolished in the British empire. At least some of the compensation money was ploughed into the development of projects such as the Great Western Railway.[5]

The 1830s was a difficult and troubled decade for Bristol: three days of riots in 1831 caused extensive damage and left a large debt to be paid off; in 1835 the port was said to be 'far below her former station'[6] and the local economy as a whole was in relative decline, along with its regional hinterland. Despite these negative factors the population was rising worryingly fast, placing a strain on existing urban infrastructure. At the same time a number of projects were begun that reflected a degree of optimism about the future, or perhaps it was desperation. So worried were Bristol's leading merchants that in 1828 the Chamber of Commerce had commissioned a report on a strategy for revival.[7] Out of this came what would today be called a branding exercise: in addition to the Great Western Railway there was the new Great Western Cotton Works at Barton Hill on the eastern edge of the city and the Great Western Steamship Company. A young and talented engineer, Isambard Kingdom Brunel, who was already employed on the construction of the Clifton Suspension Bridge and to advise the Dock Company on problems with the floating harbour, was appointed to take charge of building the Bristol to London railway. He also built the innovative steamship, the *Great Western* in 1838, and then the even more original *Great Britain*, launched in 1843. His biographer, Angus Buchanan, noted that Brunel's arrival in Bristol did seem to be associated with 'a spirited commercial revival'.[8]

Also in the 1830s the ancient, self-selecting and corrupt Corporation was replaced by a more democratic town council, although at the first elections, at the end of 1835, 20 of the men elected had been members of the old Corporation, and the council continued to have a Tory majority throughout the remainder of the century. The new body consisted of 48 members representing 10 wards covering an area of nearly eight square miles, five times larger than the old city as defined by the charter of 1373. Extension of the administrative boundaries of the city and county embraced for the first time the parishes of Clifton, St James, St Paul and St Philip and St Jacob, together with the Redland part of Westbury-on-Trym and part of Bedminster. In all of these areas there was at that time plenty of undeveloped land into which the built up area could expand, as it did, and there was no further extension of boundaries until 1897.

Uneven Development

Accurate population figures are not readily calculable for the whole of the built up area because of the way the data were collected, but one widely quoted source suggests that the population was 61,153 in 1801 when the first national census was taken, and that by 1841 it was 125,146.[9] Over the next sixty years the population reached 328,945 by 1901. In the early Victorian period, between 1841 and 1861, population growth was relatively slow, but much faster thereafter and Bristol was still the seventh largest city in England in 1901, behind London, Manchester, Liverpool, Birmingham, Leeds and Sheffield.

The population figures are one sign of the unevenness of Bristol's development in this period, highlighting the sluggishness of the twenty years up to 1860. It is a remarkable feature of Victorian Bristol that nothing much happened until after 1860, when the pace of change noticeably quickened. Although the arrival of the railways in the 1840s improved communications with the rest of the country, and the municipal takeover of the Dock Company in 1848 implied the possibility of better management of the port, in fact the local economy remained less than dynamic. If Brunel's presence and enthusiasm was at least partly responsible for the optimism of the 1830s, it was not long before he became disillusioned with the prospects for Bristol. He remained the Dock Company's consultant engineer but relations were strained by the company's half-hearted response to his proposals for dealing with the silting up of the floating harbour and by the difficulties encountered in getting the huge bulk of the *Great Britain* out of the harbour. In 1844 Brunel seemed to write off the possibility of Bristol becoming a major port for ocean going steamships.[10] He was certainly correct in one respect: his vision of Bristol as a major passenger port linking Britain to the United States never came to fruition.[11]

Once the basic rail routes were in place by 1845 little was done to develop the system until the line from Temple Meads was extended to link up with the docks in 1867. In 1861 the first of a number of proposals for a central station appeared, but none actually resulted in such a station, and instead an enlarged and remodelled Temple Meads station was finally opened in 1878. The docks were similarly starved of investment for years after the municipal takeover, and it was left to private investors to build the outer docks at Avonmouth and Portishead in the 1870s. The entrance locks at Cumberland Basin were much improved in the early 1870s and over the next few years new quays were built within the floating harbour to increase capacity and to make facilities better for the growing numbers of iron steamships. Eventually, by the late 1880s, the centre of gravity within the harbour had moved sufficiently downstream for the authorities to bow to demands for a fixed bridge over St Augustine's reach, the upper part of which was then covered over. The fixed crossing should be seen as the last link in an improved road route between Temple Meads and Clifton. Earlier parts of this project included the construction of a new road, Victoria Street, south of Bristol Bridge, and the straightening of Baldwin Street (which hitherto had curved along the line of what is now St Stephen's Street). The idea of Victoria Street had emerged in 1841, only six months after trains started running from Temple Meads to London, but work did not start until 1865. The town council carried out several other important street improvement projects, but their work was concentrated in the years 1865 to 1881, when the newly straightened Baldwin Street was opened. There was a lot of other work of a much more minor nature, but the major projects were almost all concerned with routes between Clifton and the centre and Temple Meads station.[12]

Industrial Restructuring

One of the weaknesses of the port of Bristol in the first half of the nineteenth century was its historic over reliance on sugar from the West Indies and the old protectionist system that sustained the Atlantic trade. It was a long time before the city's merchants and industrialists came to terms with the collapse of that system and the rise of competitive capitalism.[13] In the second half of the century timber and grain grew to be staple import commodities, both producing distinctive impacts on the landscape around the docks. However, despite the growth of the tobacco industry in the city it was not until after 1900 that tobacco was imported directly into Bristol. Away from the quaysides the economy was always more diverse; although the long established woollen industry declined, the cotton industry never really took off in the city and iron founding was hard hit by the recession of the early 1840s. Heavy engineering, including shipbuilding, also declined, as did sugar refining and glass bottle making. The overall balance in the local economy shifted towards consumer goods.[14] 'Although not in the forefront of industrial pioneers, Bristol managed to catch the 'second wave' and build up a considerable number of port-related industries, mainly in the food, drink, tobacco, boot, shoes, printing and packaging sectors. Thus from the 1860 the town caught up with the industrial age by concentrating on the production and marketing of modern consumer goods.'[15]

By the end of the century the clothing industry, including footwear, provided around 15,000 jobs.[16] Derham Brothers employed 1500 people making boots in their large multi-storey factory in Barton Street, St James's, built in 1866. Nearby the long established Fry's cocoa works was transformed in 1878 by a new building extending from the bottom of Pithay to Nelson Street. The company grew from 193 employees in 1867 to around 5,000 by 1914.[17] A small number of businesses, in particular those that were most adept at exploiting new production machinery, experienced very considerable growth in this period. The paper and packaging firm ES and A Robinson was one but the star performer in terms of growth in the latter part of the century was WD and HO Wills, the tobacco manufacturer based in Redcliff Street. In the 1860s Wills was just one tobacco firm among many in the city, albeit already the largest. In 1880 it had 600 employees but by 1900 it had expanded to 3,000 workers, with one enormous factory on East Street in Bedminster, plus a further 14 acres at Ashton Gate about to be developed.[18] Although Robinsons and Wills were well known and profitable firms, leaders in their respective fields, their industries were not the largest employers of labour in Bristol. In the context of a book about housing it is appropriate to point out that in 1901 the largest employment category for men and boys was housebuilding, with nearly 11,000 jobs, and the largest category for women and girls was domestic service, with nearly 12,000.[19]

Professor Alford summed up Bristol's economic development like this:

> after a period of uneven but somewhat sluggish growth over the early nineteenth century, in the 1840s the local economy moved into a period of stagnation which lasted until the 1860s, and which might even have included a shorter period of absolute decline; in the 1860s, however, there was a sharp recovery which lasted through to the 1880s, and even though the tempo slackened from then until the end of the century the trend remained upwards, so that over the whole period from the 1860s to the turn of the century Bristol compared very favourably with the economy as a whole.[20]

Who ran Victorian Bristol?

The Municipal Corporations Act, 1835, abolished the old unelected Corporation and replaced it with an elected town council. It would be wrong, however, to think of the Act as creating a modern, democratic local government system, but it did begin to lay the necessary preconditions for the emergence of such a system. It would also be a mistake to depict the council as running the city, not least because it was dominated throughout the Victorian period by people whose inclination was not to accept responsibilities that could be denied, postponed or minimised.

> Bristol was never in the forefront of cities adopting the great legislative and administrative changes of the second half of the nineteenth century which were to transform the duties of local government.[21]

Despite this entrenched stance, by the end of the century the town council had acquired an impressive list of responsibilities, including the docks, a range of public health functions, street improvement, public parks, libraries and museums, swimming pools, electricity supply and, somewhat indirectly, elementary education. Alongside the council the Bristol Corporation of the Poor continued to administer the Poor Law within its original 1696 boundaries, while the surrounding suburbs were the responsibility of the Bedminster Union and the Barton Regis Union. Eventually, in 1897, one Poor Law authority for Bristol was established.

Rather than looking at institutions it is more fruitful to consider the individuals who had the power to get things done. The term 'community capitalism' was coined in the 1980s to refer to the idea that there existed in late Victorian Bristol a close knit group of businessmen who formed an economic elite with powerful social and political connections.[22] They constituted a community of capitalists, but the idea can be extended to highlight the extent to which businesses in that period were, in most cases, small and locally based, thus emphasising the links between the capitalists and the localities in which they operated. Thus, the answer to the question, who ran Victorian Bristol? is that it was largely an oligarchy of leading citizens, all men, who lived, worked and worshipped locally. Two thirds of councillors serving in the period 1835-51 were classed as merchants, manufacturers or professionals,[23] and until 1887 all councillors were members of the middle class.[24] Throughout the period as a whole 15 families of merchants and industrialists provided 56 councillors.[25] Both WD and HO Wills served together on the council between 1846 and 1860, there were six members of the Hare family of floorcloth manufacturers and three from the Fry family. Some other notable figures included Elisha Robinson, founder of the successful paper and packaging firm ES and A Robinson, William Proctor Baker, grain merchant and influential chair of the Docks Committee, William Killigrew Wait, grain merchant who served for nearly twenty years on the council and also became MP for Gloucester, and George White, stockbroker and transport systems entrepreneur, who gained control of Bristol's tramways.

All of these men lived in or very close to Bristol, made business decisions that affected how the local economy worked and also sat on the council deciding how to allocate ratepayers' money. They were not, of course, all of one mind and the argument has been made by, for example, Helen Meller and Spencer Jordan, that as the century wore on the hitherto Tory Anglican hegemony was challenged by an emergent group of non-conformist Liberal councillors, including the Wills, Frys and Robinsons, who injected a different, more socially concerned, element into debates in the council chamber.[26] However, given the perpetual Tory majority, these Liberals were never in control of the council, and Meller conceded that, 'On the whole, Bristol's town council was parsimonious and extremely conservative in its view of its role.'[27] An interesting aside here is that housebuilders seem to have been on the margins of the ruling oligarchy, for only three found their way onto the town council, all representing the Liberal cause.[28]

Two further points to make under this heading concern the relationship between localities like Bristol and the outside world. First, what happened in Bristol was shaped by a wider set of economic, political and cultural influences. Even though the industrialisation of the economy was led by the dynamic manufacturing towns of the north, Bristol nevertheless benefited. As the economy grew so did the opportunities for Bristol businesses to sell their goods and services; and as trade with the empire expanded it created more traffic passing through the port – grain from Canada would be a good example. In this sense the growth of the city was being buoyed up by the rising prosperity of the country as a whole. In terms of government policy, it is pretty clear that, to take two examples, Bristol would not have adopted public health powers when it did without pressure from the centre, and the same was true in relation to elementary education in the 1870s. Culturally, Bristolians were of course aware of widely circulating ideas about what sorts of institutions and grand buildings were expected in a great city. Having said that, they managed to resist the temptation to build the sort of imposing town hall found in cities like Manchester, Leeds and Bradford. Nevertheless,

Meller refers to the idea that Bristol experienced a civic renaissance in the period – one product of which was the establishment in 1876 of University College, created with financial backing from the Fry and Wills families, among other local enthusiasts.

Second, the ruling oligarchy retained not only considerable freedom to determine what happened within the city, but also they were responsible for making things happen. When the merchants of Bristol decided that they needed a railway line linking them to London in the 1830s they had to take the initiative. This was an era when townspeople were left very much to their own devices and the development of the urban fabric, broadly defined, was in their own hands. As subsequent chapters reveal, the way the housing of the people was sorted out was almost entirely the result of individual landowners, builders and property professionals on the one side and the pattern of consumer demand on the other. In the absence of any sort of plan, the only co-ordination of the process was provided by market forces. Collective action was almost entirely absent.

The Approach and Structure of the Book

This book is about housing in Victorian Bristol, which gives it a clear focus on a specific period and a particular geographical area. Within that frame of reference, it aims to be comprehensive, without, of course, trying to describe in detail the development of every neighbourhood and every street, let alone every house. Comprehensiveness here means thinking about the housing of all the people, rich and poor. On the issue of housing production, questions arise about who owned the land, who built the houses and how it was decided what to build, when and where. On the consumption side the questions are about who got what, when and where. A key issue here is the question of how well the people were housed. Tackling these various questions involves study of aspects of the housing market. A different set of questions arises in relation to the role of non-market based housing activities: what did the local authorities and charities do to address evidence of failure of the market to provide decent and affordable housing for the least well off?

How can these sorts of questions be answered? The nineteenth century has now receded into the historical past, well beyond the recall of any living person, and only a diminishing number can remember conversations with people who could speak with first hand experience of those days. Although Bristol is rich in historiography, little has been written specifically on housing in the Victorian period. The book by Lobell and Carus-Wilson provides a good introduction to the earlier urban development of the city, and Roger Leech's book on town houses is essential reading in relation to the medieval and early modern periods but stops short of the Victorian era.[30] Several works on architectural history make reference to the houses of the wealthy and the people who designed them,[31] but the housing of the working class has been largely neglected.[32] A number of authors have touched on housing in the context of studies of particular neighbourhoods,[33] but the Victorian housing market as such has not been systematically investigated.

In addition to the works just cited it turns out that there is a wealth of material on Victorian housing, and much of what is written in subsequent chapters derives from extensive research in the archives, building on a broader study published in 2019.[34] The main sources of information are the records held at the Bristol Archives and Central Reference Library, augmented by the invaluable website Know Your Place (maps.bristol.gov.uk), and many hours spent walking around the remaining Victorian neighbourhoods. These places are familiar to the tens of thousands of people in Bristol who today live in houses built in the nineteenth century, but it is important to remember two things: no-one now lives in a Victorian house in its original form (no central heating, no electricity, no broadband, primitive plumbing), and the houses that remain are not a representative sample of what was built.

The attempt to develop a comprehensive account of housing in Bristol in the Victorian period implies a certain shape and structure: chapter two considers different ways of thinking about the notion of the 'housing problem' in the nineteenth century, and chapter three looks at how the various neighbourhoods developed around the ancient centre. Chapter four looks at the key actors, the landowners, builders and professionals, involved in converting green fields into streets and houses, while chapter five turns to the process of housebuilding. Chapter six examines the different kinds of houses built in different parts of the city, for different sorts of people: essentially, terraces for the workers and semi-detached villas for the middle class. Chapter seven focuses on aspects of consumption, considering questions of tenure and security, what people paid for their houses and what they got for their money. An important theme in this chapter concerns the distinction between house and home. Chapter eight deals with the politics of housing in the city, highlighting the slow and reluctant response of the town council to the revelations of squalor and deprivation, and the similarly small scale response of well meaning individuals acting together on a charitable basis. The final chapter reflects on the changes and continuities across the Victorian period and considers the legacy bequeathed to the twentieth century in terms of the continuing utility of much of the housing stock but also the burden of crumbling old houses that had to be replaced. It also looks at the influence of the Victorian city on thinking about urban planning.

CHAPTER TWO

Understanding the Housing Problem

> One house has four families; the housekeeper has four children, the eldest girl grown up; lodgers on the first floor, man and wife, and two babies in one room. Second floor, mother and grown up girl; two others, 12 and 17 years old; these have one room; all sleep in one bed. On the second floor is a widow and son of 16, in one bed also.

This account of 15 people in one house in Hotwells comes from a report written in 1843 by Dr William Kay, senior physician to the Clifton Dispensary. Evidently outraged by what he had seen Kay put his finger on the nub of the problem:

> And why, let me ask, should persons be allowed to erect human habitations, in situations and in construction, so palpably at variance with every principle of health or convenience? What right has any man to crowd human beings, poor though they may be, into space utterly incompatible with wholesome, not to say comfortable, existence?[1]

Here Dr Kay was posing a moral challenge to the inviolability of property rights. This was to be a prolonged struggle, for these rights were formidably well protected.

Throughout the 1840s and subsequent decades similar circumstances, and worse, were to be found among the rapidly growing populations of Bristol and other large towns, with the result that today it is uncontroversial to say there was a housing problem in Victorian Britain. At the time, however, recognition of a distinct housing problem was slow to emerge, and when it did it was understood in rather narrow terms, almost exclusively focused on the conditions endured by the poorest people in the most rundown areas, 'the slums'. The housing problem was, and still is, generally seen in terms of the difficulties faced by people who want somewhere to live that is conveniently located, suitable to their needs and yet affordable. This consumption side perspective naturally leads to a focus on the least well off and those who are trying to enter the market, to get started on the 'housing ladder'. It seems rather artificial to talk about a housing problem facing the well off and well housed, especially when, as now, their houses represent such a significant store of wealth. It is not that the consumption perspective is wrong, just inadequate. It needs to be complemented by an understanding of the production side, specifically the problems facing builders trying to make money by selling products that are inevitably too expensive for most people to buy out of regular income.

This book is based on the view that the housing problem needs to be understood in terms of the fundamental nature of housing as a commodity and the implications of providing it through the mechanism of the market. Markets are created by people who see an opportunity to make money for themselves by responding to other people's need for goods and services. As long as they go on making money they will be disinclined to change, except in ways designed to increase their profits. Others, however, may look at aspects of the market, in terms of the processes involved, the quality of the products or the outcomes created for consumers, and conclude that all is not as it should be, that there is a need for reform, which may be defined as changes other than those willingly undertaken by businesses themselves. It is these people, reformers, who play a crucial role in defining social problems. In other words, whether one perceives an opportunity or a problem depends on where you stand and how you look at it.

Public Health and Housing
During the middle decades of the nineteenth century housing was subsumed within a much wider debate about public health, defined more broadly than it is today, to include not just the filthy and stinking state of towns and the threat of infectious diseases, both epidemic, such as cholera, and endemic, such as typhus and tuberculosis, but also the moral condition of the working class, especially those crowding into the rapidly expanding towns and cities. The growth of urban populations in the early decades of the century overwhelmed the pre-existing physical infrastructure for supplying water and removing waste, and undermined what might be called the social infrastructure of restraints on behaviour imposed by traditional patterns of authority and deference that were believed to persist in the countryside. The term 'slum' then had both physical and social connotations, referring to concentrations of squalid housing, often labelled 'rookeries', occupied by people who were seen in popular discourse as the criminal and destructive class, the undeserving poor, the abject poor and the demoralised poor (a term that was intended to be taken literally, to refer to an alleged lack, or loss, of morals). It is telling

Samuel Loxton's drawing from the end of the century of Jones's Buildings, Hotwell Road. This appears as Jones's Court on the 1828 map, and was still occupied at the end of the century. (Courtesy: Bristol Reference Library)

East Street, St Paul's, a turning off Newfoundland Street built before 1828 and now beneath Cabot Circus carpark. (Courtesy: M Hooper)

that there were so many ways of referring to this group.

By the late 1830s it was becoming clear that Britain was moving towards an urban crisis, and that something would have to be done to make towns cleaner and healthier.[2] The measures adopted were heavily influenced by Edwin Chadwick, secretary to the Poor Law Commissioners, and leading campaigner for a particular version of sanitary reform. After 1841 Chadwick and other reformers shifted their focus from measures to improve houses to external sanitation and drainage.[3] One of the great Victorian administrators, Chadwick produced a *Report on the Sanitary Condition of the Labouring Population of Great Britain* (1842), a landmark in the development of public health policy. He went on to be one of the main authors of the report of the Royal Commission on the Health of Towns in 1845, and one of four commissioners of the General Board of Health when it was set up in 1848. His great achievement was to redefine the problem of public health as one to be tackled through prevention, engineering and public administration, not through curative medicine.

Strange as it may seem to twenty-first century observers, until the 1840s house drains were not supposed to connect to public sewers, and it was an offence to allow sewage to enter such a sewer. Traditionally the sewers had been reserved for land drainage, discharging into the rivers and streams from which people drew their water. Keeping these water courses clean and healthy was, therefore, a wise policy, but in practice rivers such as the Frome and the Avon in Bristol were heavily polluted, so much that in the mid-1820s the Bristol Dock Company lost a court case brought against it because of the disgusting state of the water in the floating harbour.[4] Chadwick became convinced that if the sewers and house drains were improved then water borne sewerage would allow waste to be instantly removed from houses and that this was the best way forward. Such a system obviously had two basic requirements, first that people had access to sufficient water and second that houses were connected to a comprehensive network of main sewers that would efficiently remove household waste. Unfortunately for the people of Bristol, in the mid-1840s it was noted that, '…the [water] supply is most inadequate, probably more so than any town of equal size in England'.[5] Fewer than 5,000 people out of a total population of about 130,000 had a piped water supply. The urgent need to take action to improve the public health was sufficient to overcome resistance and inertia within the city and in 1846 the privately owned Bristol Waterworks Company was formed. Reservoirs were built, water was piped from the Mendip Hills and over the next twenty five years or so most parts of the city were provided with a mains supply, which is not to say that every house was connected. Over the same period, starting in 1853, the Town Council, acting as the Local Board of Health, built miles of new sewers, although, again, existing houses were not necessarily connected.

The Public Health Act, 1848, which was the first legislative response to the campaign for reform, has often been criticised for its weakness and limited impact, largely because it conferred powers on local communities rather than imposing duties. In many places, including Bristol, the authorities were reluctant and slow to act. Chadwick's favoured sewerage system never really worked as he intended. In practice in places like Bristol the new sewers merely moved sewage more rapidly and efficiently into their local rivers, displacing the waste a little further downstream rather than processing and recycling it. Another consequence of the Chadwick system was that the country as a whole became committed to using expensively purified clean water for flushing away waste material. Nevertheless, despite, or perhaps because of, the limitations of the public health legislation and the measures taken by local authorities, they serve to highlight the abject failure of housing reformers both to talk the issue up the agenda of public debate and to secure effective policy action.

For various reasons it was in the 1880s that 'the all too real housing 'problem' began to take shape as a public issue'.[6] What this means is that although there had long been much to deplore and complain about it was only then that housing was recognised as a problem that had to be addressed. Locally a key factor was the collapse of the late 1870s housebuilding boom, which, along with a series of business failures in the city, meant that there was much distress among the labouring population. The dire housing conditions of the poor, in many cases just as bad as those revealed in Dr Kay's report forty years earlier, were described at length in a series of articles in the *Bristol Mercury* in November 1883.[7] At the same time Andrew Mearns published *The Bitter Cry of Outcast London: an inquiry into the condition of the abject poor*, which has been credited as one of the main reasons for the appointment of a Royal Commission on the Housing of the Working Classes in 1884. Overcrowding in London was reaching crisis point as the population of the central area increased faster than housing supply and there was concern about the ineffectiveness of existing legislation designed to tackle unfit properties. The Artisans' and Labourers' Dwellings Act, 1868 (usually referred to as the Torrens Act after McCullagh Torrens, the Liberal member for Finsbury, who promoted it) gave powers to local health boards to close and remove individual unfit houses. The Artisans' Dwellings Improvement Act, 1875, (the Cross Act, named after Sir Richard Cross, Liberal member for South West Lancashire and Home Secretary, 1874-80) gave powers to deal with areas of unfit housing. Both Acts were amended but still failed to make any real impact, largely due to lack of enthusiasm among councillors, whose stance was partly justified by the argument that clearance of slums without planned rehousing of the displaced population simply made matters worse.

The setting up of the Royal Commission came after two parliamentary select committees reported in the early 1880s on the poor implementation of the Acts. A sign of the seriousness attached to the subject was that the Prince of Wales was appointed to the Commission, which was chaired by Sir Charles Dilke (Liberal MP for Chelsea and president of the Local Government Board). Between March 1884 and February 1885 the Commission heard from a wide range of witnesses, including four from Bristol (whose evidence is quoted extensively in later chapters), but for current purposes the most important point concerns the Commission's implicit definition of the housing problem. Their terms of reference specified an investigation into the housing of the 'working classes', a group then constituting at least 80 per cent of the population, so that was hardly constraining, but the Commissioners themselves focused heavily on overcrowding and what they referred to as 'cognate evils', including threats to the physical and moral wellbeing of the poor. In other words, they were concerned about the poorest people living in the worst housing conditions, not the housing of the working class as a whole. They discussed the causes of bad housing, including the possibility (which they did not deny or reject) that responsibility lay with tenants themselves, especially those who drank too much, ran up rent arrears and inflicted damage to their houses: 'It is sometimes said, that if a certain class of the poor were put into decent dwellings, they would forthwith wreck them and reduce them to the condition of the most miserable'.[8] However, the Commission also recognised that a major cause of overcrowding was poverty and, crucially, the proportion of low and irregular incomes that had to be devoted to rent, but the 'wage question' was deemed to be outside the scope of the enquiry.

Overcrowding implied that either there were not enough houses in the areas where they were needed, or that, even where there were enough houses, rents were too high for families to afford a whole house. It was admitted by Bristol witnesses that the town had been 'over built' in recent years and that there were many vacant houses, but rents had not fallen sufficiently to prevent sharing. Nevertheless, the Royal Commission made no recommendations about increasing supply or regulating rents. The rights of property owners and the sanctity of the market mechanism were, apparently, taken for granted, except in relation to dwellings that were so deficient as to be unfit for human habitation. This formulation of the housing problem left the basic structures of housing provision unquestioned and unexamined. All the emphasis was on the poor at the bottom end of the housing market. The poor were, to borrow a term coined much later, flawed consumers.[9] That is, the problem did not lie in the housing market itself but instead resided among those who were not able to participate properly in that market. If they could not afford decent housing that was due to 'the wage question', the poor management of household budgets or outright deviancy. This is seen in its most explicit form in the intrusive, moralistic style of housing management associated with the prominent moral entrepreneur, Octavia Hill (see also chapter eight), and in the observation that blocks of model dwellings were intended to provide 'a controlled environment of enforced respectability'.[10] Such blocks were often sheltered from the outside world by railings and gated entrances and overseen by a resident superintendent, usually a man recruited from the armed forces.

The Royal Commission's view of the housing problem can be seen as an elite formulation, designed to give comfort to the comfortably housed: there was no need to do anything radical or expensive. In a memorandum added to the Commission's Report, Lord Salisbury, a future prime minister, went so far as to say that apart from the special difficulties in central London, he felt that overcrowding in the suburbs and provincial towns 'may probably be cured by the ordinary sequence of supply upon demand'.[11] Nothing could be more reassuring to middle-class opinion than that, and the outcome of the Royal Commission was little more than an Act to consolidate existing legislation in the hope that it would be more effectively applied.[12] In the event the agitation around housing in the 1880s was 'a turning point that failed to turn'.[13]

Rethinking the Housing Problem

The elite formulation of the housing problem prevailed beyond the end of the century and is reflected in the academic literature, which is heavily skewed towards the study of working-class dwellings rather than the housing market as a whole. Thus, on the first page of her otherwise excellent book, *Cruel Habitations*, Enid Gauldie wrote that the 'core of the problem' was the group at the bottom of the income distribution, 'the casuals, the unemployables, the aged and the sick'.[14] A little later David Donnison and Clare Ungerson asserted that, 'Most housing problems are really problems of unemployment, poverty and inequality.'[15] But this suggestion that housing problems are merely symptoms of other problems is to misrepresent the nature of housing itself, especially when it is a commodity provided through the mechanism of the market. By the Victorian period very few people indeed were building their own houses (see pages 42-44 for a rare example in Bristol) and the great majority relied on the market, and herein lay the true housing problem.

While Lord Salisbury may have believed in the efficacy of market forces, 'the ordinary sequence of supply upon demand', in fact housing was unlike other goods and services supplied through the market mechanism: from the consumer point of view, it was both essential and too expensive to buy out of regular income, and this was true of almost everyone, not just the poor. From the supply side point of view, housing was an attractive business opportunity simply because it was essential – there would always be a need for it – but it had three particularly awkward characteristics: its production required large amounts of money to be laid out on labour and materials, and production inevitably extended over time, meaning that money was tied up for months or years. Then came the problem of selling something that was beyond the pocket of nearly everyone.

Builders needed to have, or be able to raise, sufficient money to pay for construction, and then they needed to dispose of completed houses as quickly as possible, in order to repay their loans or finance further production. The scale, profitability and sustainability of their businesses depended on their creditworthiness and the rapidity with which they could circulate their capital, converting it from money into buildings and back again. There was thus a tension at the heart of the relationship between builders, who needed to sell quickly, and consumers, who needed to spread their housing costs over a long period. The standard way of relieving this tension in the Victorian period was for builders to sell new houses to the few people who had capital that they wished to invest for the long term. These investors then became housing landlords, drawing a regular income in the form of rent. This meant that the builders were able to withdraw the money spent on production, consumers were able to spread their expenditure over an indefinite period and owners of capital had a secure form of investment ('as safe as houses'). Despite their reputation for being cruel and grasping parasites living off the backs of their tenants, landlords as a group played a valuable enabling role in the Victorian housing system.[16]

The housing market was not a comfortable place for many of those taking part, whether as consumers or providers, or both. On the consumption side the rental housing market varied from squalid hovels in inner city courts and alleys to opulent mansions in the leafy suburbs. Market forces allowed some people to put physical distance between themselves and people they saw as their social inferiors, but of course looking at the same situation from the point of view of the socially aspirant, and the self-consciously respectable working class, the market was a barrier to advancement. Like all consumer markets, the housing market worked best for those with the most money, and for those at the bottom of the resource distribution it effectively failed to work at all, producing the sorts of conditions described and complained about by Dr Kay and others. For the poor there were acute problems of high rents, lack of security and poor value for money, together with the risks to health from the surrounding environmental degradation. There is a tendency in the literature to assume that the working class as a whole lived in slums, but this was not the case. It is important to differentiate between the new streets built for the respectable artisan fraction of the working class and the older, subdivided, houses or backyard infill developments occupied by the poorest. In his research in York in 1899 Seebohm Rowntree divided working-class houses into three categories: class one comprised the 'comfortable houses of the well to do artisans', class two houses were 'for the most part four roomed, principally occupied by families in receipt of moderate but regular wages' and class three was defined as all those houses not good enough to be included in classes one and two. Class three, he calculated, made

Vyvyan Terrace, Clifton, built between 1832 and 1850, one of the last monumental terraces in Bristol. (Courtesy: Bristol Region Building Record)

up a quarter of all houses in the city, and only some of these, dating mainly from the first half of the century, he counted as slums.[17]

From the supply side point of view, sustained population growth implied plenty of demand, creating attractive opportunities to make money out of land development, housebuilding or investment. But each of these came with its own pattern of risks as well as rewards. Despite the numbers of people who needed houses, the rate of new building fluctuated alarmingly from year to year. Owning a row of rented houses may have been a safe investment, but there is plenty of evidence of the risky nature of housebuilding; it has been calculated that almost two thirds of building firms started in Bristol in 1865 failed to survive as long as five years.[18] It might be expected that it would be the least well resourced and undercapitalised small builders of terraced houses for the working class who would be most at risk, but difficulties were not confined to the bottom rungs of the market, and builders of high quality, expensive houses in Clifton sometimes struggled to raise the capital they needed, and then struggled to sell completed houses. The saga of Victoria Square, which took more than twenty five years to build, provides a salutary reminder of the difficulties routinely encountered in the business of property development.[19] Nearby was Vyvyan Terrace, which was under construction for about eighteen years. Even ordinary suburban roads could take twenty or more years to be built out. Inevitably some projects started when market conditions were propitious ended up being caught by slumps in demand. The largest and richest landowners sometimes struggled to get their timing right; Sir Greville Smyth, who owned several hundred acres of Bedminster, started to develop his land in Southville when the market was in recession in the 1880s and then sold land just when demand was picking up in the mid-1890s.[20]

In an important contribution to the literature Dyos and Reeder put forward a corrective to the assumption that had prevailed since the Royal Commission of 1884-5, namely that the housing problem could be understood by an exclusive focus on overcrowding and cognate evils at the bottom of the market.[21] Whereas the Royal Commission had acknowledged the 'wage question' but then set it aside, Dyos and Reeder argued that the distribution of income and wealth lies at the heart of any explanation of the housing situation. In the same way that poverty cannot be understood in isolation from wealth, the housing problems faced by the poor cannot be separated from an understanding of the wider housing system. Dyos and Reeder made two specific points of relevance to the present discussion. The first is that, 'As the manipulators of capital, the middle classes helped to make possible the expansion of housebuilding in the suburbs, the parts of the city in which they were shaping their own environment, but in diverting resources for these purposes they also helped to determine the environment of those left behind in the city centre'.[22] By removing themselves to the suburbs the middle class not only used wealth generated in the city to take advantage of lower priced land on which to develop their villas but they also abandoned houses in the centre that were too large for single working-class families to afford, and which, according to the brutal economics of the market, therefore degenerated into multi-occupied slums. Thus the suburbs and the slums need to be seen as two ends of the same process.

Their second point concerns the argument that the results of suburbanisation could have been different, if the fruits of economic growth had been more evenly distributed, and if the workers had won higher wages. In the aggressive political economy of the Victorian period real wages were kept low for a large proportion of the employed working class because of a combination of factors: Dyos and Reeder cite the rather flimsy argument that wages costs had to be kept down in order to protect the competitiveness of Britain's exports. They see this as an unconvincing argument in view of Britain's dominant position in the production and international trade in manufactured goods. In addition, wages reflected low productivity per capita, not least because of the low level of capital investment in plant and machinery; employers chose to take a substantial proportion of profit for themselves (not least to pay for their suburban mansions) or for expansion of their businesses, and the workers were not well enough organised to demand a different pattern of distribution. Dyos and Reeder conclude that, 'The slums...embodied some of the most burdensome and irreducible real costs of industrial growth that might be imagined'.[23] While the middle classes were sympathetic to arguments that blamed the poor for causing their own plight through their dissolute behaviour, they were themselves in control of the local authorities that had statutory powers to adopt remedial measures, powers that they chose to largely ignore. The inference here is that it was the middle class, as the group with most economic and political power, who must bear responsibility for the slums, rather than the poor.

It follows from what has been written above that this book is based on a rejection of the elite formulation of the housing problem as a way of approaching the question of how the people were accommodated in Victorian Bristol. Whereas in that period the market was seen as the taken for granted, unquestionable, solution, here the Victorian housing market is seen as a flawed solution, one that served only some of the people and failed others. Overcrowding, squalor and shortage were in fact merely symptoms of underlying and inherent features of the market mechanism. Here the market is the problem, in the sense that it is the object of study.

CHAPTER THREE

The Growth of the Town

Bristol has existed for about 1000 years and during that time it has grown from a tiny settlement covering just 20 acres into a city whose administrative boundaries today cover 26,500 acres, or 40 square miles. It is unsurprising that over such a long time growth has been uneven; prior to the twentieth century there had been three periods of particularly active growth and outward expansion of the built up area: the early years up to about 1250, from about 1660 to the late eighteenth century and in the second half of the nineteenth century. Although Bristol was recognised as a rich and important town from at least the twelfth century it remained small both in population and extent. Indeed as late as the middle of the eighteenth century, the population was no more than 50,000[1] and buildings hardly strayed beyond the tightly drawn boundaries of the city and county set by the charter of 1373.[2] Everything changed in the nineteenth century and although a significant proportion of the increased population crowded into the ancient city the great majority were accommodated in surrounding areas as the urban frontier advanced unevenly into the rural hinterland.

The aim of this chapter is to provide a descriptive account of the physical growth of Bristol in the nineteenth century, in terms of three dimensions: first, the spatial dimension, indicating where new houses were built; second, the temporal dimension, recognising both that different areas were developed at different times and that rates of housebuilding varied considerably over time; and third, the social dimension, showing how some areas acquired a distinctly working-class character while others were equally obviously middle class.

'An ancient town surrounded by a modern'[3]
It was in 1794 that William Matthews observed that the old town of Bristol had become, as he put it, surrounded by a modern one. The same point could have been made a century later, for by then it was even clearer that Bristol was again encircled by a ring of new and expanded neighbourhoods. Matthews was writing in the immediate aftermath of a frenzied speculative building boom that had added fifty new streets in just ten years up to 1793,

including some of the best known and grandest of Bristol's terraces and squares, such as Royal York Crescent, Cornwallis Crescent and Prince's Buildings in Clifton, plus Berkeley Square, large parts of Kingsdown and the area around Portland Square, St Paul's. Some 3,000 new houses were built before the boom suddenly collapsed, ruining at least a third of the speculating builders.[4] Reference to this episode is relevant to a discussion of Victorian housing for two reasons. First, most of the activity in the boom years was concentrated to the west and north of the old town, in areas that were already favoured by the better off citizens, and these were areas, especially Clifton, that became entrenched as middle-class suburbs of privilege in the Victorian period. The building boom added few if any new dwellings for people with low incomes, but as the population swelled in the early nineteenth century this was precisely the area of the market with the greatest shortage. Second, so dramatic was the collapse that 500 houses still stood unfinished in 1798, and Royal York Crescent and Cornwallis Crescent were not finished until the 1820s. But the longer run impact was even more significant: the available evidence suggests that apart from the completion of houses begun before 1793, fewer than 100 new houses were built in Clifton between 1793 and 1831. And what was true of Clifton seems also to have been true of Bristol itself. Comparison of Matthews's map of 1794 and Ashmead's 1828 map reveals that the built up area expanded very little in this period, with few new streets being developed. Another indicator of slow growth is that no new Church of England churches were built between 1800 and 1820, and only two (St George's, Brandon Hill and Holy Trinity, Hotwells in the 1820s).[5] All this suggests that the collapse of the property boom in 1793 was followed by a prolonged recession in the building industry in Bristol, at the very time when the population was rising as fast as at any previous period.

Housebuilding was left entirely to private enterprise and market forces. There was therefore nothing systematic about the way the town grew: it all depended on the perceptions of landowners, developers and builders of the level of demand, and because houses took a long time to build it was always difficult to be sure that demand would be there when houses were completed – as the speculators in the early 1790s had discovered to their cost.

In about 1838 John Chilcott wrote that

> Bristol is nearly eight miles in circumference...including its suburbs, it measures from east to west, that is, from the top of St Lawrence Hill to the colonnade at the Hotwell House, considerably more than three miles;

from north to south, or from Stoke's Croft turnpike to the end of the building on the Bridgwater road, or the Ashton Turnpike, the distance is about two and a half.[6]

By 1901 'the built-up area stretched for almost six miles east-west and five miles north-south'.[7] The clearest and simplest way to approach the growth of the built up area in the intervening period is to conduct a survey of the ring of new and expanded neighbourhoods, from Clifton round to Bedminster. But before embarking on such a tour there are one or two general points that need to be made. First, the starting point for understanding any area is landownership, for the owners of the land played a key role in determining how and when it was developed, ie, converted from agricultural to non-agricultural uses. Even today, the urban and suburban landscape, in terms of street patterns and property boundaries, is still heavily influenced by who owned what in the middle of the nineteenth century. All around the city (as the historic maps on Know Your Place reveal) there are traces of ancient field boundaries, reflecting the tendency of individual owners to build without reference to what others nearby might be doing.

Landowners were not entirely free to do as they pleased because they were often constrained by the precise nature of their legal title to the land; for example, much land around Bristol was leased out to farmers, sometimes for long periods and could only be developed once the leases ran out or were otherwise terminated. Landowners were also constrained by the extent of their estates and their location, in particular in terms of proximity to the old town, elevation and aspect. Owners were limited by market forces, which affected not only the appropriate time for development but also what it was possible to sell; there was no point in trying to develop land when demand was weak, and no point in trying to sell big expensive houses in areas where the better off preferred not to live. Third, the way the city developed in the nineteenth century was influenced by topography and the way that earlier generations had responded to the physical advantages and disadvantages of different areas.[8] Bristol and its immediate hinterland already had an emerging pattern of socially distinct neighbourhoods, with the better off generally choosing the higher ground, and Victorian expansion merely accentuated the tendency for middle-class and working-class families to live in different areas. Fourth, these socially distinct areas were also physically different from each other. Whereas the neighbourhoods where the working class lived were effectively urban extensions, the middle-class areas developed into true residential

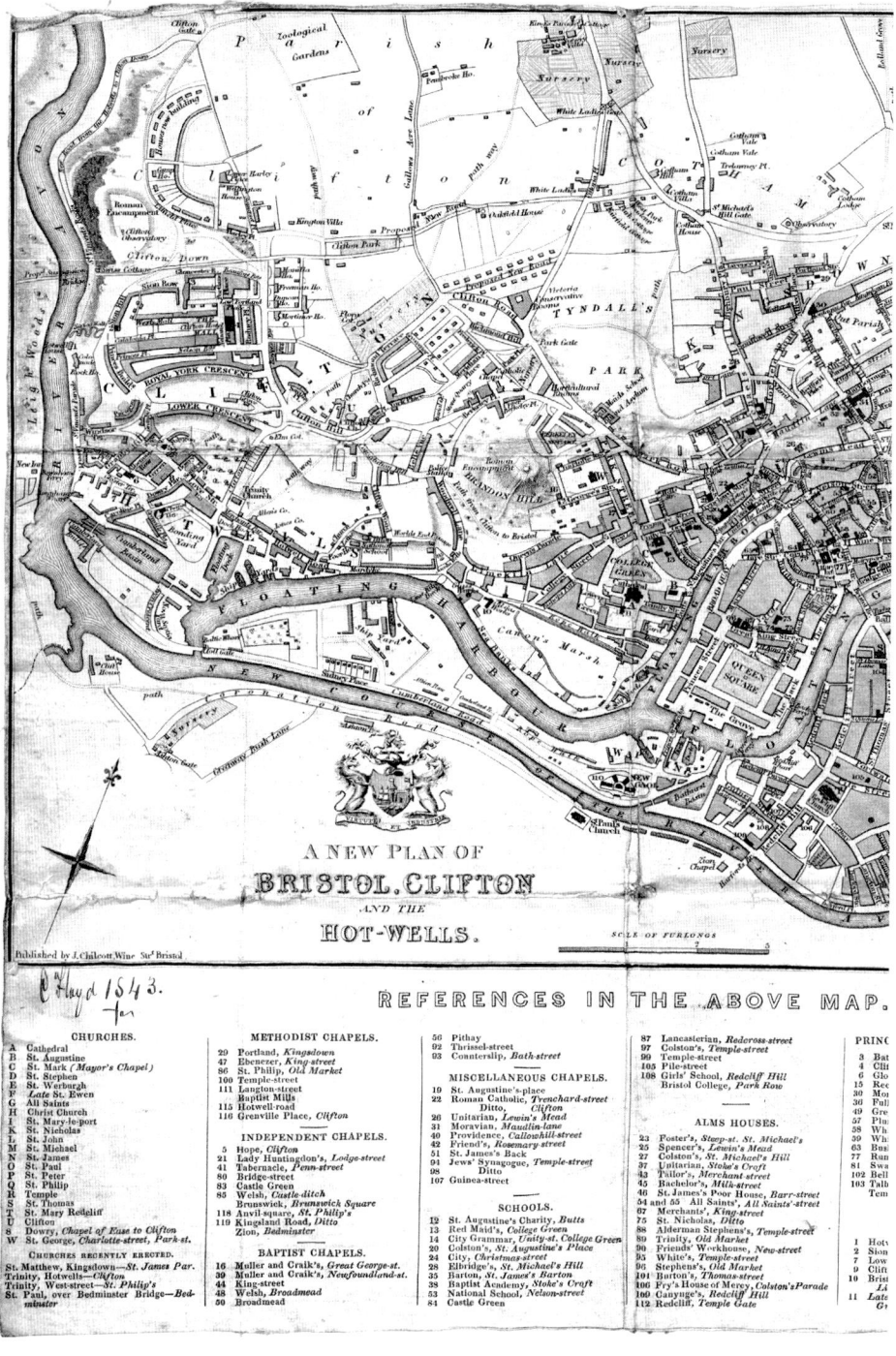

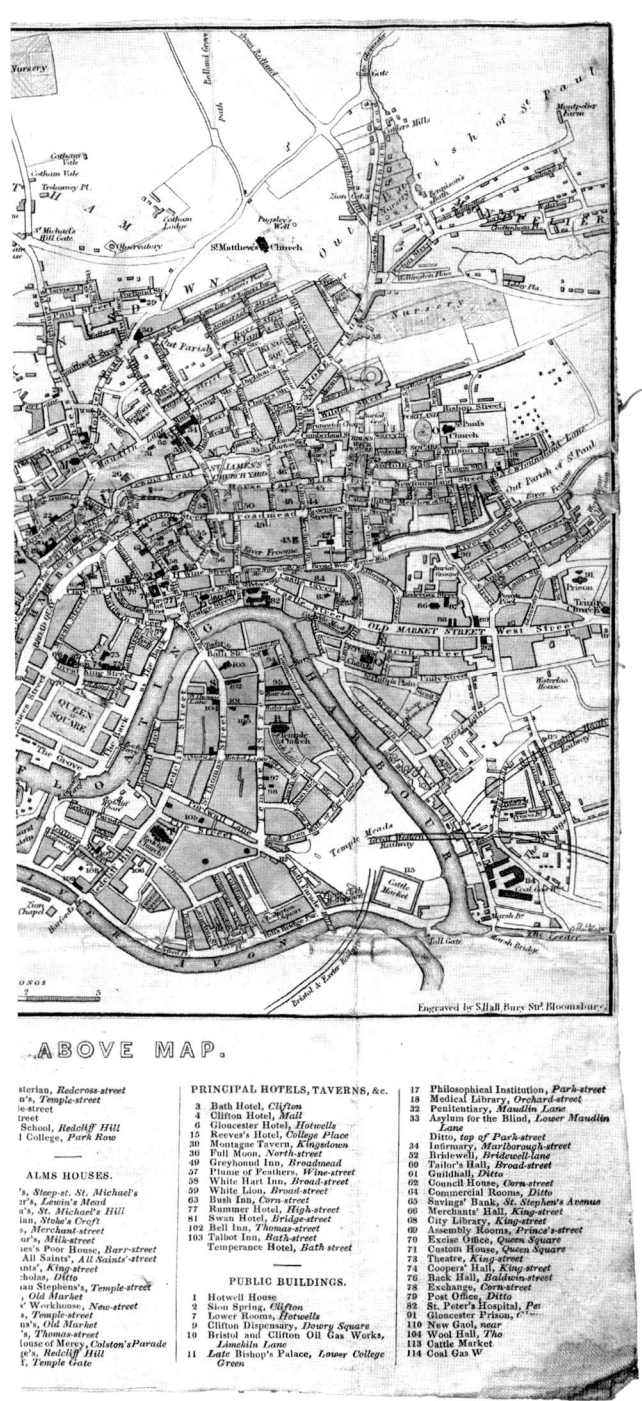

Chilcott's map of Bristol, about 1838. Note the lack of attention to development south of the Avon

suburbs. The new working-class areas were essentially the same as the pre-existing parts of town in the sense that houses, shops, pubs, warehouses and factories were all mixed together at high density, with little open space and few trees or other greenery. The houses were almost invariably built in continuous terraces with their front doors opening straight onto the street; at best they had a small enclosed front area, but front gardens were rare. The middle-class suburb, by contrast, was exclusively residential (apart from a few shops and many churches), and the houses were built at lower density, predominantly detached or semi-detached, with generous front gardens, and often more ground at the back.

The Western and Northern Residential Suburbs
From at least the seventeenth century St Michael's Hill, just north of the old town, had been a favoured resort of well-off citizens (including people of gentry status) seeking an escape from the congestion and pollution down in the town itself.[9] In the 1730s the high ground to the north east of St Michael's Hill began to be developed and from the 1750s Kingsdown became a popular and affluent suburb.[10] According to Latimer, in the 1760s Kingsdown remained a more favoured area than Clifton among those who could afford a suburban house.[11] Although Clifton had been central to the 1790s building boom, as late as the mid-1850s there was very little development north of the line between the Victoria Rooms (dating from 1838), at the town end of Whiteladies Road, and Christ Church (labelled New Church on the 1844 tithe map) on Clifton Down Road. Until 1835 Clifton had been a separate settlement, outside the boundaries of Bristol, but for much of the Victorian period it was the city's premier residential suburb, the location of choice for the city's wealthiest citizens, for obvious reasons: it already had an established reputation among the better off, having enjoyed a period of prosperity in the eighteenth century due to the popularity of taking the waters of the Hotwell.[12] Although as a resort the Hotwell was in decline well before Victoria came to the throne Clifton had other advantages, including its up-wind location to the west of the town, and the fact that much of the parish lay on high ground, some 300 feet above the river Avon. In short, Clifton was recognised as a healthy and prestigious place to live.

The largest single landowner in Clifton at the time of the tithe survey of 1844 was the Society of Merchant Venturers (SMV), which, as a body composed of and representing the interests of the city's elite citizens, could be relied upon to ensure that as and when its land was developed it was done in a way that would protect and enhance its attractiveness to those with the deepest pockets. For example, in the 1850s the Society bought and removed a brewery adjacent to land that it was converting into Victoria Square. The Society's historian, Patrick McGrath, claimed that it acted as a sort of planning authority,[13] in the sense that it policed the quality of new houses built on its land. But the Society was not in any sense a strategic planning body and any plans it produced related only to its own fields. As a result Clifton was developed by the initiative of the various landowners acting more or less independently of each other. The Society had been the owner of land in Clifton since the late seventeenth century, including the 250 acres of Clifton Downs, but by 1844 it had reduced its holding to 74 acres, plus the Downs. The other main owners of open land with the potential for development at that time were Francis Adams (80 acres), John Hurle (36 acres), Thomas Goldney (24 acres 2 roods*) and George Farnall (21 acres 2 roods). Goldney's land remained largely undeveloped and Hurle died in 1855 so he did not make a significant impact, but the others were all actively involved in transforming the northern part of the parish into a suburb of privilege.[14] Adams and Farnall were both absentee landowners who had inherited their Clifton property. There was a certain amount of tactical collaboration between landowners but there is also evidence on the ground to this day to show how they were often inclined to build without reference to the actions or intentions of owners of adjacent land.

Adams in particular, but also Farnall and the SMV, concentrated on building houses that ranged from large to enormous, although towards the end of the century there was a tendency for new houses to be of rather more modest proportions. By the late 1880s most of the available building land in Clifton had been developed, the Downs having been saved as a public open space for the people of Bristol. At that stage the really huge houses were being built on the far side of the Downs, in Sneyd Park and Stoke Bishop, then still outside the city boundary.[15] For the wealthiest families looking for a new house in an exclusive location Clifton was no longer exclusive enough. Sneyd Park is interesting because its development had required a private Act of Parliament, in 1853,[16] in order to dispose of building plots, but because at that time the distance from the built up area was still considerable and it was many years before demand increased.

Much nearer to the town, sandwiched between Clifton and Kingsdown was Tyndall's Park, covering almost 70 acres, which remained undeveloped

---

* A rood is a quarter of an acre, and there are just under two and a half acres to a hectare.

Detached villa, Priory Road, Tyndall's Park. (Photograph: the author)

at the start of the Victorian period, when, it is not unreasonable to say, the countryside started at the top of Park Street. Thomas Tyndall proposed in 1844[17] to build on his estate but it was not until the early 1850s that houses started to appear on the Whiteladies Road edge of the Park. Development continued throughout the rest of the century, by which time the Park had acquired not only a set of grand villas (with up to ten bedrooms), but also a number of important cultural institutions: the Royal West of England Academy, Bristol Grammar School and the University College (soon to become the University of Bristol).

To the north of Kingsdown lay Cotham, which in the 1820s consisted of just a few houses at the top of St Michael's Hill, but by the 1840s houses were

North-east side of Fremantle Square, Kingsdown. (Photograph: the author)

being built on fields owned by Sir Thomas Fremantle, another absentee landlord. Fremantle Road and Fremantle Square give a sense of where his land lay, together with Nugent Hill – named after his wife who was born Louisa Nugent. Fremantle also had inherited land in nearby Redland. Today the boundary between Cotham and Redland is not very clearly defined but at the start of the Victorian period there was open ground in the valley between the two settlements. Redland lay to the north east of Whiteladies Road, which was for much of its length the boundary between the parishes of Clifton and Westbury-on-Trym. The tithe map of 1841 shows that there were only about 100 houses in Redland, most of them substantial villas that were home to some of the city's leading citizens, including, for example, Charles Ludlow Walker, merchant, manufacturer and mayor of Bristol in 1833-4, and William Edwards, banker. The largest holding, 166 acres, belonged to yet another absentee, James Evan Baillie, a banker and West Indies estate owner. His land, centred on Redland Court, stretched from what is now Westbury Park right down to Cotham Brow. Further west the ownership was more fragmented

Redland Court, rebuilt by John Cossins in the 1730s and owned by James Evan Baillie 1829-63. (Courtesy: Bristol Culture – Museums, Galleries and Archives)

and it was here that development began in the 1840s, first with the construction of large terraces (eg. Burlington Buildings) and then, as fashions changed, substantial villas in roads at right angles to Whiteladies Road. Thomas Fremantle, for instance, owned a single field facing Whiteladies Road, on which he developed Westfield Park in the 1850s. At the same time Benjamin Stickland was developing land he had purchased in the 1840s adjacent to what is now Hampton Road. It was not until after Baillie's death in 1863 that part of his estate, between Cotham Brow and the newly laid out Zetland Road, was sold for housebuilding, and only after 1883 was Redland Court and the surrounding 11 acres sold. The purchaser was James Dole, a provisions merchant from West Street, Old Market. The sale of Redland Court triggered the final phase of development in Redland, during the boom conditions of the 1890s, largely filling the open ground between Redland Road and Cranbrook Road.

These four areas, Clifton, Tyndall's Park, Cotham and Redland, were the fashionable middle-class suburbs of the Victorian period. Taken together they constituted a landscape dominated by semi-detached villas designed to appeal to the servant keeping classes. They were suburbs in which there was little employment apart from domestic service, although some jobs were available in the few rows of shops and in the private schools. Developers made sure there were plenty of churches, but few pubs.

Horfield, Montpelier and St Paul's
The north eastern edge of Redland was defined by the stream that ran in a deep gulley parallel to what is now Cranbrook Road, down to meet another stream behind the Gloucester Road. Until 1897 these two water courses were part of the city boundary, and the land between them was part of the parish of Horfield which lay outside the city, while to the east of the Gloucester Road Montpelier was within. Taking Horfield first, the ancient manor of Horfield was wholly owned by the bishop of Bristol from the creation of the diocese in 1542 right through to 1841 when over 300 acres were sold to raise capital to pay for a new bishop's palace at Stapleton. At that time there were fewer than 50 houses in Horfield and in the opinion of bishop James Monk, 'not a single house of a superior class [had] been erected'.[18] Monk explained this in terms of the archaic system of land tenure, known as copyhold, under which most of the land in the manor was leased and sub-leased for lives (ie. each lease would be for a term defined by the longest lived of three named people). He hoped that by modernising the system, essentially by converting copyhold tenure to freehold, Horfield would become an attractive place for developers. The story of how this goal was achieved is long and complicated but by 1852 most of the land belonged to the newly created Bishop Monk's Horfield Trust, Henry Richards, the local vicar, Anthony Storey, an absentee landed proprietor with an estate near Swindon, and two members of the Shadwell family who were based in Bath.[19]

One of the first parts to be built on was the area around Berkeley Road and Egerton Road, where in 1852 Richards sold 30 acres to the National Freehold Land Society, which had been formed in 1849 to enable working men to obtain the right to vote by acquiring a small patch of freehold land. For this reason the plots were not laid out with housebuilding in mind: they were very long and narrow, so that after 1857 when houses began to be built it was often necessary to combine two plots. Richards also built a church, St Michael and All Angels (now demolished), on his land next to the Gloucester Road, and in 1862 a new parish known as Bishopston was created, taking in the southern part of Horfield parish and part of the only recently created

Shadwell Road, Bishopston, built on land owned by John Shadwell in the 1870s. Gloucester Road is visible in the distance. (Photograph: the author)

parish of St Andrew. Bishop Monk's Trust was slower to build and did not produce a coherent plan (for the area around Bishop Road and Monk Road) until 1886. Meanwhile John Shadwell, who inherited in 1858, had begun developing his land from the late 1870s. The majority of houses built on Shadwell land were small terraced houses, at, for example, Wolseley Park (including the inevitable Shadwell Road) and further north at the Thornleigh Park estate (on the Gloucester Road at its junction with Ashley Down Road). But by the 1890s John Shadwell was attempting to build for a more middle-class clientele in the Claremont Road area. And when Herbert Story-Maskelyne began to build on the area previously known as Russell's fields (the area around Morley Square and Brynland Avenue) in the late 1880s he too aimed at that segment of the market. The OS map surveyed at the end of the century shows a finger of development reaching as far as the Wellington hotel at the top of the Gloucester Road, with plenty of undeveloped land to the west, in the direction of Henleaze, and also to the east towards Lockleaze.

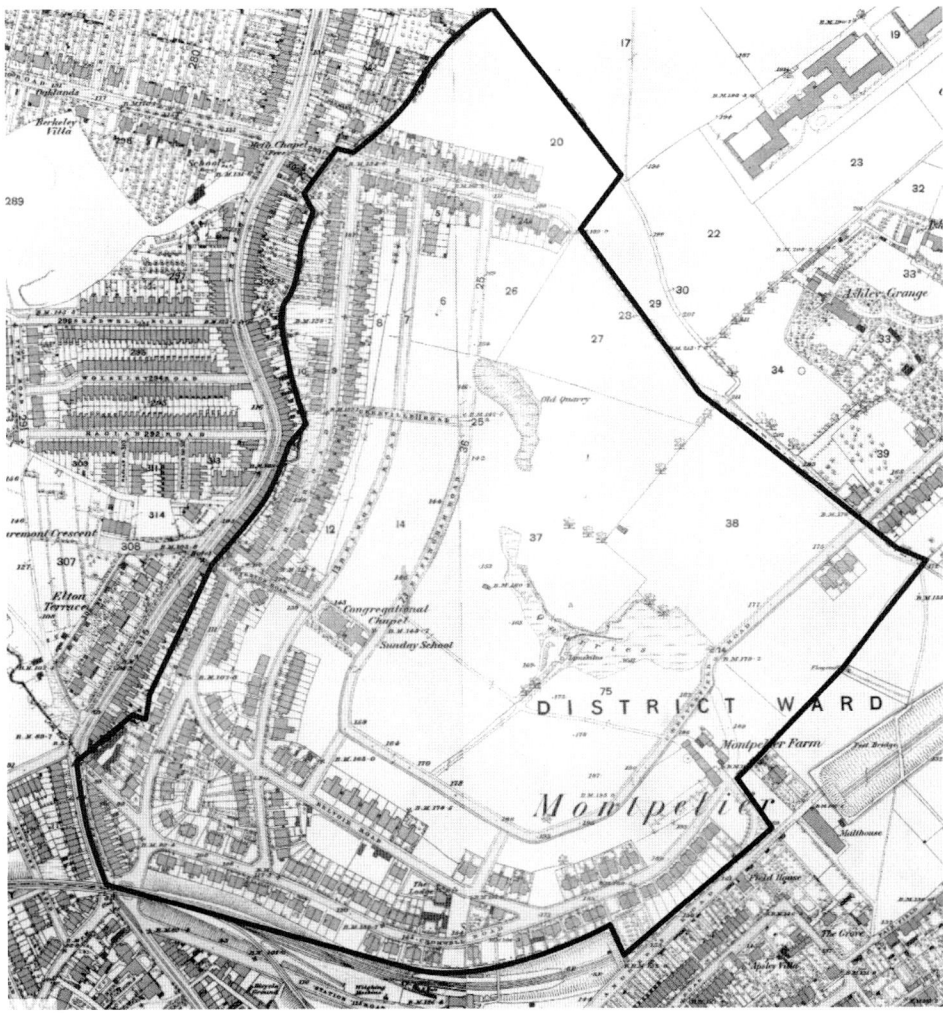

The St Andrew's estate. The black border defines the land acquired by William Baker and James Derham. (OS)

In the same way that the southern part of Horfield became known as Bishopston, the northern part of Montpelier, to the east of the Gloucester Road, was re-labelled the St Andrew's estate after an area covering some 93 acres was acquired by James Derham, a successful Bristol boot maker. The background to this further example of a businessman turning to property development is that the estate was previously owned by a Mary Jackson, of Sneyd Park, who in 1810 left it to distant relatives, John and James Martin, living in Worcestershire. It was a grandson of James Martin who, in 1853, sought the power to create building plots in Sneyd Park, but not, at that stage,

Montpelier. The connection between the Sneyd Park deal and the development of Montpelier is that William Baker, a Bristol builder, was involved in both. It was in 1873 that he and Derham acquired their first lease of 17 acres of land in what was to become the St Andrew's estate. Further tranches were leased in 1876 and 1877, and in 1884 the final parcel was sold to Derham, who took over as the main developer of the whole estate after Baker was incapacitated by illness in 1878.

Building proceeded slowly, so slowly that Derham was able to offer to sell 22 acres 2 roods to the Town Council for a park in 1882 and when that was declined he still had 29 acres 3 roods to offer seven years later.[20] The estate remained under construction at the end of the century, and indeed a few plots were left unbuilt in 1914. The area proved to be more attractive to rather better off customers than much of Bishopston and semi-detached villas were the norm. Whereas Bishop Monk's Horfield Trust had failed to secure offers to build houses valued at more than £200 in the 1880s, in St Andrew's Derham agreed in 1883 to build houses of at least £300 on Belmont Road and £360 on North Road.

There was more to Montpelier of course and several streets, notably Picton Street, St Andrew's Hill (now St Andrew's Road), Richmond Road and York Road, dated from before Victoria's accession. The steep slope and the construction of the railway line in the 1870s served to divide the area still known as Montpelier from St Andrew's. To the south of Ashley Road, where City Road was later to be built, there was an extensive area of nursery garden, supplying Bristol with vegetables, although in 1850 it was unflatteringly described as a low spongy valley.[21] St Paul's parish church dated from the 1790s and was located on a square otherwise surrounded by large terraced houses: the tobacco manufacturer William Day Wills lived at number 2 until his death in 1865, but the low lying location to the east of the city meant that in the long run the area struggled to attract well off residents and by the latter part of the nineteenth century a majority of the houses in Portland Square had been converted into boot and shoe factories.[22] Between Grosvenor Road and Newfoundland Lane, was an area, unique in Bristol, that had originally been let out as garden plots, but, in the words of Rev. Ernest Fuller, a local vicar, 'The garden ground had been squatted on a good deal, and the people had run up little cottages here and there'.[23] It seems that as long as the inhabitants contented themselves with a single storey dwellings and did not try to build any higher they were left alone. 'Upwards of a hundred cabins and cottages were erected, and the colony gradually increased to 500 or 600

Davey Street, once part of the Forlorn Hope estate, built in the late 1870s, looking towards St Agnes Park. (Photograph: the author)

Albany Place, Montpelier, built in the 1870s. (Courtesy: Bristol Region Building Record)

people, who bred fowls and ducks and pigs, and were famous for monster vegetables.'[24] They were referred to in contemporary sources as belonging to 'the roughest class of the population'.[25] The area as a whole was known as Newfoundland Gardens, but one part went by the evocative name of the Forlorn Hope Estate, owned by the vestry of the ancient central Bristol parish of St Nicholas. The Forlorn Hope Estate was originally 13 acres and 3 roods, purchased by the vestry in the late sixteenth century to generate income for the relief of the poor of the parish. At some point in the nineteenth century part of the estate, probably a field known as Knapp's Close (now Burnell Drive and Ludlow Close), was sold to the trustees of Trinity Hospital, and most of what remained was developed into the streets between St Nicholas Road, Grosvenor Road, Newfoundland Road and St Agnes Park.[26] The low lying site was chronically prone to flooding from the nearby river Frome but nevertheless over a period from the late 1860s to the early 1880s it was redeveloped and covered in rows of small terraced houses. However, the flood threat was not removed and the people of the area suffered terribly in the inundations of October 1882 and March 1889.

South and East of the Frome
The river Frome marked an important boundary in Victorian Bristol: to the north and west development was predominantly residential, with little industrial activity; to the south and east, however, there were coal mines, tanneries, brickworks, a pottery, two gas works, metal and chemical industries and eventually extensive areas were given over to the railways and railway-related industries making locomotives and wagons. One of the first planned urban extensions in this quarter had been built as early as 1711-12:

> A considerable extension of the eastern suburb of the city took place...by the construction of Wade Street, Great George and Great Anne Streets etc [ie Eugene Street and New Street]. The owners of the ground, Nathaniel Wade and Abraham Hooke, built a bridge in 1711 over the Frome, at Wade Street, for the development of the estate.[27]

On low-lying ground, adjacent to the river Frome and down-wind of the city this area lacked the advantages of more elevated locations such as Kingsdown and Clifton to the north and west,[28] but this new district added some 560 new houses, mostly of the smallest kind, occupied by artisans and craftsmen.[29] In the nineteenth century the area was known as St Jude's and was notorious

Mrs Sarah Tucker at her front door in Tyler Street, the Dings, in the 1920s. (Courtesy: Peter Insole, Know Your Place)

for overcrowding in its many common lodging houses. In 1865 one local paper wrote

> ...we believe the cheapest thing the city could do would be to purchase the whole district of St Jude's, and level with the earth the squalid abodes that crowd it and which do not deserve the name of human habitations.[30]

Further south, before the arrival of the railways in 1840 numbers of small houses were built in the Dings, an area separated from the river Avon by a strip of heavy industry and eventually enclosed by railway lines. Near the Dings the

Part of the Goodhind estate, on the northwest side of Stapleton Road. (Courtesy: Peter Insole, Know Your Place)

Front elevation of houses to be built in King Street, Goodhind estate, 1871. (Courtesy: Bristol Archives)

Anvil Street area consisted of little houses tightly packed together and virtually surrounded by industrial sites – Avonside works making engines, Barley Field iron works and the Phoenix glass bottle works. For rating purposes the houses in this most heavily industrialised part of Victorian Bristol were given some of the lowest valuations anywhere in the city, and so it is safe to say that this was always an exclusively working-class area. The same was true of the settlement that emerged around the Barton Hill Cotton Factory after 1838.

By 1847 streets of houses were beginning to appear between the main roads fanning out eastwards from the old town, namely Pennywell Road, Stapleton Road, Easton Road and Lawrence Hill, and in the second half of the nineteenth century, especially after 1860, the wedge of land between the rivers Frome and Avon to the east of Bristol's ancient core, experienced very significant change in terms of population growth, industrial investment and urbanisation of the landscape. Much of the urban growth of east Bristol in the Victorian period was concentrated within the ancient out parish of St Philip and St Jacob, which stretched from St Werburgh's church in the north down to the river Avon in the south, embracing Baptist Mills, Upper Easton,

Newtown, from the 1880s OS map.

Newtown, the Dings, Barton Hill and St Philip's Marsh. Further east less extensive building occurred in Lower Easton, Russell Town, Redfield and Whitehall, which were in the parish of St George and as such remained outside the city until 1897.[31]

The St Philip and St Jacob tithe map of 1847 revealed a pattern of landownership that was much more fragmented than in the north western suburbs: 74 individuals owned at least one acre but no-one had more than the 41 acres owned by James Duffett, a brick and tile maker based in St Philip's Marsh. One of the larger owners was Samuel Goodhind, a Bristol solicitor who later gave his name to the Goodhind estate, 21 acres between Stapleton Road and Pennywell Road.

Although neither Goodhind nor his trustees were quick to develop their land, further south an area that became known as Newtown was being actively built up from the early 1850s. Indeed, at that time Newtown, which occupied an area of some 25 acres between Lawrence Hill and the Bristol and Gloucester (later the Midland) railway line, was the most active building site in Bristol. In 1851-52 alone 7 landowners and 32 different builders were involved in developing Newtown, indicating the fragmented and small scale of the land and housing market at that time. Nevertheless, by the mid-1870s a coherent pattern of streets had been established and the whole of the Newtown enclave had been built up. The overwhelming majority of houses built here were narrow fronted, two-up-two-down, opening straight onto the pavement. It was a densely populated neighbourhood, with very little open space.

Newtown undergoing redevelopment in the 1960s. (Courtesy: D Cheesley)

The remaining half dozen streets of the Goodhind estate, between Stapleton Road and Goodhind Street, are but a remnant of an extensive and heavily built up area of exclusively working-class houses that used to cover the eastern neighbourhoods. The final area to be considered, however, St Philip's Marsh, between the Feeder Canal and the Avon was quite different in the sense that much of the land was used for industrial purposes or remained undeveloped. As the name suggests this was another low lying area and throughout the Victorian period there were no more than a dozen or so streets of working-class houses.

South of the Avon
In 1805-09 a new course, the New Cut, was excavated for the tidal river Avon, from what is now the Underfall Yard in the west to Temple Meads in the east, a distance of 1¾ miles almost entirely through the ancient parish of Bedminster, which was then outside the city boundary, in the county of Somerset. By the time the northern part of the parish was incorporated into Bristol in 1835 the built up part of Bedminster consisted of a settlement clustered on both sides of Bedminster Parade and extending on East Street half a mile south-west from Harford's bridge (now Bedminster bridge) over the New

Mount Pleasant Terrace, built on a field so narrow that there was room for houses only on one side of the road. (Photograph: the author)

Cut. The boundary extension of 1897 brought in more of Bedminster as well as Knowle, where there was a certain amount of housebuilding, mainly to the east of the Wells Road, but Victorian urbanisation south of the Avon was concentrated in Bedminster parish, including areas that came to be known as Southville, Ashton Gate, Windmill Hill and Pylle Hill.

Land ownership in Bedminster was dominated by the Smyth family of Ashton Court and their relatives the Gore-Langtons of Langton Court, Brislington and Newton Park, Newton St Loe, near Bath. The tithe map of 1843 shows that Sir John Smyth owned 321 acres of Bedminster within the city, and Colonel William Gore-Langton owned 27 acres, but the two men together, as joint lords of the manor, owned a further 194 acres. It was this manorial land, let on copyhold tenure, that was most heavily built up at that stage, while the Smyth and Gore-Langton land remained largely agricultural. The buildings on the manorial land were described as 'cottages, gardens etc' and the great majority were small terraced houses, mostly on flat and low lying ground. In 1850 Bedminster was described in the most unflattering terms:

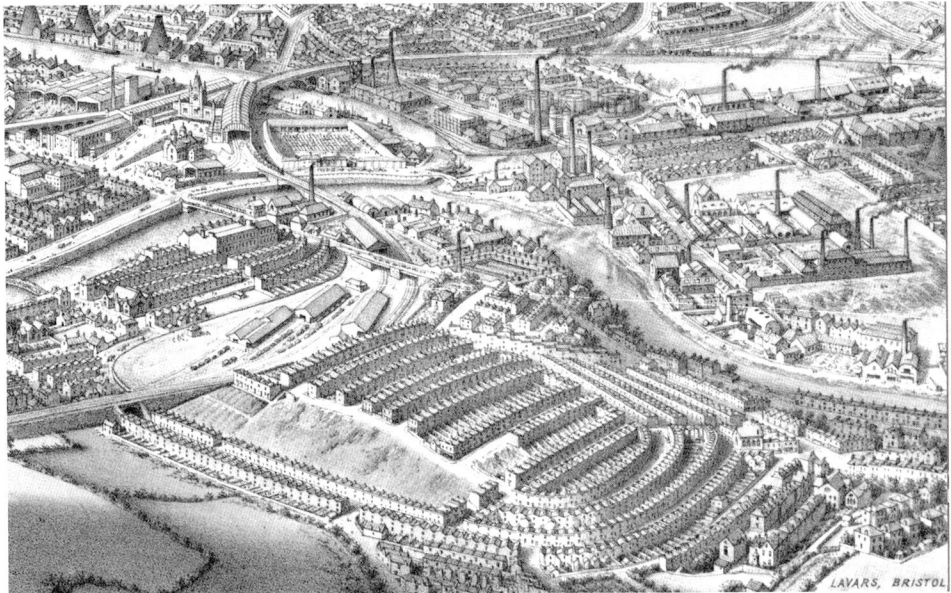

Pylle Hill, Totterdown, from Lavar's projection of 1880, showing houses all round the hill with the railway goods yard to the north.

> In fact, it is difficult to convey in words, a correct impression of the condition of a place in which the houses are, for the most part, low, ill-built and crowded together; a large proportion of the inhabitants are poor; in which there are very few sewers, and scarcely any house-drains; of which the more densely peopled parts are the lowest and worst drained; of which the turnpike roads are in bad order, and the side roads, and most of the streets have never been made or metalled at all; and which, to crown it all, is miserably supplied with water, and without public lights at all.[32]

The four tanneries located in close proximity to the houses added nothing to the attractiveness of the neighbourhood. However, in the second half of the century conditions in Bedminster undoubtedly improved, although parts near the Malago brook remained prone to flooding and the river remained heavily polluted. New industries appeared, including a large smelter, several coal mines, a rapidly expanding tobacco industry and printing and packaging works. In east Bedminster, below the steep slope of Pylle Hill, there was also a large railway goods depot. At the same time the population increased considerably to more than 69,000 by 1901. This obviously implied a corresponding increase in housing supply, and by the end of the century streets

Oxford Street, Pylle Hill in the 1970s, with Victoria Park in the distance.
(Courtesy: Peter Insole, Know Your Place)

of terraced houses covered not only much of the flatter and more accessible land but also some of the slopes of Windmill Hill and Pylle Hill.

At the time of the tithe map survey Lord Methuen, of Corsham, Wiltshire, owned land at Pylle Hill, having recently sold 6 acres for the construction of the Bristol and Exeter Railway. Methuen died in 1849 and a subsequent Chancery court decision led to 60 acres of his Bristol estate, including 30 acres at Pylle Hill, south of the railway, being put up for auction in July 1853.[33] The purchaser was Henry Green, a Bristol maltster, but he was not the developer; in 1865 he entered into an agreement[34] to sell the land to Thomas Morgan, a builder, and William Vowles. Later Vowles bought out Morgan's share thereby becoming the sole developer of the land over the next 25 years (for more on Vowles see chapter four).

Further west housebuilding was more or less continuous, but often slow: in almost seven years between August 1851 and May 1858 plans were submitted for only 226 houses in Bedminster. In the 1860s an area known as Whitehouse Mead and Ragg Acre was prepared for development, but, probably because of its low lying position and the fact that it was hemmed in by the Malago brook, two tanneries, a smelter and the railway line, it did not excite the interest of builders and this 11 acre site took at least 12 years to be developed.

In 1852 the Ashton Court estate had passed to Sir John's nephew, Greville Upton (who later became Sir Greville Smyth) and he remained the owner until his death in 1901. He was a major landowner: in addition to the extensive tract of parkland attached to the Ashton Court mansion itself he owned over 1,000 acres in Bedminster beyond the 1835 boundary, plus 1,620 acres in Gloucestershire to the east and north of Bristol. In that context Bedminster was a small part of the overall estate but it was also the part closest to the advancing urban frontier of Bristol and therefore had the greatest potential for profitable development. For reasons unknown Smyth and his estate manager, Thomas Dyke, were slow to seize the opportunity, although they engaged in a prolonged sequence of land deals that can be interpreted as the strategic assembly of sites for development. It was not until the early 1880s (just when housebuilding levels in Bristol were at their lowest, see below) that plans were announced for the development of Greville Town, about 30 acres of what is now Southville, between North Street and Beauley Road. However, progress was extraordinarily slow and eventually, in 1896 (just when housebuilding rates were increasing rapidly), the estate began to sell off the land to others who injected more energy and momentum into the process. Among those who became involved at that time were builders such as Harry Rossiter and William Kingston, both of whom were able to operate on a much larger scale than those who had built places like Newtown earlier in the century. Kingston, for example, was able to buy 10 acres of Greville Town for £13,000 in 1896 and a further 11 acres of Smyth land for £16,925 in 1899.

Ups and Downs in Housebuilding

So far this survey of urban expansion around Bristol in the Victorian period has concentrated on the geography of housebuilding, identifying areas of new housing that came to encircle the ancient city. Although it has not been possible to go into detail about each new or expanded neighbourhood, it is clear that in some areas, such as Clifton and Bedminster, housebuilding was more or less continuous throughout the period after about 1840; other areas, including Newtown, were full by the 1880s, while in Horfield and St Andrew's activity was much slower to get going and large tracts of open ground remained until the 1890s. Another way of approaching the subject is to look at overall fluctuations in housebuilding over time. This is easier said than done, because information was not collected in a readily accessible way and the town council issued no figures for annual building rates until the late 1890s. There is no information on houses completed, only plans submitted to the council after August 1851. The surviving plans are an invaluable resource but not perfect: there are gaps, some plans were not carried through and houses built in areas just beyond the existing city boundaries are less well recorded. Another problem is that the various building plan volumes cover quite different lengths of time, making it difficult to calculate annual rates of construction. Nevertheless, by counting the numbers of houses proposed in each volume it is possible to estimate the monthly average. These estimates should be treated as such, not as definitive figures, but they do provide an idea of how building activity rose and fell over time.

In the first decade of the collection the monthly average never rose above 30 but then it climbed to 40.5 in 1862-65, and continued its upwards trajectory in 1867-69 to reach 59.4. This rise is reflected in Latimer's observation that, 'During the summer of 1867, building operations were carried out with unusual vigour in the suburban districts'.[35] The rate then fell back to 30 in 1872-74 only to rise again with even greater strength to 121 by 1877-78. This was the greatest housebuilding boom since the 1790s and was followed by a similarly severe slump in activity: in the early 1880s the monthly average was just 11.4 (in 1883-85), or less than 10 per cent of the boom years.[36] In 1884 the Royal Commission on housing was told by Bristol witnesses that the city had been 'over built' in the 1870s, resulting in a glut of unsold houses and a steep decline in new building.[37] In the spring of 1881 there were said to be more than 3,500 empty houses in Bristol, and considerable distress among the families of workers in the building trades.[38] The un-named author of *The Homes of the Bristol Poor*, 1884, wrote of '…the great want of work and the immense surplus of unskilled labour at present in the city'.[39] Activity slowly recovered, with the monthly average exceeding 50 between 1889 and 1892. There was a sharp acceleration in 1896-7 when the average rose to 94.8, falling back a little in the following year but then a new boom emerged in 1898 (176), reaching an unprecedented 236 houses per month in 1899, followed by 190 in the next year. The 1890s was thus the most important decade in terms of the total numbers of houses added, estimated to be 10,367.[40] This figure may be compared to the estimate of 2,621 in 1851-62. The late 1890s building boom finally ran out of steam in about 1905, and there are many streets in Bristol where building began during the boom but where vacant plots remained until after the First World War; these are readily identified by the marked stylistic differences between pre- and post-war houses.

Explaining this pattern is not straightforward, but it is clear that Bristol was far from alone in witnessing such instability, unrelated to the underlying

These two houses in Northumberland Road, Redland, illustrate the stylistic changes often seen in roads that were started before 1914 but finished in the 1920s, or, as in this case, the 1930s. The pre-1914 house is on the right of the picture. (Photograph: the author)

needs of the population. Different towns, with different economic structures displayed different peaks and troughs in housebuilding, different in terms of both amplitude and timing.[41] Bristol, however, was known as a town with a diverse industrial base, not heavily reliant on a single dominant industry, and therefore expected to be better able to respond to economic vicissitudes.[42] The low level of housebuilding in the 1850s can be seen in the context of Bristol's still relatively poor economic performance; after 1860 the local economy began to pick up and the trough in building in the early 1880s was a reaction to the exuberance of speculating builders in the late 1870s; it was arguably made worse by the collapse of Finzel's sugar refinery and the Avonside Engineering Works.[43] Bristol's late 1890s building boom needs to be seen in the context of the boundary extension of 1897, which doubled the area of the city and thus meant that houses that would previously have been counted by neighbouring authorities were now attributed to the city. However, this was probably of minor significance, given that the building boom took place alongside economic growth and optimism in Bristol, fuelled by the rapid expansion of the tobacco maker WD and HO Wills, the chocolate manufacturer JS Fry and the paper and packaging firm ES and A Robinson. But it is also true that the late 1890s witnessed a major housebuilding boom on a national scale.

Who Lived Where?

Earlier parts of this chapter have referred to the way that the west and north Bristol was predominantly residential, with little industrial activity, whereas the south and east was much more mixed. This had a powerful influence on who lived where: those with sufficient income and/or wealth generally chose to live in the more exclusively residential areas, while those with less spending power lived where they could. The central parishes had already, before 1840, been largely abandoned by the better off, who chose to move to the leafier suburbs, thereby vacating large old houses that were either occupied by the poor or redeveloped for warehouses and, less often, factories. After the mid-1860s the central area became less populated as the working class who could afford to do so also began to leave. This left the poor, some of whom were also squeezed out of their dwellings by higher value land uses, thereby adding to the overcrowding in the remaining courts and alleys. Market forces effectively distributed people around the city in ways that mapped onto the urban landscape the inequalities generated by the industrial economy. This section looks in a little more detail at the evidence on socio-spatial segregation in Victorian Bristol.

From at least the 1770s it was possible to make a distinction between what Elizabeth Baigent called the artisan parishes, such as St Philip and St Jacob, and the fashionable parishes, such as St Augustine (which included Park Street, Brandon Hill and Berkeley Square), within the ancient city.[44] As the population grew in the early decades of the nineteenth century social segregation became more obvious and entrenched.[45] This can be demonstrated in several ways. Following the creation of the town council and the widening of the boundaries in 1835 there were ten wards each returning a number of councillors in proportion to rateable value. Clifton represented 43 per cent of the additional rateable value brought into the city and it had nine councillors while St Philip and St Jacob and Bedminster had three each. Moreover, voters in these latter parishes were highly likely to be represented by someone who preferred to live in Clifton: in the period 1835-51 161 councillors lived in Clifton, but only one lived in Bedminster.[46] In 1845-46 just over a third of all councillors lived in Clifton and by 1875 the proportion had risen to two thirds.[47] Another source says that,

> From 1852-1882 of the 48 elected councillors a percentage ranging from 46% to 52% at the beginning of each decade dwelt in Clifton and a further percentage ranging from 18% to 27% lived in Redland, Cotham, Tyndall's

Park or the Park St – Berkeley Sq area. All of these localities were indisputably the haunts of Bristol's well-to-do middle class.[48]

Given that the council was entirely composed of middle-class men, who needed to be able to demonstrate ownership of an estate worth at least £1,000 or own property rated at a minimum of £30 per year, it is clear that the western suburbs exercised a powerful attraction to the city elite.

Social segregation can also be inferred from a study of the rateable values attached to properties in different parts of the city. The Bristol Archives contain several invaluable documents detailing the results of valuation surveys carried out between 1837 and 1871.[49] These surveys indicate not only the wide variation between the highest and lowest value properties but also their distribution across the city. The survey of 1837 includes large numbers of houses (sometimes referred to as tenements) rated at less than £5 per year, the very cheapest being £2 (for example, Willmott Crescent, off Rose Street in St Thomas parish, near to Temple Meads). Contrast that with the £335 per year valuation placed on Manilla Hall, Clifton, the home of William Miles, a banker, ship owner and West Indies plantation owner. In 1850 George Clark, the government inspector who carried out a survey of the sanitary conditions in Bristol, compiled a table analysing the situation in different parishes: in Clifton 10.7 per cent were rated at under £5 and 30.48 per cent under £10, whereas in the out parish of St Philip and St Jacob the equivalent rates were 60.8 and 89.69, and in the east tything of Bedminster they were 48.1 and 86.23. At the same time 54.7 per cent of houses in Clifton were valued at £20 or more, but the rate was only 3 per cent in both St Philip and St Jacob (out) and Bedminster (east).[50] Looking at these figures from a different direction, only 4 per cent of the lowest rated houses were in Clifton, while 39 per cent were in St Philip and St Jacob (out). The distribution of poverty and wealth was reflected in mortality rates: in 1877 the council's Medical Officer of Health, Mr Davies, reported that mortality across the city was 22.5 per 1000; in Clifton and Westbury it was 16.7 and in St Mary Redcliffe it was 29.5.[51]

There is no reason to doubt that the general pattern of inequality persisted throughout the rest of the century. An investigation of the homes of the poor in 1883 identified many of the same locations that had been discussed by George Clark in 1850 and an earlier report by Sir Henry de la Beche, in 1845. Clark pointed to the poor conditions in the following areas: Hotwell Road, Woodwell Lane (Jacob's Wells Road), the courts behind College Street, Lewin's Mead, the courts west of St James's church, the cottages in the out parish of St Philip and St Jacob and the cottages in Bedminster.[52] The 1883 report contained harrowing accounts of poverty and distress concentrated in these and other areas. Consider, for example, this passage:

> The district of St Jude's, [within the old out parish of St Philip and St Jacob] with its thickly clustering old houses and foul rookeries, its dank courts and blind alleys, its 'dark entries' and back yard shed dwellings, common lodging houses and tramps' retreats, its thieves haunts and prize fighters' quarters, long enjoyed an unenviable reputation as the abode of the utmost squalor and misery, abject poverty, personal improvidence and social wrong.[53]

This area, previously known as Poynt's Pool (the open space in front of St Jude's church), had been singled out as a particular black spot of crime and depravity in 1854.[54] Meanwhile, the better off had been migrating further away from the city, establishing ever more exclusive enclaves, across the Downs at Sneyd Park and Stoke Bishop, and after 1864 across the Clifton suspension bridge.[55] David Large reports on the strenuous efforts made by the residents of Stoke Bishop in the 1890s to resist inclusion within Bristol, on the grounds that most of the residents had no connection with the city.[56]

CHAPTER FOUR

Housing Production: the Key Actors

The previous chapter painted, in fairly broad brush terms, a picture of when and where housebuilding added to the urban expansion of Bristol in the Victorian period. Here the discussion turns to the people involved in the business of housebuilding. Reference has already been made to individual landowners and one or two builders, but the production of houses involved a wider set of actors, including those who provided professional advice, finance and building materials. Sometimes the same people could play more than one role at the same time, or move from one role to another over time. It was also true that in many cases their involvement in housing production was not their main or sole source of livelihood: developers of houses, for example, were often people who had previously made money in some non-housing related business. The production of houses was an activity, or rather a complex set of quite different activities, that involved a variety of people drawn from across society. The actual construction work was literally in the hands of working-class men and boys, including both practitioners of a variety of trades and craft skills and those who had nothing to sell but their labour. Some of these men, often bricklayers or carpenters, undertook responsibility for organising building work, becoming employers in their own right, and if they were particularly talented, and lucky, they might find themselves in charge of large and enduring firms, accumulating enough capital to enable them to adopt the title of 'gentleman', and eventually to retire in comfort. The unlucky ones sank without trace. More firmly established within the middle class were the lawyers, architects and surveyors whose inputs were essential to the whole process. Also within the middle class were the 'fund holders' (as they often defined themselves on census returns), people who had accumulated or inherited wealth and were looking for a safe and remunerative home for their money. However, in terms of social standing they all ranked beneath members of the gentry and aristocracy, who owned much of the land developed for housing. It is a reasonable hypothesis that the higher their social standing the less direct involvement middle-class people had in housebuilding, but the more substantial was the material benefit they derived from the process. Not only was there a class dimension there was also a heavy gender bias in the business of housebuilding. This is not to say that there were no women landowners or builders, but they were very much the exception. Margaret Newsom, the adoptive mother of Samuel Goodhind, owned land off Stapleton Road in the early part of the century, and Lady Sarah Cave owned land in Redland.[1] It is also possible to find one or two cases where women are identified as builders on plans submitted to the council, for example Mrs R Jeffries who submitted plans for two houses in Newtown in February 1854. The building trades, however, were exclusively male, as were the professions of architecture, surveying and the law.

Landowners

The first group of people to be considered are the owners of the land on which new houses were built. The tithe maps drawn up in the 1840s mean that it is possible to say who owned more or less all the land around Bristol at that time (it is more difficult to say much about landownership within the pre-1835 boundaries). This is a valuable baseline of information, especially about the overall pattern of ownership, but in itself it tells us little about who the owners were at the time of development, as much as fifty years later. A useful distinction may be drawn between people who owned land by the accident of birth and inheritance, and those who consciously acquired land in order to develop it. The inheritors were more likely to be absentees while the developers were more likely to be local businessmen. Most of the land was owned by individuals, but there was a certain amount of institutional ownership, for example the Society of Merchant Venturers in Clifton and the Anglican church in the person of the bishop of Bristol in Horfield.[2] The town council was not a major owner of land in and around Bristol in the nineteenth century. Unlike some cities, including Cardiff, Sheffield and Birmingham, Bristol did not have extensive tracts of land owned by aristocratic magnates. In Birmingham, for example, the Edgbaston estate of Lord Calthorpe ran to more than 2,000 acres,[3] but in and immediately adjacent to Bristol the largest estates were not much more than 300 acres. The largest individual landowner in the area at the time of the tithe surveys was Sir John Smyth of Ashton Court, but much of his extensive estate in Bedminster and south Gloucestershire was too far from Bristol to be affected by urban expansion in the nineteenth century. The great majority of local landowners controlled estates of a very much smaller scale; as mentioned in chapter three, in the out parish of St Philip and St Jacob, beyond the eastern end of Old

Market Street, for example, 74 people owned at least one acre, but the largest holding was 41 acres. It is also important to remember that estates were often fragmented, consisting of one field here and another there, making development more difficult. In Horfield, for example, on its formation in 1852 Bishop Monk's Horfield Trust owned ten separate parcels of land, and in 1841 Sir Thomas Fremantle's 39 acres in Redland were in seven scattered lots.

The absentee landowners around Bristol were a diverse set of people. Sir Thomas Fremantle (later Lord Cottesloe) lived in Buckinghamshire, inherited a large fortune from his father and pursued a successful political career. The land in Bristol that came from his great aunt would not have occupied much of his attention. Francis Adams also inherited land, 80 valuable acres of Clifton, but lived in Cheltenham. Other absentees chose to buy land near Bristol as an investment, a good example being Anthony Storey, a Wiltshire landowner who first (in 1827) leased and later (in 1841) bought Horfield Great Farm (263 acres). In this case it seems unlikely, given the remote location of the farm in relation to the city, that Storey envisaged developing the land for housing, although his descendants certainly did well out of it. Also in Horfield was Dr John Shadwell, a medical doctor living in Southampton, whose family had a centuries-old connection to the parish, with successive generations enjoying the archaic title of Lord Farmer of the manor of Horfield. When bishop James Monk succeeded in enfranchising his copyhold tenants in the early 1850s John Shadwell was already dead but his son Henry emerged with the freehold of more than 300 acres in what became Bishopston.[4] Inheritance was an important feature but some absentee owners were opportunistic purchasers, capitalising on the troubles of others. James Evan Baillie, for example, is interesting because he purchased, for £25,000 in 1829, the mansion house of Redland Court, together with the surrounding estate, on the bankruptcy of the previous owner, Sir Richard Vaughan.[5] Baillie, who lived in London, was a partner in both Bristol's Old Bank and the family firm of Evan Baillie, Sons and Company, based in Corn Street. In the mid-1830s he received a share of a £76,000 payment under the government's slave owners' compensation scheme, and it is arguable that some of that money helped him to extend his Redland estate over the next few years, although he made little attempt to build houses on his land before his death in 1863. Baillie was the recipient of one of the larger payments received by Bristol slave owners, and he is the only such recipient for whom there is any evidence that the money might have been recycled into land in the vicinity. The total amount paid to Bristol slave owners was at least £300,000 and the lack of evidence for this money finding its way into land and housing development no doubt reflects the state of the local economy at that time: the money came long before the recovery in housebuilding.

The solicitor Samuel Goodhind was a different kind of inheritor landowner. His estate had belonged to his adoptive mother, Margaret Newton, who had lived with her first husband, John Mellsum, at Pennystone House (or Penstone Lodge) off Stapleton Road. When Mellsum died his widow married William Newton and they adopted the young Samuel Goodhind, presumably going on to set him up in the law. Goodhind himself did nothing to develop the estate and when he died in 1849 it passed to his trustees who, in the decade after 1867, built a number of streets, including Newton Street, Milsom Street and Goodhind Street, which still exist, together with others to the north west of Pennywell Road that have been replaced.

The developer landowners were local businessmen who had accumulated capital in industry or commerce and diversified into property. These people were more likely to enter the land market later in the century, when there was evidence of sustained demand for new houses. James Derham, who made his money from the footwear industry, has been mentioned in chapter three as investing in the area that became known as St Andrew's from the early 1870s.[6] Like a lot of successful Bristol businessmen, Derham was not born in the city. He and his brother Samuel came from Wrington, in Somerset, and moved their boot making business into the city, initially in Brunswick Square, in the early 1850s. James Derham served as a Liberal councillor and lived in style at Sneyd Park House, where the grounds covered more than 8 acres.

Another from the same industry was William H Cowlin,[7] who lived in Henbury but purchased 15 acres of Smyth land in Bedminster in the late 1890s. It was not just boot makers of course: in the early 1840s Benjamin Stickland, a silversmith, purchased 16 acres on the Redland side of Whiteladies Road which he developed over the next thirty years. Stickland was perhaps unusual in he lived for many years in one of his own houses at number 1 Hampton Terrace.

Many more such examples could be cited, such as John Lysaght, the owner of a galvanising business next to the feeder canal, who invested in 17 acres of land in Cotham in 1875. Both Derham and Lysaght were undoubtedly successful entrepreneurs, running businesses that were large by Bristol standards, but they serve to highlight the point that the really successful business owners (the likes of Wills, Fry, Hare and Thomas) did not invest in housing land. A further point here is that Bristol employers did not build

Sneyd Park House, home of James Derham, pictured in the 1930s.
(Courtesy: Peter Insole, Know Your Place)

Hampton Terrace, Redland, built in the 1840s on land owned by Benjamin Stickland.
(Photograph: the author)

houses specifically for their workers, although Thomas Baynton, the owner of the Ashton Gate Brewery, was an exception, almost certainly because of the isolated location of his business until the expansion of housebuilding in the area towards the end of the century.

William Vowles was a shrewd developer and landowner who started from humble origins in the village of Dundry and seems to have combined farming and property speculation as a route to capital accumulation. He farmed in Brislington but was involved in at least three property deals in Bristol, first in Pylle Hill (mentioned in chapter three), but also across the city in Woolcott Park and Durdham Park. At Pylle Hill he and Thomas Morgan, a builder, purchased, in February 1869, 30 acres of land on which they had held a lease since 1865, and on which they had already started to build houses (in Cambridge Street and Richmond Street).[8] This land had previously been bought at auction in 1853 for £4,840 and it was sold to Vowles and Morgan for £12,000. At the same time Vowles and Morgan took out a mortgage of £20,000 (presumably to give them some working capital). Later that same year Vowles bought out Morgan's share and proceeded to develop the area himself. He disposed of any interest in most of the land and houses there but retained the ownership of the annual rent charges on 235 houses, which generated an income of nearly £700. However, when he died in 1904 it was calculated that the capital value of his rent charges (including properties in other parts of Bristol) was £62,900, and his total estate was valued at £122,000.

At the same time as he was beginning his involvement with Pylle Hill Vowles was also party to an unusual deal at Woolcott Park, where the solicitor Edward Burges owned the land. In 1867 Burges agreed with Vowles, Morgan and another builder, James Rowe Shorland,[9] to grant them 10 acres for the trivial sum of 10 shillings per year for three years, but £310 in each subsequent year. At the end of 1870, however, Burges sold the remaining undeveloped land to Vowles and his collaborators for £1,307, but retained the rent charges on the houses already built. Vowles et al were then lucky enough to sell a small slice of the land, little more than an acre, to the company building the Clifton Extension Railway, for the sum of £3,420, thereby ensuring themselves a handsome profit. Later, in 1886, Vowles purchased what had been the garden of Redland House, Durdham Park, and collaborated with Shorland again to build four houses, one of which, Iddesleigh House, was his last home.

Given the diversity of landowners, any generalisations must be regarded as provisional and speculative, but it seems that the larger owners were more likely to be absentees, and to show rather less urgency about converting their land for housing development. The owners of smaller estates were more likely to be local and motivated to press ahead with development.

Builders

Housebuilders, on the other hand, were a more homogeneous group, not least in that they were all locally based – there was no such thing as an absentee builder. Builders were also uniformly working class, which is not to say that all builders were the same; most operated on a small scale, often a very small scale, and were famously prone to bankruptcy, but a few were able to establish large and enduring businesses.[10] One indicator of the precarious nature of building is that, as mentioned above, successful businessmen diversified into landownership, not building, whereas successful builders tended to diversify out of their industry. In the early Victorian period there was little demand for housebuilding and inevitably the majority of firms remained very small and ephemeral, even if they survived long enough to complete the houses they started. In Newtown in the period September 1851 to September 1852, for example, the building plan evidence suggests that seven landowners employed 32 different builders. James White, who was responsible for half the 92 plans submitted in the period, used 18 different builders, none of whom worked for any of the other landowners. In January 1852 White had to auction five unfinished houses, presumably because the builders had failed.[11] Moreover, 14 of the 18 builders working to develop White's land only submitted one set of plans in the year, and most built only one or two houses. Over 70 per cent of plans submitted were for just one or two houses, and none was for more than nine. At this time there were approximately 200 men listed as builders or carpenters in the local *Mathews's Directory*, but more than 80 per cent of the builders in Newtown were not listed.

It might be objected that an area like Newtown, where the houses were all small and simple structures, would attract small and insecure builders, and that elsewhere things would be different. In Clifton in the 1840s some very large houses were being built, presenting a much greater challenge to the builders. On the road now called the Promenade, but then known as Clifton Road, eight enormous houses were built, in pairs, starting in 1845. One pair was erected by William Baker, starting in 1850; he then went on, from 1853, to build four pairs of similarly huge houses on the nearby road now called Clifton Down. Baker was clearly a man of great ambition. Born in Bristol in 1820, he is first recorded as a slater, plasterer and painter in Trenchard Street

Cavenham House (now Tellisford House) and Trenmore House, Clifton Down, built by William Baker from December 1852 on land belonging to Francis Adams. (Photograph: the author)

in 1844 and it was obviously a big step up from there to building mansions in Clifton. By 1846 he had premises in Canon's Marsh and later documents refer to him as a builder from Canon's Marsh. He is said by Latimer to be the owner of the Sneyd Park estate from 1855, but this is incorrect, for Baker later leased plots of land (for example, in 1864)[12] for housebuilding from the owners, James Thomas Martin, of Weymouth, and Joseph John Martin, of Ham Court, Worcestershire. It is true, however, that in 1853 Baker had been involved with the Martins in securing a private Act of Parliament to enable houses to be built on the 220 acre estate, and he was certainly living there in 1861, when his address was given as Sneyd Park Villa, where he lived with his wife and seven children, together with four servants.[13] He was still there in 1871, a widower at the age of 51 with eight children, together with his elderly mother in law and three servants. He wrote on his census return that he was a builder employing 70 men and 8 boys.

William Baker must count as one of the most successful builders in Bristol between the late 1840s and the late 1870s, but his career ended sadly. He collaborated with James Derham to acquire the Montpelier estate, also owned by the Martin family and by 1873 in the hands of George E Martin. In 1871

Sneyd Park Villa (now The Well House), William Baker's house on Ivywell Road. (Photograph: the author)

Baker built the first row of houses to be erected on what became the St Andrew's estate, on North Road, but by 1878 he was suffering from mental health problems and was declared to be of unsound mind and removed to an asylum at Brislington. He died in 1882, but in 1881 James Derham and his brother Samuel paid Baker £10,250 for his fifty per cent share in the St Andrew's project.[14]

Other successful builders included William Coates, who built over 200 houses, mostly substantial semi-detached villas, in Clifton, Redland and Cotham. He was born in Devon in about 1816 but by 1851 he was a carpenter in Bristol, living in Edward Place, a street of small houses between Pennywell Road and Lawford's Gate in the parish of St Philip and St Jacob. His business success and upward social mobility can be measured in terms of the houses he built for his family to live in, first in 1851 in Picton Street, Montpelier, then in the late 1850s a larger semi-detached house on Cheltenham Road, where he also had a yard and workshop.

Another measure of Coates's success is that on his census return in 1861

Hebron Villa, Cheltenham Road, built by William Coates for himself in the late 1850s. (Photograph: the author)

he described himself as a builder employing 23 carpenters, 16 masons, 2 plasterers, 3 boys and 13 labourers. Ten years later he reported that he employed 59 men, and by that time he had built himself a substantial detached villa, Rockleigh, on a half-acre site on Redland Road (now occupied by the Elmgrove building of Cotham Gardens primary school). Over a number of years Coates built (or at least submitted plans for) 61 houses on the land being developed by Benjamin Stickland in west Redland. In most cases he submitted plans for two houses at a time, and never more than eight at a time. In 1865, after the death of James Evan Baillie, his trustees sold off land between the newly laid out Zetland Road and Cotham Brow, and Coates bought 6 acres 3 roods for £3640 (£539 per acre).[15] In addition he is known to have purchased at least two other parcels of land in this vicinity, but not all of it was to be developed by his own firm, for in 1868 he began disposing of plots in Eastfield Road to other builders. Unfortunately for his ambitions as a landowner and developer the Clifton Extension railway line was driven through his land in 1874, requiring the construction of a high embankment and substantially disrupting the planned layout of streets. Nevertheless, Coates was able to withstand this blow and by the time of his death in 1891 he had retired to Clevedon and was able to leave a personal estate valued at £7,537.

Across the city Henry J Rossiter carved out a similarly successful career, albeit concentrated on smaller houses, more than 90 per cent of which were in Bedminster. Rossiter was born in the Somerset village of Priddy in about 1850 and by 1881 he and his wife were at Draycott Villa, Victoria Terrace, having married at St Paul's church Bedminster in 1872. Analysis of the building plans submitted by Rossiter suggests that he began with 2 houses in Percy Street, Bedminster in October 1869 – when he was still a very young man. His business continued in a typically small way for several years, with plans for just 20 houses in ten years, but then in 1877 he submitted plans for 15 houses in one go, at Brook Street (this was behind what was then the Bedminster Tannery, and the whole street was demolished in the 1890s to allow expansion of Wills' tobacco factory). The peak period for Rossiter's business expansion was 1879-81 when he submitted plans for 50 houses. He managed to survive the collapse in demand in the early 1880s, although his output was much reduced for several years. He was more active again in the late 1880s but then throughout most of the next decade he built little. Over a career spanning more than thirty years Rossiter built more than 200 houses, but on only five occasions did he submit plans for more than 10 houses, and never more than 15. Towards the end of his working life he diversified his business; in 1896 he spent £15,000 buying land from the Ashton Court estate, and by 1901 *Wright's Directory* had him listed as a contractor, timber merchant and ironmonger, of West Street, Bedminster. By that date, however, he and his family had moved out of the city and were living in some style at the Grange, Bishopsworth. When he died in 1915 Rossiter left £24,544.

Andrew Brown provides an illustration of a different sort of successful builder: a manufacturer who diversified into land acquisition, housebuilding and landlordism. He was born in Whitechapel, London in 1810, but by 1841 he was in Bristol, living in West Street, Old Market with his wife Matilda and two small children. From 1844 he was listed as a 'wholesale dealer in Birmingham and Sheffield goods, book and print seller, varnished picture and Congreve match manufacturer'.[16] At the 1851 census he said he was the employer of 10 men, 27 boys and 26 girls in the match works, and this continued to be the family business, run by Andrew Brown junior from 1863. In his later years the father owned the Stapleton Road Tavern and his occupation on the 1871 census was given as licensed victualler. It seems that at no point did he refer to himself as a builder, although his widow did when she obtained probate after his death in 1873. What did she mean? What kind of builder was he?

Andrew Brown was different from most builders in that he appears to have had no personal experience of actual building work, but the description of his business interests, given above, suggests that he was a man prepared to turn his attention to more or less any opportunity to make money. In December 1851 Brown had submitted plans for six houses at the Rope Walk, Lawrence Hill, to be built on his own land. To be the landowner and the builder was decidedly unusual at the time. In January 1854 he submitted plans for 13 houses at Raglan Place, on Stapleton Road (opposite Armoury Square), again on his own ground. He had purchased from Jacob Strickland two small fields (511 and 512 on the tithe map), little more than an acre and a half, on which he built some of the houses and allowed others to build the rest. Altogether in his career Brown seems to have built at least 34 houses, all of them in the neighbourhood of Lawrence Hill and Stapleton Road, within a quarter of a mile of his last home. Builders living and working in the same area was the norm, but where Brown differed was that he also owned as many as 67 houses, according to the rating valuation survey of 1869. Some, for example those at Raglan Place, were houses he had built and probably kept in his ownership, but his property portfolio in 1869 was nearly three times as big as it had been seven years earlier.

To conclude this section there are two points to bring out. First, while it has been shown that builders tended to concentrate their activities within limited areas of the city, there was also a tendency to emphasise the breadth of work they were prepared to undertake. For instance, in 1872 Richard Dibbins of 31 St Augustine's Parade, advertised himself as a 'general builder, painter, glazier, slater and plasterer, estate and house agent'.[17] Second, as the century progressed a small number of builders were able to establish firms that were both larger and more robust over time than those that typified the industry in the middle of the period. The outstanding example is WH Cowlin and Son Ltd, which started in Milk Street in 1834 and grew into a firm that built many of Bristol's largest and most prominent building of the twentieth century, including the University's Wills Memorial Building and the three giant warehouses near the Cumberland Basin.[18]

The Professionals
Urban expansion in the nineteenth century created opportunities not only for landowners and builders but also for men with technical skills related to

property development, principally lawyers, architects and surveyors. It was in this period that these groups aimed to enhance their social standing by establishing professional bodies to represent their interests and to protect the public from unscrupulous practitioners: the Law Society was founded in 1823, the Institute of British Architects in 1834 and the Institution of Surveyors in 1868. Bristol architects set up their own local society in 1850, 'for the advancement of architectural knowledge…and for insuring an uniformity and respectability of practice in the profession'.[19] Although full membership of the society was open only to architects 'engaged as principals' for not less than three years (just thirteen men joined under this criterion in 1850), associate membership was, initially at least, open to 'engineers, surveyors, builders and other persons engaged in pursuits appertaining to building'. In this context it is interesting that *Mathews's Directory* had separate headings for surveyors and architects but there was considerable overlap in membership. As the century progressed, and as the market for professional services expanded, architects and surveyors worked to define exclusive areas of competence, but nevertheless in 1880 in Bristol there were still 13 names appearing in the lists of both groups.

In many cases fathers were joined by their sons and professional practices became long running family businesses. In architecture four generations of both Fosters and Popes designed buildings in Bristol throughout the nineteenth century. A less celebrated example was Henry Rumley, who was born in the Somerset village of Nunney in 1792. In 1806 he was apprenticed to a cabinet maker, and it is not known how he obtained his training as an architect, but he was entrusted with rebuilding the north side of Queen Square after the riots of 1831. He was briefly joined by his son, Henry Augustus, who sadly died young, but then Charles Rumley, his nephew, joined the firm and carried it on for two decades after the death of the first Henry Rumley in 1858.

In surveying the most prominent family firm was established in Bristol in 1799 by Jacob Sturge and his son, Young. This became Y and JP Sturge, working from offices at St James Barton from 1810, and subsequently John P Sturge and Sons of Corn Street.[20] A succession of Sturges held the post of land steward to the town council across the whole of the nineteenth century, as well as having the charge and management of a large extent of valuable property. In addition to managing property for clients the Sturges were involved in map making, including several of the tithe maps of the 1840s. Other well-known mapmakers and surveyors in Victorian Bristol

George Ashmead, surveyor and mapmaker lived at 3 Alma Vale Road until his death in 1895. His son Frederick, the City Surveyor, lived next door, in the house obscured by a later addition. (Photograph: the author)

included James Marmont, 15 Corn Street, who, for example, drew up a detailed map of the parish of Horfield in 1834,[21] and over many years provided plans and advice to the Merchant Venturers in relation to the development of their land in Clifton; and George Ashmead, 19 Small Street, whose son, Frederick, was the surveyor to the Sanitary Authority for nearly fifty years. On a small scale George Ashmead was also a landowner and developer: he bought land in Clifton where in the 1840s he developed Buckingham Vale and Alma Road, including houses for himself and his son at numbers 1 and 3 Alma Vale Road.[22]

The same pattern was found in the law. Jeremiah Osborne set up his practice in Bristol in 1748 and over the next century and a half successive generations worked closely with the chief power brokers in the city, including the Corporation, the Merchant Venturers, the Dock Company and the Great Western Railway.[23] Another dynasty of lawyers was the Burges family. The first Daniel Burges was involved in the law in Bristol in the 1770s and his son, also Daniel, served as city solicitor and later town clerk between 1822 and 1849. He had two sons who entered the law: yet another Daniel, who took over as town clerk from 1849 to 1874, and Edward who founded his own practice in 1841.[24] Daniel Travers Burges, son of Daniel III, served as town clerk from 1880 to 1900.

It was common, especially in the early Victorian period, for the town council to appoint private practitioners to provide essential services on a part-time basis. Or, looking at it from the other direction, private practitioners took such posts as a way of guaranteeing a steady flow of work and a set of influential contacts. These practitioners, therefore, had insider knowledge of the workings of the council and freedom to act on their own account, a situation that created the potential for corruption or at least conflicts of interest. For this reason the Bristol Society of Architects opposed the arrangement whereby under the terms of the Bristol Improvement Act, 1840, three district surveyors (prominent architects in the city: Richard S Pope, Samuel Fripp and William Armstrong) were appointed to part-time posts to inspect new buildings under construction (ostensibly on a weekly basis) while continuing as private practitioners. Armstrong died in 1858 but Pope and Fripp both remained in post until 1872, when the council at last reformed the system and appointed, Josiah Thomas as city surveyor.[25] Thomas described himself as a surveyor and architect and had his private office at the Athenaeum Chambers. From January 1873, however, as the city surveyor he worked from an office in Prince Street at the premises of the Local Board of Health. His appointment prompted the town council to go into a detailed explanation of his new role in relation to that of Frederick Ashmead, who had been the Local Health Board's surveyor since 1854 and was to continue in post until retirement in 1894. At one point in this explanation Ashmead was referred to as the Engineering Surveyor. Ashmead always defined himself as a civil engineer and he had overseen the construction of the city's sewerage system. However, it remains unclear how the two men divided their responsibilities on a day to day basis. The district surveyors were responsible for inspecting new buildings under the city Improvement Acts, but Ashmead's responsibilities included the building plans required by the Public Health Acts. The archives say nothing about how they dealt with the apparent overlap. After Ashmead's retirement in 1894 Thomas Yabbicom was appointed city engineer, and from Josiah Thomas's death in 1897 he became city surveyor as well.[26]

In 1841 the solicitor Edward Burges became clerk to the council's Improvement Committee, at the time when his father was town clerk. An

HOUSING PRODUCTION: THE KEY ACTORS

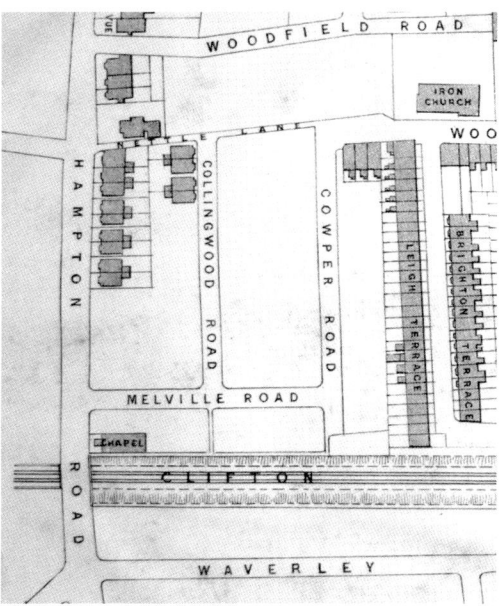

Streets in Woolcott Park, Redland. In 1876 William Hunt bought the field on which he built Cowper Road, Melville Road and Collingwood Road, together with houses facing Hampton Road. Melville Road was prevented from continuing eastwards through to Kensington Road by the recently built houses on the next field. (OS)

early example of this interest in property was that in 1841 he was the promoter of a plan to build a new street (Victoria Street) to ease congestion between Bristol Bridge and the new railway station at Temple Meads.[27] However, in 1866 he resigned as clerk to the Improvement Committee the day after a newspaper report implicated him in what was referred to as 'civic jobbery'. It was alleged that speculators had made up to £30,000 after being tipped off about properties the Improvement Committee was intending to buy. He was subsequently exonerated by a committee of councillors, but the incident must have caused embarrassment to his brother, who had succeeded their father as town clerk. He was, of course, the same Edward Burges referred to earlier in relation to the development of Woolcott Park where he was the landowner in the late 1860s.

Also involved in Woolcott Park was William Hunt, another solicitor who went into property development. He lived at Northcote House, Westbury-on-Trym, until his death in 1904, but acted as the developer of land in Redland and Baptist Mills, among other places. In Woolcott Park he purchased a field that had been part of an extensive area of nurseries, just to the west of the land owned by Burges. Here he became involved in a dispute with the town council over the widening of Nettle Lane, now Chandos Road. In June 1876 the council paid Hunt £250 for a tiny patch of ground to help create a circuitous carriage route westwards to Hampton Road via Collingwood Road and Melville Road, but less than a year later the council agreed to buy and demolish two newly built houses on Hunt's land to make possible a direct route.[28]

Before leaving the professionals it is worth noting that they tended to work from city centre offices but lived in the suburbs, unlike the much more numerous housebuilders who generally lived and worked in the same area. There were always a lot more lawyers than architects and surveyors, and it is highly likely that none of them relied on housing work for the viability of their practices. Looking at it from a different perspective, lawyers played a pivotal part in the changes of ownership of land and property, initially verifying the vendor's claim to ownership and then conveying title to the new owner, and surveyors were involved in the marking out of land for development but it is much less clear to what extent housing production generated work for architects. This is a subject explored further in the following chapter.

To conclude, in introducing some of the cast of characters involved in building houses in Victorian Bristol the discussion has inevitably been almost exclusively about men, reflecting their dominance in property ownership and related activities. It has also been largely about the owners of land and businesses of various kinds; the workers who actually dug into the ground and laboured to build houses that they could scarcely afford to rent let alone buy are no less deserving of attention but are harder to rescue from obscurity.

CHAPTER FIVE

The Housebuilding Process

The majority of houses built in Bristol in the nineteenth century were constructed according to a set of conventions that differed from most other places in England. In some towns, including London, as professor Dyos revealed in his study of Camberwell, it was usual practice to establish relatively short leases, of up to 99 years, after which the land reverted to the original owner or his/her successor.[1] Other places had a freehold tradition. But in Bristol houses were almost always freehold, or very long leasehold (999 or 1000 years), but with a perpetual annual rent charge of a few pounds (sometimes less than £2, rarely more than £20, depending on the size and location of the house). In this system landowners did not receive any money at the point of conversion but they were entitled to a fixed annual income from their land, for ever. Entitlement to rent charges could be bought and sold, much like stocks and shares.

Most houses built in and around Bristol in the Victorian period were erected on previously undeveloped agricultural land. The conversion of such land into streets and houses inevitably began with a decision by the landowner, or their advisers. Absentee landowners such as Thomas Fremantle must have relied on local professional advice and assistance. Sir Greville Smyth of Ashton Court was close to the city but he employed a full-time estate manager, Thomas Dyke, and also took advice from local surveyors. In an illuminating passage from a report to Smyth in 1866 he was advised that:

> Building land may be disposed of in larger lots by wholesale, or in smaller lots by retail. The latter is the mode of realizing most money but it involves the constant attention of an agent in Bristol, large outlay on Roads and Sewers, and advances of money either by the Vendor or his Solicitor to Builders on mortgage of their unfinished houses. A Sale in large lots will not realise on the average more than half the ultimate proceeds, but the risk, expense and delay of a sale in small Lots is thereby avoided, and on the whole we think it the better course to adopt in the present case [ie, in Bedminster].[2]

In the event, the Smyth estate tried both approaches, although the initial response to the report was to continue to assemble sites rather than to promote housebuilding. It was not until 1882 that George Ashmead was paid ten guineas to draw up a layout plan for the area then proposed to be known as Greville Town, between Southville and Ashton Gate. The plots were then offered to local builders on a retail basis. However, development was very slow and in 1896 the estate switched to a wholesale approach, selling land in larger parcels to be developed by others, including Henry Rossiter, as mentioned in the previous chapter. Another Bedminster builder to take advantage of the sale of Smyth land in the 1890s was William Kingston, who purchased more than twenty acres.

Development had to begin with a judgement about the right time to build, and of course it was not always easy to make that decision. This is well illustrated by reference to the development of the former Armoury site on Stapleton Road in the 1840s, at a time when it was largely surrounded by fields. In 1805 the small site, just 1 acre 2 roods, had been sold to the government Ordnance Office and then transferred to the Bristol Poor Law guardians in 1831 before being sold for housing in the 1840s. It was acquired in 1841 by a Rev Francis Edgeworth for £2,000 and two years later he borrowed £1,000 from the ubiquitous Edward Burges, at the same time covenanting to build eight houses. The terms of the loan required repayment, plus interest of 4.5 per cent, by February 1844. When Edgeworth failed to repay the loan Burges invoked his right to take possession of the land, which he then sold to two builders, George Wilkins and William Honeycombe, who were financed by John Whittington and Charles Castle, gentlemen, on terms similar to those between Edgeworth and Burges, and with a repayment date of September 1846. Wilkins and Honeycombe refinanced in July 1845 via a loan of £1,662 from Matthew Scott (chaplain in the Royal Artillery, Woolwich) and George Scott (captain in the 76th regiment of foot). Whether any houses were as yet under construction is hard to say, but in January 1846 Honeycombe must have seen the wisdom of pulling out for he sold his half share to Wilkins for just £337, which Wilkins financed with a further loan from the Scotts. Success was still hard to achieve and by July 1848 the Scotts were in possession, Wilkins having defaulted on his loans. The Scotts sold the site to George Burges (brother of Edward) for £2,300 (the amount of the outstanding loans), and he made an agreement with James Bridges to build three houses within twelve months. By the time of the 1851 valuations survey there were 15 unoccupied houses,[3] and Ashmead's map of about 1855 shows 42

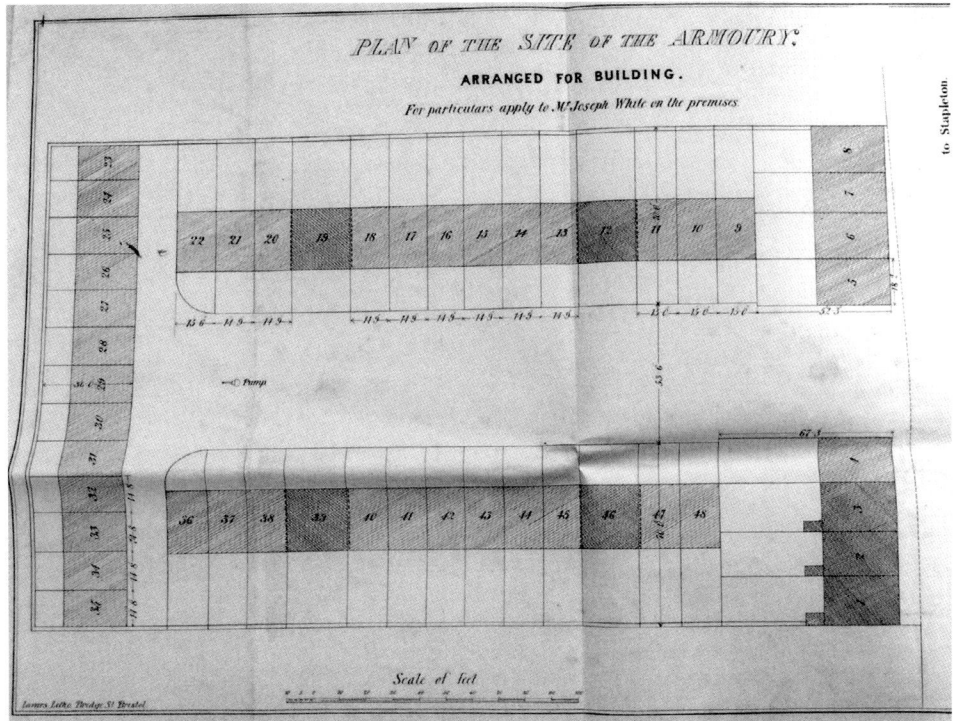

Block plan for the development of Armoury Square, 1848. (Courtesy: Bristol Archives)

One side of Armoury Square in 1966. (Courtesy: Bristol Region Building Record)

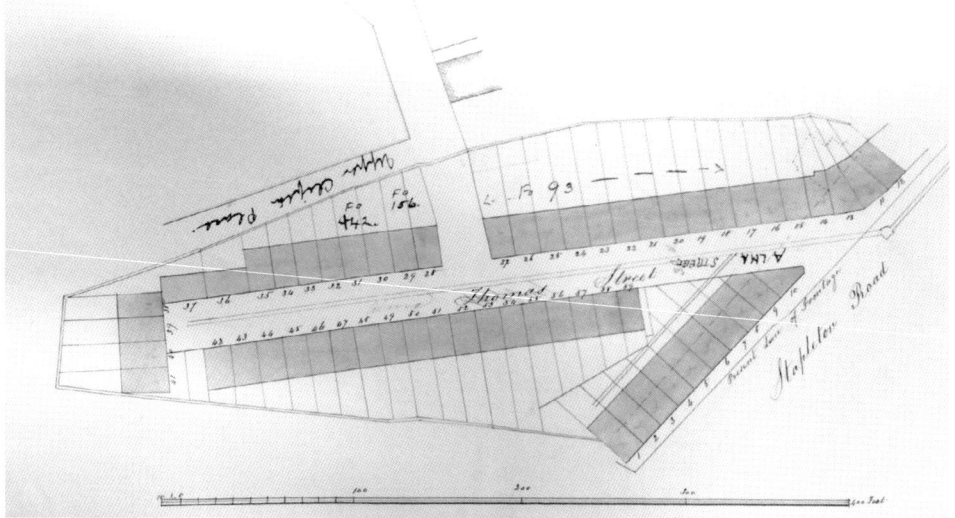

Andrew Brown's layout plan for houses on the opposite side of Stapleton Road from Armoury Square, 1854. (Courtesy: Bristol Archives)

houses on the site. It is certain that Edgeworth lost money on the Armoury, and so too did Wilkins and Honeycombe, but the money lenders seem to have survived unscathed.

Rather more successfully timed was the development of part of the Redland Court estate on the other side of the city. Here in 1865 the trustees of the late James Evan Baillie sold 32 acres between Cotham Brow and the newly laid out Zetland Road. The auctioneers, Messrs Alexander and Daniel, promoted the sale in the local press:

> The property now offered for sale affords to large and small capitalists, builders or others an opportunity seldom met with, of acquiring freehold building land close to the City of Bristol; and as building land is in great demand at the present time, there can be no doubt that by a judicious laying out of the land for building, a large profit may be realised by purchasers.[4]

One of those who took advantage of the chance to develop this land was the builder William Coates, who bought one lot in the auction and certainly acquired other sites in the vicinity at that time. It turned out that the late 1860s was a busy time for housebuilders, with new houses being built at more than three times the rate in the late 1850s to early 1860s (chapter three).

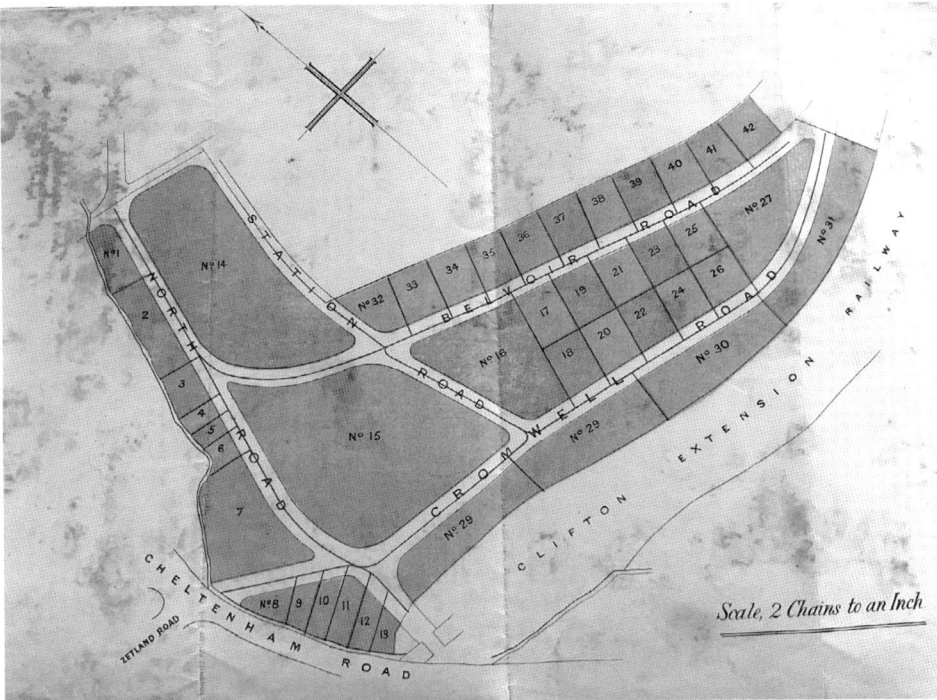

Layout plan for the first part of the St Andrew's estate, 1873. (Courtesy: Bristol Archives)

Once it had been decided to go ahead with a development the next step was to draw up what was commonly referred to as a block plan, showing the layout of the proposed roads and the boundaries of individual numbered plots. Most of these have not survived, but we know that some of them covered several hundred plots, and they have had a lasting impact on the urban landscape. Block plans also determined the sorts of houses to be built, for if the plan indicated narrow plots then terraced houses became inevitable. This was definitely the case on Andrew Brown's little development on Stapleton Road, where the plan indicated no fewer than 59 houses on a site of not much more than an acre and a half.

Landowners had to decide the terms on which land would be developed, and sometimes they would appear to test the market and/or the commitment of developers by initially agreeing a lease and only later conveying the freehold. This was what happened at Pylle Hill in the 1860s, when the land was leased, building began and only then, five years later, the freehold was sold. Something similar happened at St Andrew's in the 1870s. In 1873 the Montpelier estate was inherited by George Martin from his uncle Joseph Martin, who has previously been mentioned as the owner of the Sneyd Park estate and who had begun to work with William Baker, the builder, and James Derham, the investor, on the first phase of development at Montpelier. Initially 17 acres with a frontage on Cheltenham Road was leased to Derham and Baker for 1000 years, for £194 per annum in rent charges derived from plots already marked out on a plan which also showed the proposed roads. The plans attached to the agreements between Martin, Derham and Baker are interesting in that they were clearly marked out in numbered plots, but in most cases these did not refer to individual house plots.

Baker and Derham undertook to make the roads within three years and to spend £14,160 by January 1880 on good and substantial houses of between £300 and £360 each.[5] Two further tracts of land, of 19 acres 3 roods and 18 acres 1 rood, were leased on broadly the same terms in 1876 and 1877, with the final 22 acres 2 roods being sold to Derham in 1884, after Baker's death. Thus Derham acquired the freehold of the entire estate, but building proceeded slowly and the development was completed by his son, Henry, and nephew Walter, with the last houses being built after the end of the century. Curiously, the first building plans were submitted by William Baker to the town council in 1872, before the start of the first lease in January 1873, but it seems that Baker did not build any other houses in the area. Instead he and Derham relied on many other builders to take plots; in Belmont Road, for example, 16 different builders were involved over a 15-year period between 1874 and 1889.

Developers invited builders to take as many plots as they felt they could manage. It was usual for the plots to be taken in small numbers, between one and four, rarely more than ten, and for no money to be paid. A good example is provided by the development of a field of 5 acres 2 roods developed by William Hunt at Woolcott Park, Redland in the late 1870s. In the period October 1877 to August 1879 Hunt, granted just over 100 plots to 26 different builders none of whom took more than 4 at a time. There were 46 grants involving 1 or 2 plots, 11 for 3 and 1 for 4.[6] The question then arises as to how builders decided what sort of houses were appropriate. In the case of Hunt's field, the plots were very narrow, which had a constraining effect, inevitably producing terraced houses. The grand terraces in Clifton were designed as a whole, providing the builders of individual houses with ample guidance, at least as far as the front elevation was concerned. Elsewhere landowners rarely went into detail about the houses to be built, limiting themselves to generalisations such as 'good and substantial' houses of a specified minimum value to be complete in a 'workmanlike manner'. However, some developers were more prescriptive and in 1877 Bishop Monk's Horfield Trustees appointed RS Pope as their architect with authority to accept or reject plans put forward by builders, and two years later they decided that all plans and elevations should be submitted to themselves for approval.[7] The trustees of the Forlorn Hope estate went further and produced a standard lease specifying that houses should be completed within a set period 'to the satisfaction of the Churchwardens for the time being or their Surveyor, and according to plans and elevations previously submitted to and approved in writing by such Surveyor'.[8] The agreement went on to specify the materials that should be used for the construction, and the minimum value of the finished houses. In a different part of the market the Society of Merchant Venturers also paid close attention to the quality of building allowed on its land, and the Society's archives contain some beautiful illustrations, but it is probably safe to assume that individual landowners were not always so assiduous.

The question of who, if anyone, actually designed the majority of Victorian houses is not easily answered, although at the upper end of the market it is often possible to identify the architect responsible,[9] and existing architectural histories of Bristol are useful in that context.[10] Some of the grandest houses dating from the middle of the century were built on land belonging to Francis Adams overlooking the Avon Gorge and 'commanding an uninterrupted view of Leigh Woods' (today completely obscured by trees). An advertisement in the *Bristol Mercury*, 1 June 1844, stated that the plans and elevations could be viewed at the offices of Foster and Son, Park Street. It went on to say that 'the design now proposed…will afford favourable opportunities for the investment of capital, and speculations by builders'. This revealed not only the name of the architect but also that the design was commissioned by the landowner, not the builder or the people intending to live in the houses.

In another part of Clifton at the same time the Society of Merchant Venturers was engaged in developing what became Victoria Square. The Society had already sold the land on the north east side to a Samuel Hemmings, who had built a fine terrace, Lansdown Place, the design of which has also been attributed to the architects Foster and Son. The Society's surveyor, James Marmont, produced several possible layouts for the space in front of the new terrace, including some that ignored its existence.[11] He is also credited with the design of Royal Promenade, on the north west side of the square, and again it was the landowner that commissioned the design of

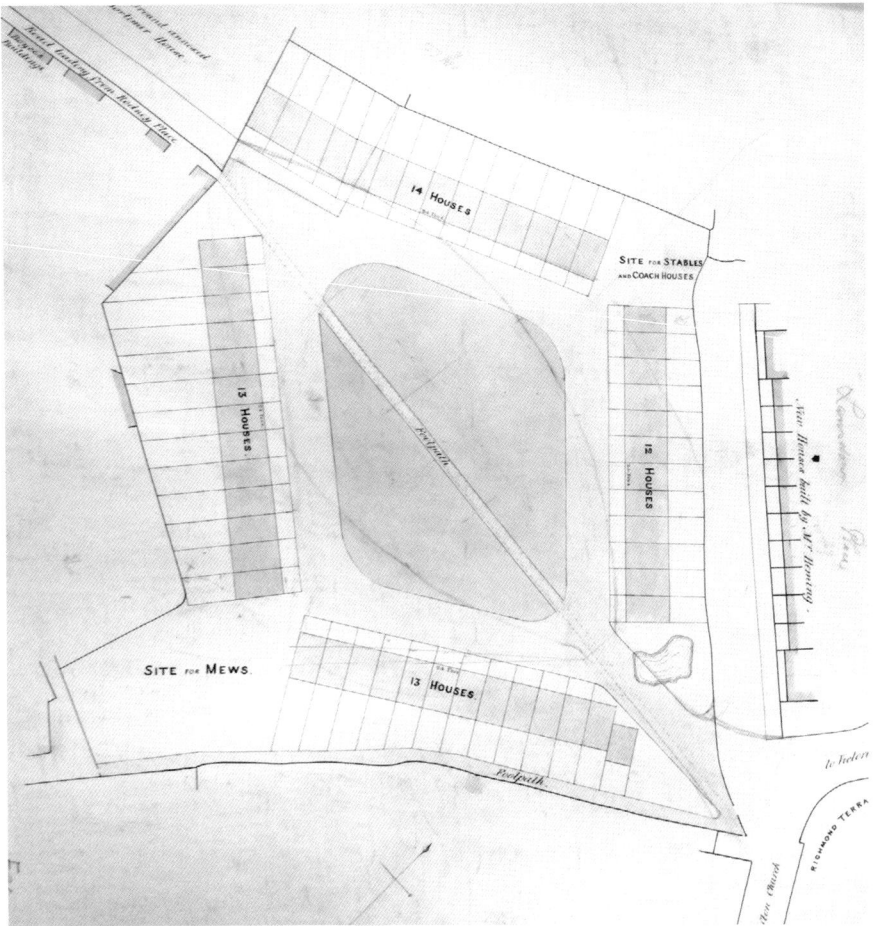

One of James Marmont's ultimately rejected plans for Victoria Square, Clifton, showing Samuel Hemming's pre-existing Lansdown Place to the right.
(Courtesy: Bristol Archives)

houses built as speculations. However, even at this end of the market, design input was lavished on the front elevations (which are also the exclusive concern of later architectural historians), leaving much of the rest of the structure to be sorted out by the builder.

It seems certain that architects had minimal involvement with housing in general,[12] although there is convincing evidence that they did produce many of the building plans now in the Bristol Archives. One architect whose name appears on building plans in the 1850s was Henry Rumley, of whom it has been written that he 'certainly built large numbers of cottages in a minimal Georgian manner in Bedminster and Southville; others are reported in the

Easton area'.[13] It is true that Rumley drew and signed a lot of building plans but whether he contributed any real design input is much less clear, especially given that Rumley put his name to plans only, with no sign of elevations, sections or details. Only a minority of building plans were actually signed by architects or surveyors but all were produced by people skilled in scale drawing. It is tempting to say that the majority of houses were not designed, merely built, but that would be unfair to the builders faced with the task of deciding what to do on any particular plot. The form, appearance and method of construction of houses continued to be heavily influenced by tradition and by what builders saw going on around them. The more successful builders tended to develop a recognisable style of their own. William Coates and Richard Cosslett both worked in Redland and Clifton at more or less the same time, yet their houses are obviously different from each other. Having said that, builders did not own their preferred designs and very similar looking houses were produced by different builders across the city. Coates and Cosslett generally built semi-detached villas, which allowed a degree of freedom to determine the appearance, but in the case of working-class housing, where narrow fronted terraced houses continued to dominate throughout the period, there was little scope for innovative design, and less money to pay for it.

The housebuilding process loaded the risks onto the builder, who had to find the labour and materials, and raise the money to pay for them. On completion it was necessary to find a buyer, not least in order to repay debts incurred during the construction phase. Labour was usually readily available, and cheap, as demonstrated by Robert Tressell in his book *The Ragged Trousered Philanthropists*, whose cast of skilled and unskilled workers employed in the building trade were lucky to earn more than 6d an hour, or 24s a week for 48 hours work.[14] In 1884 it was said that wages in Bristol were very low, with labourers prepared to work for 2s-6d per day, much less than £1 per week.[15]

Houses are expensive products to make: they require land, large amounts of raw and processed materials, and a lot of labour over a prolonged period of time. The basic structure of Victorian houses was not particularly complicated, with load bearing walls made of brick or stone, while internal walls were often derived from traditional timber construction with a covering of laths and plaster. Where possible materials were obtained from the immediate locality, but clay had to be fashioned into bricks and then fired in kilns; stone had to be quarried and dressed, at least to some extent. Roof tiles, like bricks, had to be moulded and fired; slate was a possible alternative, but that had to be brought in from a distance. Much of the timber for the roof, stairs, floorboards and window frames had to be imported from abroad and then sawed, planed and turned into shape. Then there was glass, plaster, paint, ironware, leadwork and ceramics to be purchased and fitted. All this inevitably took many men months to bring to fruition, even in the case of a small house, and then, ideally, it needed to be left to dry out for some time before being occupied.

Stone quarries were to be found in many places around Bristol, including the Downs and the Avon Gorge and there were also brickworks at Malago Vale, Bedminster, and St Philip's Marsh. If they were lucky builders found they could quarry stone and/or brick clay actually on their building sites, but they were not permitted to transport such materials to other sites. Firing clay to make bricks was a process producing much smoke pollution and understandably people living nearby objected to it; in July 1869, during a boom in housebuilding, residents in Woolcott Park complained to the Local Board of Health about brick burning close to their homes on the grounds that the bricks were not solely for use in building on the land there.[16] In 1864, James Shorland had to admit to the SMV that he had breached the terms of his agreement and sold stone quarried from his plots on Beaufort Road to the developers of All Saints church, just round the corner on Pembroke Road.[17] Of course not everything could be sourced from the immediate vicinity; timber in particular was imported from abroad in large amounts (and became one of the staples of the port of Bristol), but other components such as ceramics came from the Staffordshire potteries. Today building firms are engaged in a process that is mainly about assembling factory made components, the chief exception being mortar mixed on site. In the Victorian period builders also relied upon others to produce items such as window glass, cast iron fire grates and joinery items such as doors, window frames and sawn and turned timber. One such successful and long lasting firm was C Jennings and Co. of Pennywell Road, founded in 1878, specialist suppliers of all sorts of woodwork.

However, Victorian builders were much more likely to employ men and boys to saw raw timbers and to fashion their own window frames, staircases and so on. William Veals, who built houses in Redland in the 1890s, described himself as a 'manufacturer of every description of joinery work'.[18] WH Cowlin and Son claimed in 1893 to stock

> great stores of building materials and appliances of all sorts…In the carpenters' shop a large staff of highly skilled workmen are constantly engaged in making window sashes, frames, doors and other requisites for building operations.[19]

In the same promotional publication TW Aspinall, builder and general contractor, Nelson Parade, Bedminster, referred to his saw mill, mortar yard and recently acquired North Street brick and tile works covering 3-4 acres and capable of producing 50,000 bricks per week. And W Galbraith referred to his heavy stocks of building materials and 'the best Staffordshire drain pipes and other sanitary appliances'. He was also the proprietor of quarries at several locations around the city, all producing what he said was first class pennant stone.

One of the problems facing the individual small builder on a day to day basis was how to pay for labour and materials well in advance of any possibility of selling the finished house. Nowadays undercapitalised builders rely on bank overdrafts and credit cards, but then they had to hope that their suppliers would extend lines of credit. Working capital was just as much, if not more, a problem for builders at the top of the market, where big houses necessarily took longer to complete, and where it was difficult to sell houses in yet to be finished grand terraces, such as those in Victoria Square. In the 1840s and '50s, when the Society of Merchant Venturers was engaged in the prolonged process of developing Victoria Square, the builder William Reed borrowed £15,000 from the Society to finance his part of the work. In June 1866 John Yalland wrote to say that he had been unable to sell the six houses he had built in the Square, and moreover, he could not afford to complete the other six houses for which he was under contract. The Society agreed to lend him a further £3,000, and by November 1866 it is recorded that six houses in Victoria Square were leased to Yalland for 1000 years, from 24 June 1863.[20] It was normal practice for the Society to backdate the start of leases by up to four years, to either Lady day (25 March) or Michaelmas (29 September), indicating the formal start of building work and highlighting how long it took to bring houses to completion.

In the twentieth century building societies became closely associated with financing home ownership, but in the nineteenth century they also helped builders pay for construction. In 1876 George Hart, of Hope Terrace, St Nicholas Road, borrowed £180 from the Hand in Hand Building Society, for a house he was building nearby at St Lawrence Street, Newfoundland Gardens. The Society agreed to pay £80 initially and the balance on completion of the building work, which was already well advanced.[21] Another example, from Redland in the 1890s, illustrates both how building was funded and confirms that prolonged building time was not just associated with very large houses. In July 1892 William Veals submitted plans for six houses to be built in Salisbury Road (numbers 6 to 16); the deeds for number 8, dated December 1892, refer to the house being in course of erection and specify completion by 25 March 1894, at which point the rent charge would become due. Veals borrowed £385 as a privately arranged mortgage from a Mrs Alice Mariette, of Leicester, to enable him to erect number 8, which he later, in June 1895, sold for £525. Thus it was three years before Mr Veals saw any return on his investment.[22] One reason for long construction periods was that the building industry remained unmodernised, retaining traditional labour intensive craft based practices, in marked contrast to the technological innovations then being developed in other industries. Another reason was the amount of plaster work that needed to dry out thoroughly before a house was ready for occupation.[23]

Private mortgages, such as the one arranged by William Veals, seem to have been quite common. Another example from the same period in St Andrew's involved £350 being lent by a Mrs Margaret Chrystal of Claremont Road to the builder Charles Bond who was building 9 and 10 Burghley Road, which pair of houses he sold for £800 on completion in 1897.[24] Sometimes, as in this case, lenders were local people with capital to be invested, but not always, as revealed by Veals's lender living in Leicester. Often, as Gilmore Barnett told the Royal Commission on the Housing of the Working Class in 1884, solicitors were the brokers of such arrangements,[25] but people also advertised in local newspapers that they had money to invest on mortgage.[26] A rather different approach was adopted by William Hunt, mentioned above in connection with Woolcott Park. He lent his builders small sums, typically £60 at a time, as 'equitable mortgages'.[27] This is not to imply that all builders relied on small loans: William Kingston, for example, built more than a hundred houses in Bedminster in the latter part of the century, and as his business grew he was able, in 1893, to borrow £2,500 by mortgaging houses already built.[28]

Conclusion

The chapter has looked at the building process as a sequence of opportunities and challenges. The demand for houses was an opportunity for successful businessmen to invest some of their spare capital, for apart from owners who had inherited their land the main group of developers seems to have consisted of people – lawyers, grocers, boot-makers and so on – for whom it was a sideline, an afterthought, or a retirement project. There is little or no evidence that 'housing developer' was a career in itself, unlike house builder. Housing development was an opportunity for those who were already financially secure, whereas being a house builder was a role associated with high levels of risk and insecurity. While housebuilding was transforming the extent and appearance of the city, it remained a craft based industry, rooted in tradition and consisting of a multitude of small and often ephemeral enterprises. Although a number of firms grew in size and managed to survive the rigours of a notoriously cyclical industry, none compared with the successful manufacturers of consumer goods such as cigarettes, chocolate and footwear. These consumer industries expanded rapidly in the last third of the century, and the rate of housebuilding also increased in that period, but the point has been made above that houses did not spring out of the ground as quickly as is sometimes suggested.[29]

CHAPTER SIX

The Houses and their Settings

It might seem that Victorian houses are easy to identify, and they often are, not least because of the stylistic differences between the Georgian and Regency periods preceding Victoria's accession and the rise of modernism in the early twentieth century. It has been argued, particularly by Donald Olsen, that, 'Nothing can have been more conscious and deliberate than the Victorian reaction against all that it thought the eighteenth century stood for. The Victorian city displayed its rejection of and contempt for the Georgian city not merely in its architecture but in its total layout'.[1] Similarly, the twentieth century witnessed a reaction to and rejection of visual and functional aspects of the Victorian city. It might also seem that there was a wide diversity of houses built in the Victorian period, given that, 'The new Victorian aesthetic sought variety as an end in itself: in form, colour, texture, size and in intellectual and emotional content'.[2] However, it will be argued in this chapter that continuity and similarity were just as important as change and variety. This is based partly on the simple point that the dates of Victoria's reign have no particular relevance and partly on the observation that much change was more apparent than real, in the sense that while the external appearance of new buildings changed, what lay behind was often very similar to, or derived from, what had come before.

A theme of this chapter is that it is necessary to see houses in the context of the neighbourhoods within which they stood. Chapter three hinted at the difference between working-class areas that were essentially urban in character and the middle-class residential areas that constituted a new kind of suburb. The working-class areas in south and east Bristol were, on this view, urban in terms of both the form of the dwellings and the layout and character of the surrounding neighbourhoods. It will be shown that working-class houses displayed considerable continuity of form and layout over time. Middle-class houses, by contrast, underwent a genuine and enduring change in terms of design and internal arrangement, and it is impossible to understand the Victorian detached or semi-detached villa apart from the exclusively residential character of the suburbs in which they stood. The chapter takes it to be axiomatic that there was a basic distinction between urban and suburban forms: the characteristic urban form was narrow fronted houses built in rows, or terraces, opening straight (or almost straight) off the street. The predominant suburban form was wider fronted detached or, more often, semi-detached villas invariably with a front garden of more than just token proportions.

Over time, of course, fashions and preferences changed, and so early and late Victorian houses, both urban and suburban, can be readily distinguished from each other, as this chapter will demonstrate. It will also show that the majority of houses built in Bristol during the period as a whole either conformed to or were variants of just a few basic house types. Having said that, at the start of the Victorian period there was already a wide variety of dwellings, accumulated over a long period. At one end of the spectrum were the eighteenth-century mansions around the parish church of St Andrew in Clifton, while at the other end there were one room hovels, built literally back to back in the inner parishes, for example off Redcross Street and Temple Street, and there were the self-built single storey huts of Newfoundland Gardens.

The Early Victorian Housing Stock

In the early 1840s there were about 18,000 houses in Bristol,[3] although almost a decade later it was estimated that there were, 'about 635 streets, 506 courts and lanes, 14 squares and about 23,000 houses'.[4] New building typically makes only marginal additions to the existing supply of houses in any town; in Bristol in the early 1850s, the first period for which it is possible to make a reasonably accurate estimate, the increase was only about one per cent per year, and therefore it was only in the latter decades of the century that a majority of people occupied genuinely Victorian houses. According to Lobel and Carus-Wilson, 'it is probable that [in the sixteenth and seventeenth centuries] the centre of the medieval city was largely rebuilt'[5] and they also suggest that 'Many Elizabethan and Stuart houses remained until the nineteenth century as witnesses to the architectural splendour of the time.'[6] Harvey, writing in the early twentieth century, noted that,

> Until quite recently, Bristol possessed a singular wealth of high-gabled half-timber houses and picturesque streets, and resembled the quaint old-world towns of northern Germany or Normandy rather than a prosaic English commercial town. It consisted of a central portion of houses of the earlier part of the seventeenth century, with here and there among them a house of earlier date...'.[7]

Seventeenth-century timber-framed houses at 1-5 King Street, in about 1930.
(Courtesy: Herbert Tarring collection)

Old timber-framed houses in East Street, Bedminster, 1870.
(Courtesy: George Elliott collection, Bristol Archives)

Eighteenth-century elite migration away from the central area resulted in greater variety; on the one hand, the new houses built on the advancing urban frontier in places such as Queen Square and later Brunswick Square and Portland Square not only added to the stock of large houses but also introduced new layouts, designs and materials. This is vividly illustrated by comparing the high gables and timber frames of late seventeenth-century houses on King Street with the brick and stone houses of Queen Square, just around the corner but built forty years later. On the other hand, as the elite abandoned the central area opportunities emerged for the gardens and spaces behind the street frontage to be more intensively developed into long, narrow courts of small dwellings, just one room deep but up to three storeys in height. Such ill-ventilated and insanitary courts, teeming with the urban poor, were a feature of Bristol much commented on in the reports of mid-nineteenth-century health reformers.

Plans of some of these courts are to be found in Roger Leech's book on medieval and early modern town houses in Bristol, a book that is essential reading for an understanding of both what the pre-Victorian housing stock consisted of and the extent of continuity and change in the subsequent period.[8] Amongst much else he shows that,

> From the 1740s onwards, new developments of houses for artisans were largely small, two-room deep houses. As in London the one-room plan was less acceptable by the end of the eighteenth century; artisans' aspirations were now set higher.[9]

Leech also suggests that the typical narrow fronted terraced house of the Victorian period was derived from the earlier form that he calls the shophouse, that is, a house built above and behind a one room shop facing onto the street. The room that would have been the shop became the front parlour.

The architectural historian Andor Gomme observed that, 'Until about 1840 almost everyone living in Bristol, as in every other city in the country, lived in a terraced house of some sort'.[10] This was true, but of course there was an immense difference in the size of houses occupied by people according to their position in society and their ability to pay. It is also important to distinguish between houses that were merely contiguous with those on either side, which was the majority case, and those that were part of a true terrace. Houses in continuous rows were, and are, the characteristic urban form; this was how towns developed, with houses close-built and opening straight off

Royal York Crescent looking west, showing stables beneath the raised walkway. (Courtesy: Bristol Archives, PicBox/2/BSt/49)

the street. Later, when purely residential streets emerged the houses were sometimes separated from the pavement by a small enclosed area, with steps down to the basement. Examples from early-eighteenth-century Bristol included Queen Square and Orchard Street. Both Queen Square and Orchard Street were accumulations of individual houses, slightly different one from another, but a true terrace was designed as a coherent whole, and stood on a raised pavement, the terrace, as exemplified in extreme form by Royal York Crescent, where the walkway is at least ten feet above the level of the road. Both Lansdown Place and Vyvyan Terrace were designed as complete entities in the sense that they were not simply rows of similar houses, indeed the individual houses were subordinated to the overall design, and the end houses were designed, as Gomme says, as independent villa fronts, pieces of architecture in their own right.[11] See also Vyvyan Terrace pictured in chapter one.

To reinforce the point that terraced houses were aimed at the middle class, here is an advertisement from 1854 for number 1 Apsley Place, off Whiteladies Road:

> This desirable dwelling house commands delightful and extensive prospects, and stands almost unequalled for salubrity of air and beauty of position. Its frontage is noble, and its interior arrangement excellent. It is entered through a noble hall which leads to a capital dining room, with sitting room adjoining. A substantial stone staircase, with iron balustrade, conducts to a large size drawing room with another adjoining. There is as

Victoria Square in about 1855, showing Royal Promenade on the left and Lansdown Place on the right. (Courtesy: Peter Insole, Know Your Place)

water closet on this floor. Above are seven good dormitories with closets. The offices, including china pantry, are extensive and convenient, affording every accommodation for a respectable family.[12]

True terraces were never part of the working-class experience, and what we commonly refer to as terraced houses in working-class areas were actually just rows of houses. True terraces were built for the upper reaches of the Bristol housing market for only about a century, between 1740 and 1850,[13] after which the middle class discovered the advantages of the detached or semi-detached suburban villa.

As mentioned, terraced houses could be large or small, although almost all were built on a narrow footprint. In working-class areas the standard width was 16 feet, but even much larger houses, such as those in Worcester Terrace, were no more than 20 feet wide. Terraced houses for the better off were not only narrow but also tall, normally on three or four storeys, plus a basement, and sometimes with an attic floor for the servants' quarters. In such houses the kitchen was located in the basement, along with the wine cellar and the

Woolcott Street, Redland, standard plan terraced houses from the 1850s.
(Photograph: the author)

St Paul's Road, Clifton (previously Victoria Park Road) terraced houses
built in the late 1840s on land owned by Francis Adams.
(Photograph: the author)

South Parade, off Whiteladies Road, built in 1845 on land owned by Francis Adams. (Photograph: the author)

housekeeper's room. However, the terraced form did constrain the internal layout of the house, in particular requiring the entrance door to be located on the street facing façade and the circulation space was generally aligned with the long axis, running from front to back. Back lanes were not common in Bristol, which meant that access to the back garden or yard was through the house, with unpleasant implications when the cess pit was being emptied.

While it is true that most people in 1840 lived in terraced houses, there were already signs of increasing demand for suburban villas standing in their own grounds. At that time this was if anything more apparent in Redland than Clifton, but as mentioned in the previous chapter William Baker and others were soon at work on new mansions between the zoo and the as yet unfinished suspension bridge.[14] And George Ashmead was pioneering the development of large Italianate villas on his land at Gallows Acre Lane (Pembroke Road).[15] It was a period of change and transition, with landowners such as Francis Adams in Clifton building both terraces and mansions at the same time. A further sign of transition from urban to suburban forms is that some large terraced houses, such as Burlington Buildings in Redland, were provided with both a railed-off front area (giving light and access to the

Seven-bedroomed detached house at 26 Victoria Square, built in about 1870 by John Davies, of Lower Redland Road, on land owned by the Society of Merchant Venturers. This beautifully drawn and coloured elevation was produced simply to illustrate the proposed porch. (Courtesy: Bristol Archives)

basement) and, that quintessentially suburban characteristic, a front garden. In a different way the Merchant Venturers' Victoria Square also epitomises the transition, with the first three sides being terraces and the delayed fourth side consisting of villas. Before long the middle-class preference for detached and semi-detached houses came to dominate supply in the new suburbs.

The housing stock in early Victorian Bristol, then, was highly varied in age, size, design, materials and method of construction, reflecting the durability of ancient structures and a natural preference for retaining buildings that were of enduring utility and expensive to replace. Gradually, as Leech has documented, ideas about what was desirable in a house changed. For the middle class the demise of the terrace reflected not just a rejection of the Georgian terrace but also its setting: whereas the true terrace, with its colonnades and pediments, overlooking a communal square, subordinated the houses to the overall architectural conception, the suburban villa set in its own grounds celebrated individuality and privacy.[16] For the workers, however, the terraced form prevailed.

The Standard Plan Terraced House and its Variants

Pre-Victorian working-class houses in Bristol are now vanishingly scarce; it is only possible to determine the external appearance of such houses from photographs and drawings but there is nothing to suggest that the start of the Victorian period coincided with a change in design or method of construction. The building of timber framed houses had long ago been abandoned, overtaken by brick and stone, often covered by render. In her book on Victorian buildings in Bristol Clare Crick suggested that,

> ...on the whole terracing between Lawrence Hill and Montpelier evolved from a debased eighteenth century form now built in brick, faced with stucco and decorated with coarse stone lintels.[17]

Building plan evidence indicates that after 1851 there was very little building of new courts and that infilling of that kind had effectively come to an end. By that time new building for the working class was predominantly in the form of two up, two down terraced houses on newly laid out streets. Despite the fact that there were many different builders, each operating within a restricted area of the town, the houses they produced, whether off Stapleton Road in east Bristol, in Bedminster to the south or even the rare examples of working-class houses in Redland to the north, were remarkably similar, to the extent that it makes sense to talk about a standard plan.[18] This consisted of a front parlour, a back parlour, or kitchen, and beyond that a single storey extension often labelled wash house. This was invariably a rather flimsy structure with just a single thickness of brickwork. Beyond that again was an outside privy, connected to a buried cess pit in the garden, or in an adjacent garden (the construction of the city's modern sewerage system did not begin until 1853).[19] In the first volume of building plans, covering the period August 1851 to October 1852 61 per cent of all proposed houses conformed to the

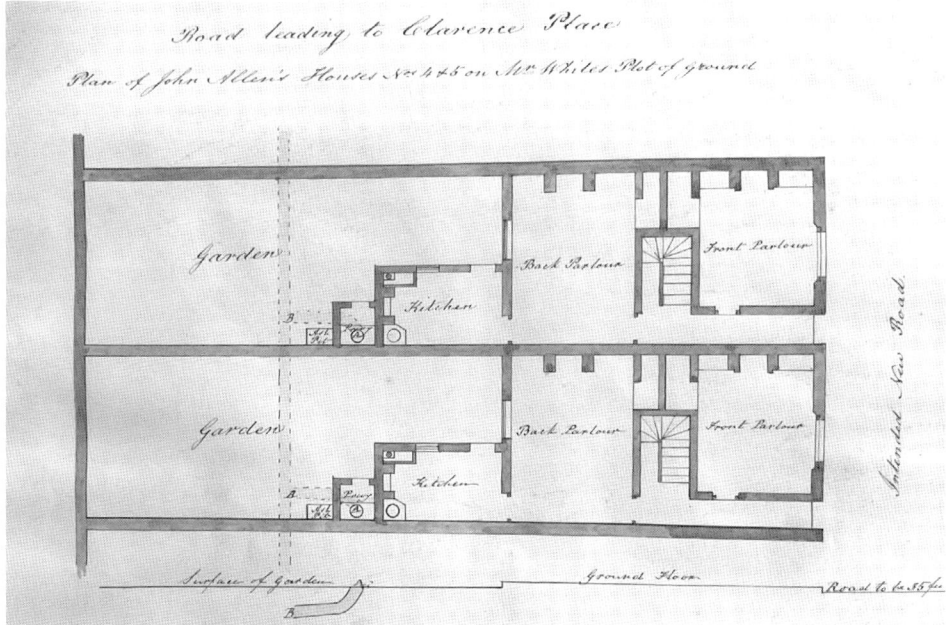

Plan submitted in September 1851 for two standard terraced houses to be built in Clarence Place, Newtown, by John Allen on land owned by James White. (Courtesy: Bristol Archives)

standard plan. The standard plan indicated houses 16 feet wide and about 36 feet from front to back, with the front door opening from the street into a passage, not directly into the parlour. The working-class terraced house was essentially a pared down version of the middle-class terraced house, usually without the basement or second and third floor – there being no need to provide for servants.[20] In the early Victorian period the stairs were located across the main axis of the house, between the two rooms. The deposited plans are all drawn to the same scale, one eighth of an inch to one foot, so it is possible to derive room sizes, but occasionally dimensions are included on the plans, a typical example being the plans submitted by Samuel Sage for two standard plan houses and a corner shop in Regent Street, Newtown, in December 1851: the front parlour was 11 feet by 12 feet, the kitchen 11 feet by 10 feet and the back extension 6 feet by 9 feet. In this case the passage went right through from front to back, but in some versions it opened into the back parlour, making that room a little wider.

In the early part of the period the fronts of houses of all classes were flat (no bay windows) and constructed with a parapet wall obscuring the roof

Flat-fronted houses in Regent Street, Newtown, built in the 1850s. (Courtesy: D Cheesley)

Berkeley Street, Lawrence Hill, with the Bristol Wagon Works at the end of the street. (Courtesy: Bristol Region Building Record)

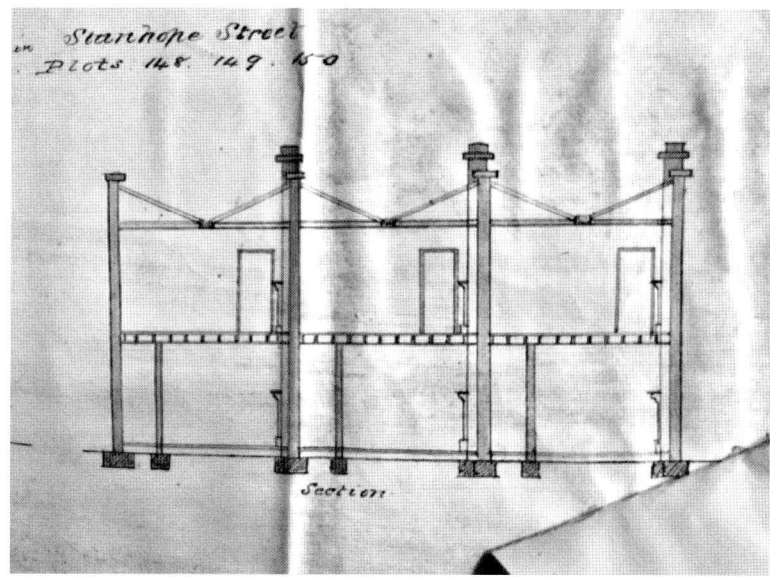

Valley roofs shown in a drawing submitted for houses at Stanhope Street, St Philip's Marsh, in 1879. (Courtesy: Bristol Archives)

Valley roofs at Pylle Hill, Totterdown. (Photograph: the author)

Back extensions at Langton Park, Bedminster. (Photograph: the author)

Back extensions at Devonshire Road, Westbury Park. (Photograph: the author)

structure, which featured a central valley gutter (later to be notorious for chronic leakiness). This type of roof had been used since the eighteenth century but later in the Victorian period different roof structures were adopted, first by placing the ridge above the middle of the house, with a high gable at the front. Later the ridge was turned through ninety degrees, resulting in a roof that drained away from the house rather than into it. This meant that the roof was now a prominently visible part of the house instead of being concealed.

Over the years the standard plan remained the basis of working-class housing provision, but it did evolve in a number of ways. One key dimension that did not change was the width of 16 feet, which was still very common as the late 1890s building boom played itself out in the early 1900s. Internally, the transverse staircase gradually gave way to stairs aligned to the long axis (although isolated examples can be found from the early 1850s). The reason for the increasing popularity of aligning the stairs in this way was probably related to the need to arrange access to a third bedroom, located over what had previously been the single storey back extension.

Building plan evidence strongly suggests that working-class houses continued to be built with outside WCs and without bathrooms until well into the 1880s. Fitting these facilities into the narrow fronted house posed difficulties not just in terms of arranging the plumbing but also finding space for two extra rooms, albeit small ones. This accounts for the increased scale of back extensions by the end of the century. Whereas in the 1850s back extensions had consisted just one room, on the ground floor, by the end of the century that one room, ground floor extension had been, in effect, pushed away from the main body of the house by the insertion of a two storey addition. This created, therefore, a six roomed house, plus kitchen and bathroom.

The early Victorian terraces, in places such as the Dings, to the east of Temple Meads, had no back extensions at all. Then, by the time that the building plans start in 1851, small single storey extensions were standard. In this period it was usual for a run of houses to be handed in the same way, that is, all having the front door and the back extension on the same side. Later, however, it became much more common for houses in a terrace to be built in pairs, where one was a left handed house and the other right handed, with the front doors and back extensions next to each other. This was because the adoption of deeper and higher back extensions encouraged builders to economise by constructing adjacent houses so that their extensions shared a party wall.

Another significant development was the increased frequency, after about 1865, of bay windows at the front, either just on the ground floor or on both ground and first floor. By the 1890s bay windows were common on new terraced houses across the city from Horfield to Southville. The bay window is a characteristically British feature, designed to admit maximum sunshine in a cool cloudy climate; the opposite is the case in the warmer European countries where bay windows are generally absent and external shutters keep the sun out. The growing popularity of bays implied the provision of a small patch of garden to accommodate them, although an exception is Upper Perry

Typical late-Victorian /early-Edwardian terraced houses, in Southville and Horfield. (Photograph: the author)

Upper Perry Hill, built on a narrow field resulting in houses with bay windows but no gardens. (Photograph: the author)

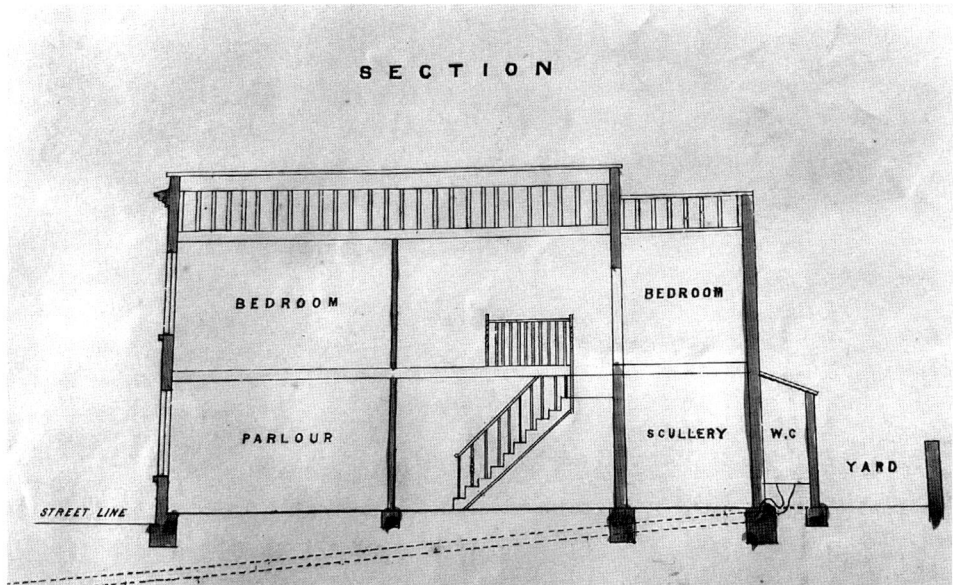

Section through houses at Byron Street, Earl's Mead, 1873 showing how the third bedroom was accommodated over the back extension. (Courtesy: Bristol Archives)

Hill in Bedminster, where the builders were confronted with a road down the middle of a narrow field, leaving no room for front gardens of any kind. This street, built after 1886, shows how bay windows had become a necessary feature, despite the awkwardness of the site. In general front gardens for working-class houses were either completely absent or mere tokens throughout the Victorian period.

To sum up the development of the standard plan terraced house, the early Victorian two-up-two-down house was succeeded first by a five-roomed version, with a small third bedroom over the scullery, and then a six-roomed house with a larger third bedroom over an additional ground floor room. By the end of the period these larger terraced houses were being built with an upstairs bathroom and WC, and were designed to appeal to the better off members of the working class, 'foremen, shop assistants and others of similar social standing'.[21]

Some writers, notably Martin Daunton, have suggested that the forty to fifty years up to 1914 can be seen as the era of building bye-laws, established by local authorities in accordance with the terms of the Local Government Act, 1858.[22] Daunton sees this as a discrete phase in the history of working-class housing, a phase that he criticises for its monotonous grid-iron layouts and narrow fronted houses. The question therefore arises as to the extent to which local authority building bye-laws affected the design and layout of houses in Bristol. It was noted in the previous chapter that under the Bristol Improvement Act, 1840 (and indeed, an earlier Act of 1788) the town council took an interest in regulating new building activity and employed surveyors to check that builders complied with the regulations (about things such as the construction and alignment of external and party walls and the prevention of jettied upper storeys). The building plans that have been mentioned many times were a requirement of the Public Health Act, 1848, which was mainly concerned with proper drainage and sewerage. The 1848 Act also set out minimum specifications for allowable cellars or basements. Compared with places like Liverpool, Bristol did not have a significant number of cellars occupied as separate dwellings, but the provisions of the Act did have an impact on the construction of basements, which were required to have a minimum ceiling height of seven feet, the ceiling to be at least three feet above ground level; there was also to be an external space at least two feet six inches wide to provide light and ventilation. Evidence of houses built in conformity with these provisions is readily available in Bristol.

Bristol town council did not issue its first set of building bye-laws until 1871.[23] The first part covered the level, width and construction of new streets and the notices required of developers before work began. In addition to the drainage plans that had been required since 1851 builders were now to supply sections through their proposed houses. Every new roadway was to be at least 30 feet wide and no building was to be erected that exceeded in height the distance between it and the opposite side of the street. Section two specified that there was to be a minimum of 150 square feet of open space at the back of every house and internally the minimum ceiling height was 8 feet 6 inches. And section three dealt with drainage: 'No cesspool shall be allowed, except when unavoidable' – fortunately, by the early 1870s the basic mains drainage system in Bristol was nearing completion. It seems quite clear that rather than constraining local builders these bye-laws were a description of what was already standard practice, and had been so for a couple of decades. As emphasised here, the habit of building narrow fronted terraced houses with small back gardens was deeply entrenched in Bristol, and other towns. It was not a product of the bye-laws. Daunton and other critics of the visual monotony of bye-law housing may have a valid point, but in Bristol it is hard to discern any real difference attributable to the bye-laws between areas built before and after 1871. Improvements in the specification of new houses towards the end of the century, in terms of bay windows, an extra bedroom and a bathroom, were due to rising incomes rather than official guidance designed to raise standards. It is important to be clear that the town council did not require new houses to be equipped with either inside WCs or bathrooms. There is evidence from building plans that houses in, for example, Greville Street, Bedminster, in the early 1880s were to have neither bathroom nor inside WC and as late as 1897 houses in Upton Road, Southville, had neither bathroom nor inside WC, but at the same date these facilities were provided in houses in nearby Leighton Road.[24] According to Daunton, 'The general design of the modern water closet emerged around 1890 in a form which was cheap, reliable and clean, although it was unusual before the First World War to risk locating the closet inside the house rather than the yard'.[25] In addition to the risk associated with inside WCs there was a view that it was simply undesirable and that outside was the proper place for them.

Extensive areas of standard plan terraced houses eventually existed in east and south Bristol, in a great arc from St Werburghs round to Southville and Ashton Gate, embracing neighbourhoods including St Agnes, Easton, Redfield, Barton Hill, Totterdown and Windmill Hill. Much of these neighbourhoods can be described as consisting of bye-law houses because of the dates of their construction. No-one, however, would apply the term to houses in the middle-class suburbs in north and west Bristol, even though they were built at the same time and the bye-laws applied everywhere.

The Middle-Class Villa and the Residential Suburb

Although most Bristolians lived in terraced houses in 1840 the first pair of semi-detached houses seems to have been built at Redland Hill as early as 1761.[26] The semi-detached form, together with the somewhat less frequently found detached variant, eventually came to dominate the residential suburbs beloved of the middle class and the economic elite of Bristol in the Victorian period. It is important to establish that the term 'semi-detached house' identifies the genre by reference to one key feature that distinguishes it from the terraced house, but there were several other ways in which it came to differ from its dominant predecessor. Before looking at the different kinds and sizes of villas it is necessary to say something about the creation of 'suburbs of privilege'.[27] Historically, suburbs, the areas outside the walls, had been populated by the poor and excluded, and by offensive industries such as tanning. The elite had lived within the walls, although as Leech has demonstrated, in Bristol by the seventeenth century they tended to have second homes in the form of 'garden houses' outside the built up area, on the healthy slopes of Kingsdown, for example.[28] Whereas the growth of south and east Bristol represented the advance of the urban area into the rural hinterland, the middle-class residential suburbs were new and different from anything that preceded them. It was not just that the people who moved to Clifton, Redland and Tyndall's Park after 1850 chose to live in different sorts of houses. These suburbs represented a much more profound change in the nature of the city.

One of the most convincing explanations of the emergence of middle-class suburbs, in Britain was written in the 1980s by an American professor, Robert Fishman, who described them as bourgeois utopias. For Fishman the importance of the residential suburb is that it represented a thoroughgoing re-imagining of the city:

> The suburb as we know it…did not evolve smoothly and inevitably from the premodern city; …The emergence of suburbia required a total transformation of urban values: not only a reversal of the meaning of core and periphery, but a separation of work and family life and the creation of new forms of urban space that would be both class-segregated and wholly residential.[29]

He argues that the new suburbs grew out of the urban crisis produced by unprecedented demographic and economic growth, which on the one hand generated the wealth of the burgeoning merchant class but, on the other hand, created conditions that became increasingly intolerable to those same people. They were tied to the city by their lucrative businesses but at the same time repelled by its congestion and environmental degradation. The solution was not simply to move to the edge of town but to make a more radical and decisive move to the countryside, while remaining close enough to be in easy reach of the Exchange and their warehouses around the harbour and in regular face to face contact with the other members of their business networks. Naturally the people best placed to move out of town were the wealthiest merchants and manufacturers, and in Bristol they were attracted to healthy but not too distant opportunities for social exclusivity and domestic comfort, initially in Clifton and Redland, later further out, in Sneyd Park, Stoke Bishop and after 1864 across the suspension bridge in Leigh Woods. Fishman makes the point that the pioneers of the bourgeois residential suburb were people with income and wealth equivalent to the landed gentry,

Early semi-detached house in Acraman's Road, Southville, built after 1843 on land owned by Elizabeth Acraman. (Courtesy: Bristol Archives)

whom they sought to emulate, while remaining tied to the city and to a middle-class style of life.[30] Thus the first suburban houses tended to be large, detached and in extensive grounds, reflecting the spending power of these pioneers. But they were followed by people with more modest incomes, the employed middle class and independent professionals, keen to share in the respectability and exclusiveness of the suburbs.

This discussion focuses on the sorts of houses built in the middle-class residential suburbs of north and west Bristol, but this is not to imply that semi-detached and detached houses were not built elsewhere. Indeed, some early semi-detached houses were built on higher ground south of the river Avon, in Alpha Road, before 1828 and also in the nearby Acraman's Road, both in Southville. Later in the century some large semi-detached houses were built elsewhere in south Bristol, for example on the Wells Road.

While it would not be right to say there developed a true mass market for middle-class villas, it is important to acknowledge the way landowners and builders began to accommodate changed patterns of demand by building for families of more modest means. The residential suburb gradually evolved throughout the Victorian period, key changes being the emergence of a limited array of more or less standard plans and the adoption of smaller plots with smaller houses (typically five-bedroomed houses on a tenth of an acre). This is not to say that demand for huge houses declined: it simply moved further out of the city. Meanwhile, in parts of Redland and Clifton some of the older mansions were actually demolished and replaced by quite large numbers of villas for the salariat. Examples from the 1890s include the construction of twenty houses on the site formerly occupied by Manilla Hall in Clifton, and at least 58 houses on the four acre site of Redland Manor.[31] Architectural historians such as Andor Gomme and Tim Mowl[32] tend to deplore the arrival of what they disparage as 'villadom' but these houses clearly appealed to people with sufficient resources to choose where and how they wanted to live.

As has been mentioned above, no more grand terraces or squares were started in Clifton and Redland after 1850, and as time went on the layouts of new roads tended to be less regularly orthogonal and more sinuous, but always with plenty of space and numerous trees. Sneyd Park, developed from the 1860s, is the best exemplar. These places were not known as leafy suburbs for nothing. Whereas in the east and south the houses were packed in at high density, together with lots of corner shops, beer houses and industrial buildings of various kinds, in the north and west the density was much lower and non-residential buildings (apart from churches) were scarce. A measure of the difference in density is that whereas it was noted in chapter four that in the mid-1850s Andrew Brown built 59 houses on a plot of little over an acre and a half off Stapleton Road, in Clifton individual houses built at roughly the same time often sat on plots of between a third and two-thirds of an acre, occasionally more (James Derham's house in Sneyd Park, mentioned in chapter four, was on a plot exceeding 8 acres).

Apart from the low density perhaps the most striking feature of the early Victorian semi-detached houses is their sheer size. They were huge, and the largest ones, on the Promenade on Clifton Down are said by Gomme to be 'up to thirty rooms and more'.[33] Gomme speculates that these enormous houses were built as pairs because the developers could not secure plots large enough to allow for single houses of the desired dimensions. However, this explanation seems unlikely because the plots are about 64 feet wide, four

Number 7 Apsley Road, Clifton, built in the late 1860s by Richard Cosslett on land owned by the Society of Merchant Venturers.
(Photograph: the author)

times the width of the standard plan terraced house, and it is now known that it was the landowner, Francis Adams, who commissioned the architects, Foster and Son, to draw up the designs in 1844.[34] These massive houses and their near neighbours at Clifton Down were too big to provide any sort of template for subsequent builders aiming at a wider market. The pair of houses known as Trinmore and Tellisford House, for example, built by William Baker in 1859, are 40 feet wide and 70 feet deep.[35] Not far away, however, on newly laid out roads in Clifton and Redland rather more modest, but still large, houses were being built on quarter acre plots according to designs that could be readily reproduced, albeit not quite on a mass scale. In the 1850s and '60s semi-detached houses with eight bedrooms were built on three storeys, plus a basement, in Redland Park and Westfield Park (two roads off Whiteladies Road), and on Apsley Road, Clifton. Number 9 Apsley Road, built by Richard Cosslett and Son on Merchant Venturers' land in 1868, was conceived as an 11 bedroomed house on three floors and a basement. The same family firm built number 8 in 1873 and when this was put up for auction in 1884 it was described in these terms:

Downside, Pembroke Road, built in 1862 by Richard Cosslett on land owned by Francis Adams. In the 1860s and '70s it was the home of Henry Overton Wills III. (Photograph: the author)

> The house…has all the requirements of a gentleman's residence. And is situate in a very favourite road in the best part of Clifton. It contains on basement – breakfast or billiard room, two capital kitchens, wc and usual offices; on ground floor – drawing room, dining room, library and smoking room, cloak room and china pantry; on first floor – large bathroom, three large and two smaller bedrooms and a dressing room; on the second floor – six bedrooms and a dressing room; hot and cold water are on every floor.[36]

Apsley Road is a good example of the reproducibility of the designs where at least six different builders were at work on houses that are broadly similar in size and external appearance. The same point was made by Gomme who notes that, 'In the upper reaches of Pembroke Road, between 1860 and 1877, at least eight builders were working according to one basic formula with variations which are haphazard or accidental and hence insignificant'.[37] Meanwhile, similarly large houses were being built in Tyndall's Park; here again there is a certain amount of repetition of designs for detached houses, for example on Tyndall's Park Road and Priory Road.

The larger town houses in Bristol had always been built on three or more storeys, with a basement, and this continued to be the case with suburban villas, although it is perhaps better to think in terms of three and a half storeys, given that mid-century basements were not truly subterranean. The really big houses were built with correspondingly extensive basements: at Francis Adams's Promenade in Clifton the plans for Fern Villa and Auckland House, dated August 1852, indicate that the basements contained scullery, kitchen, entrance hall, two pantries, servants' hall, housekeeper's room, WC and three rooms without labels. Also in 1852 George Ashmead submitted plans for a pair of houses on Gallows Acre Lane, where the basements were to contain the butler's room, housekeeper's room, kitchen, scullery, two pantries, larder, rainwater tank, coal house and privy. Reference to a rainwater tank here is interesting, first as a reminder that it was not yet the case that even substantial villas were provided with piped water, and, second because collecting soft rainwater for laundry purposes was common practice in Bristol on account of its naturally hard water. Nineteenth-century advertisements often referred to houses having 'both kinds of water'.

A number of features that became embedded in the design of villas in this period were, first, wider plots, which gave outside access to the rear without going through the house; this might seem so obvious as scarcely to warrant a mention, but in a city where back lanes were not usually provided it represented a real improvement in functional utility. In Redland, for example, the use of plots 30 feet wide became widespread, although many, especially in Clifton, were wider still, in excess of 40 feet. Second, greater width within the dwelling itself encouraged the adoption of different plan forms. Third, the main entrance was positioned on the side elevation (although in many cases the addition of a porch enabled the front door itself to face forward). This allowed for transverse, rather than longitudinal, internal circulation space. These changes facilitated the adoption of a square floor plan, two rooms wide and two rooms deep, rather than the one-room-behind-another layout found in the standard terrace plan. Fourth, the kitchen migrated from the basement to the ground floor, and basements were either

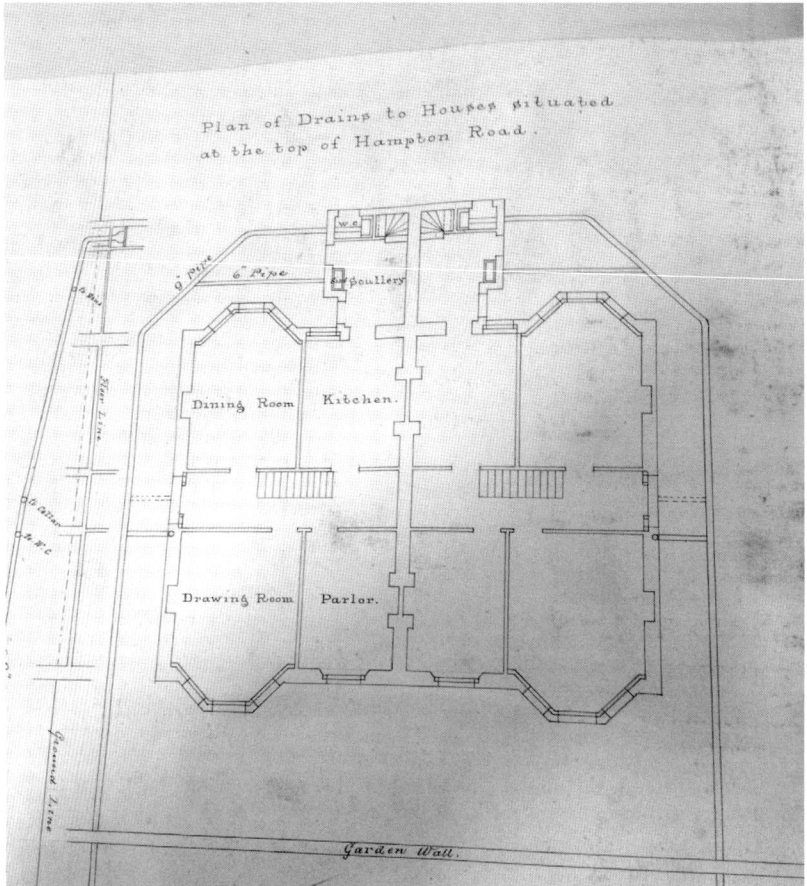

Plans of 'houses at top of Hampton Road', Redland, March 1868. A typical four-room layout of the period. (Courtesy: Bristol Archives)

omitted altogether or of diminished proportions and reduced significance. Fifth, virtually every house had a front garden that was more than a mere strip, and finally, by the latter part of the century houses for the middle class were increasingly often built with bathrooms and inside WCs.

There was, of course, plenty of scope for variation and some of the features listed above arrived as innovations at different times in the Victorian decades. The earliest semi-detached houses, such as the pair at Redland Hill and another at Clifton Hill, had the entrance doors on the front elevation, with rooms on both left and right. It is particularly clear in the Clifton example that, as Sir John Summerson commented in relation to similar houses in London, they were, in effect, ordinary terrace houses, just built as a terrace of two.[38] There was nothing in the design to prevent repetition to left and right, whereas when the front door moved to the side this option was removed. In the case of the pair at Redland Hill, the two houses were mirror images of each other, and this was to become a defining feature of the semi-detached form. The access way to the rear of the house was sometimes wide enough to accommodate a carriage but more often it was a path three or four feet wide. In some cases adjacent pairs of semi-detached houses were actually joined by their porches and access to the rear was through the porch. Although it became normal on a thirty foot plot for villas to be two rooms wide, where plots widths permitted it builders were naturally inclined to increase the sizes of those rooms.

As mentioned at the start of this chapter, despite appearances there were in fact very few basic house types in Victorian Bristol. Here that proposition is developed into an argument that there were just three generic types of semi-detached villas, and that it is possible to trace the evolution of these three types from the tall narrow fronted Georgian terraced house. The first was a tall, narrow house with a basement kitchen. The second was a wider version, ultimately with a square, four room plan, still with three floors and a basement; and the third was similar to the second, but without the basement or top floor, and with a ground floor kitchen. This is not to suggest that all new villas conformed to one or other of these types, but a great many did.

In 1858 William Coates built four houses on Cheltenham Road, including one for himself, Hebron Villa (illustrated on page 67). This particular house and it partner were not the first of their kind, for the records show that Coates had proposed identical houses in Hampton Road in 1856.[39] Nevertheless, they were among the first of what became, and remains, a familiar style in the area. No architect is credited on Coates's deposited plans and so it not possible to say whether he was an innovator in house design or merely the instrument of its promotion, but he was clearly a shrewd businessman who understood that there was profit to be made from repeating a successful design. He went on to build dozens of houses that either look just like his Cheltenham Road house or can be shown to be basically the same.

Coates's house looks different from the traditional terrace in three ways: it has a ground floor bay window, the concealed valley roof has been replaced by a prominent gable, and of course it is part of a pair of left and right handed houses, with the front door at the side. Nevertheless, it can be argued that this sort of house was derived from the terraced houses built in earlier years: it is tall, on three and a half storeys, with the kitchen in the basement,

These two houses in Ashgrove Road, Redland, are in many ways identical but the one on the left illustrates how the semi-detached form permitted sideways extension. (Photograph: the author)

and it is narrow, just one room wide at the front – in fact the width at the front is 16 feet, exactly the same as the standard plan terraced house. Several variants of this type can be found, especially in Cotham and Redland, not always built by William Coates. In the case of the evolution of the terraced house it was seen that back extensions became larger over time. But these tall semi-detached houses did not have back extensions; instead they tended to acquire side extensions, as can be seen on Hebron Villa. The minimal side extension was a simple single storey porch, half way down the side of the house, with a forward facing front door. This could be made larger by building backwards and upwards, or, indeed forwards. In this way the two room plan evolved towards the second basic type, the four roomed plan.

The houses in Redland Park, Westfield Park, Ashgrove Road and other roads off Whiteladies Road, sometimes then referred to collectively as Whiteladies Park, built in the 1860s were all faced with Bath stone and had a different roof structure (a transverse valley instead of a front gable), but on close examination they can be shown to belong to the same family as Hebron Villa. These two adjacent houses in Ashgrove Road nicely illustrate the scope

A pair of large semi-detached houses in Westfield Park, Redland, built in the early 1860s probably by William Coates, on the field owned by Sir Thomas Fremantle.
(Photograph: the author)

A pair of houses in Chertsey Road, smaller but otherwise very similar to the large houses in Westfield Park. Note how the basements in these houses are really semi-basements with good daylighting, reflecting the impact of the Public Health Act, 1848.
(Photograph: the author)

A pair of semi-detached houses in Elgin Park, Redland, built in the late 1860s by Richard Cosslett. Note the stylistic similarities with his much larger houses in Apsley Road (page 111) from the same period, but here there is no habitable basement or second floor. (Photograph: the author)

for variation. They are basically the same as each other, with identical fenestration and other detailing, but the one on the left has a larger side extension that has been brought right out to the front, and it is easy to see how a four room ground floor plan could be achieved, if space permitted the door to be located at the side. This is what happened in the case of the very large pair at 7 and 9 Westfield Park (almost certainly built by Coates, in 1864), which can also be seen to be, in effect, extended versions of the otherwise identical pair built in nearby Chertsey Road.

In Apsley Road, pictured earlier, on the other side of Whiteladies Road, houses of similar size to the largest of Westfield Park but built a little later, from 1868 onwards, illustrate how the plan could be tweaked, with the bay windowed drawing room being switched to the outside wall and the smaller room being moved to the party wall. This arrangement may have proved popular because it positioned the main reception room closer to the entrance where visitors came into the house. Receiving visitors in the socially correct way was important, and the layout of the Apsley Road houses certainly provided for that, for it has been suggested by John Burnett that three reception rooms were considered necessary for respectability.[40] Whatever the reasons, putting

Detached house in Woodland Road, Tyndall's Park.
(Photograph: the author)

the drawing room on the outside wall became standard practice.

One of the builders in Apsley Road was Richard Cosslett, and it is possible to see similarities between his very large houses and those that he built in Elgin Park and Clyde Road, Redland, also from 1868 onwards. The Redland houses are in many ways simply smaller versions, sharing a number of basic plan features and design details. The key differences are that in Redland Cosslett omitted both the deep basement and the top floor. These houses epitomise the third basic form: square four room plan, two storeys, kitchens on the ground floor and drawing room on the outside wall. By the late 1860s recently built houses in Elgin Park, were advertised as having cellars, rather than basements, and the kitchens were on the ground floor. These houses had two WCs, one on the ground floor and one upstairs, but no bathroom.[41] Houses of this sort came to be built in large numbers in Redland, Clifton, St Andrews and elsewhere in the last thirty years of the century. The migration of the kitchen from the basement to the ground floor can be seen in plans submitted from at least the late 1860s.[42] The wider floor plan made it possible to accommodate the kitchen but it became normal to add a back extension with the scullery and a WC, the latter accessed from outside (previously

Two-storey villas in Alma Road, Clifton, built by Richard Cosslett junior in 1872. Houses like this, with the same double bay spanning the full width of the room, were built by different builders in different parts of west and north Bristol for at least thirty years. (Photograph: the author)

middle-class villas generally did not have back extensions). At the same time as the kitchen was being moved basements became less common. That is to say, basements that were designed to be used for living and working were less often included in plans. New houses continued to be provided with basements where the lie of the land made it appropriate, but these were for storage, not meant for everyday use.

It is necessary to recognise that detached houses did not necessarily follow the same sort of plan found in semi-detached. A beautiful illustration (see page 97) of a square plan detached house with the door on the front is number 26 Victoria Square, built by John Davies. The plans, dated 1869, were signed by Davies and the surveyor to the Society of Merchant Venturers, James Marmont, who may also have been responsible for the design.[43] This house was forty feet wide and forty feet deep, on three floors plus a basement. It had eight bedrooms, and the 'master bedroom' (to use modern estate agents' language) had not only an en suite dressing room but also a bathroom, albeit one with no sign of plumbing. There was one WC on the first floor and almost certainly another one in the basement for the servants. To twenty-first century observers this may seem to be a serious deficiency of bathrooms and toilets but in its own time this was a fine example of the sort of house aimed at the social and economic elite. Interestingly, it seems to have been purchased as an investment by a man named James Fraser Hore, a barrister and retired Indian judge living in Sneyd Park.[44]

Having considered the evidence for thinking in terms of three basic house types, it must be acknowledged that builders were skilled in creating the illusion of difference. The great majority of villas were stone faced, at least on the front elevation. As has been illustrated above, Bath stone was common in the 1850s and '60s, after which pennant sandstone became more frequently used. Bricks were used but rarely left exposed. Fenestration also gave builders much scope to create distinctive front elevations. Windows came in different shapes and sizes. Most were simply rectangular, but some were topped by rounded or pointed (gothic) arches, or put together in double or triple forms. They were invariably given more or less elaborately carved surrounds of freestone, the local pennant sandstone being less amenable to a dressed finish. Bay windows also came in different forms: many, especially early ones, were shallow and rounded, others were much deeper and still rounded while eventually the majority were angled rather than rounded. A popular form of bay, built over at least thirty years, spanned the entire width of the drawing room while others were narrower. Bays on the ground floor only were common, especially in the earlier years of their popularity, but by the end of the century they were usually two storeys high, the so-called double bay.

Roof structures allowed builders to give variety to the external appearance of their houses. The shallow pitched roofs hidden behind parapet walls of the early Victorian period gradually have way to roofs that were much more visible. Gabled roofs of varying proportions reappeared, in some cases spanning the width of the house (this form was more common on smaller, terraced houses) and in others providing cover over the projecting bays beneath. Gables allowed the inclusion of attic rooms in what were otherwise two storey houses. The larger villas tended to have a floor area that demanded a complex roof, often involving low ridges and valley gutters in order to keep the height down. In general, roofs became more visible as the century wore on.

Conclusion

This chapter has reviewed some of the evidence, both material and archival, relating to the sorts of houses built by and for the people of Bristol in the Victorian period. It has been shown that there was considerable similarity across large parts of the city and over time, especially in terms of working-class terraced houses, where it is possible to talk of a single standard plan. There was a certain amount of modification of the standard plan as time moved on, mainly in the form of bay windows at the front and larger extensions at the back, only latterly accommodating indoor WCs and bathrooms. The ubiquitous two-up-two-down of the 1850s had become a six-roomed house by the 1890s, reflecting higher living standards.

In the case of suburban villas, it has been argued that change over time was more profound, and that true suburbs pioneered by the economic and social elite have to be seen as a rejection of urban living. And yet what this chapter has shown is that changes in house design were not derived from the mansions of the wealthiest suburban residents, the weekend aristocrats, as Robert Fishman called them.[45] The different types of villas that eventually gave the suburbs their distinctive character were in fact derived from traditional urban forms by gradual, incremental changes as builders modified their output in response to their understanding of consumer demand and preferences. The key point here is that they were seeking to accommodate a widening market, not just the truly wealthy, and therefore they had to take their lead from what these newer arrivals in the suburbs could afford. This helps to understand why new houses in both Redland and Clifton in the 1890s were smaller than those built in earlier decades, but it does not obviously explain the key design changes, principally the abandonment of basements and the relocation of kitchens to the ground floor. Which way does causality run – were kitchens forced up by the abandonment of basements, or were basements abandoned because people preferred ground-floor kitchens?

CHAPTER SEVEN

House and Home: the consumer experience

The great eighteenth-century economist Adam Smith wrote that,

> Consumption is the sole end and purpose of production; and the interest of the producer ought to be attended to only so far as it may be necessary for promoting that of the consumer.[1]

Houses, of course, are not literally consumed in the way that food is; nevertheless, they are designed to be lived in, and the act of dwelling in a house is a form of consumption. Indeed, consumption of housing is a basic human requirement, especially in the British climate. Builders and consumers have quite different relationships with houses: for builders, they are simply products to be disposed of as soon as possible for the best obtainable price, but from the consumers' point of view a house is potentially a home to be occupied over a long period. Builders construct houses but families make homes; the distinction between house and home is fundamental, and one aim of this chapter is to explain the importance of the home for an understanding of the Victorian consumer experience of housing.

In general terms the consumer experience of housing can be summed up as, first, what the house does for its occupants, and second, what they do in and to the house to make it their home. The basic function of a house (used here in a generic sense to mean a separate self-contained dwelling, whether that be a house or a tenement, the more common nineteenth-century terms for a flat) is to provide both shelter from the elements for people and their possessions, and an arena, a space or set of spaces in which domestic life can be played out. In addition, a house is an address, a signifier of the social and economic status of its occupants – a vital piece of information in an unequal and hierarchical society, in which people are acutely aware of where they stand in relation to others both above and below them in wealth and status. The concept of home is more complex and requires a little more discussion. Familiar phrases such as 'home sweet home', 'home is where the heart is' and 'there's no place like home' all conjure up warm and positive images of a place of familiarity and deep emotional attachment, together with privacy, safety and security. This suggests a degree of permanence, or at least somewhere that is not understood as merely temporary, such as student accommodation or a hotel room. Home is a place of privacy and relaxation, where it is unnecessary to 'keep up appearances', and the invitation to 'make yourself at home' can be seen as an expression of tolerance of behaviour that would not be welcomed or appropriate in a more public setting, as can be seen by considering the opposite, the admonition sometimes administered to a misbehaving child: 'you're not at home now'. However, although the idea of home is routinely invoked in a positive way it should not be forgotten that for some people some of the time home is associated with misery, conflict and danger. Thus, while it can be argued that a house needs to meet certain minimum requirements for it to have the potential to become a cherished home, it cannot be inferred that a house that does meet those requirements will become such a home; that all depends on the inter-personal behaviour and affinity of the occupants.

How well people got on with each other and the quality of home life in that sense is beyond the scope of this discussion, which instead focuses on home making in terms of how people across the range of housing experiences set up the spaces at their disposal to produce a sense of homeliness. Home making activities can be thought of in terms of two sets of behaviours, one primarily inward facing and the other outward facing. The first includes the cultivation of personal relationships, the raising of children and the regular round of quotidian routines (preparing and eating food, washing and cleaning etc) that have to be gone through in any household. Home making also entails the accumulation and display (or concealment) of particular sorts of possessions, on the one hand those with special sentimental value, such as family photographs or children's paintings, and on the other hand iconic or fashionable, 'must have', items that help the household to fulfil perceived social expectations and identify it with a certain position in society. One such signifier in Victorian front parlours was the upright piano, irrespective of whether anyone ever actually played it. In this sense there is a degree of overlap with the outward facing activities or displays, projecting an image to the world at large. A good illustration of image projection would be the way that people who bought their council houses in the 1980s often made great efforts to advertise their change of tenure status by modifying the outside appearance of their property, by fitting a new front door or external cladding – anything that said 'this is no-longer a council house'. Whatever it may be –

an image of modest respectability or brash opulence, of humble conformity or robust individualism – everyone does something of this kind, albeit more or less consciously.

A basic assumption underlying this chapter is that the nature of the house has implications for home making, and that some circumstances are more conducive to it than others. In particular it can be taken for granted that sharing is not conducive to home making. In 1852 it was noted that,

> The possession of an entire house is…strongly desired by every Englishman; for it throws a deep, and well-defined circle round his family and hearth – the shrine of his sorrows, joys and meditations.[2]

Different people will of course have different aspirations, but the idea is that it is easier to build a home in a house that has adequate space for the number of people living in it, is capable of being kept warm and is not in itself a threat to the health of its occupants. It is also easier if the household has a degree of security of tenure and does not live in fear of the rent collector's weekly rap on the door. There are, therefore, two sorts of questions to be addressed when thinking about the consumer experience of houses and homes in Victorian Bristol: first, how and to what extent did the houses of people in different parts of the city, and different parts of the market, allow, limit or enhance the possibility of home building? And second, how did people express their idea of home in and through their houses?

The consumer experience of housing in Victorian Bristol was largely determined by the market, which acted as a powerful mechanism for distributing people to dwellings and locations across the city. Market forces set a price for each dwelling, which, for most people, meant the rent money they had to find each week to satisfy the demands of the landlord or the landlord's agent. The rent was a distillation of the values attached to features such as the size, quality and position of a house. The relationship between price and affordability was the key factor in deciding who lived where. The price was externally set by market forces, whereas affordability was, at least in principle, a subjective judgement made by the consumer about what proportion of their income they wished to devote to housing. The market mechanism allowed, again in principle, consumers to make choices based on their preferences in terms of the attributes of a property and the money in their pockets. Markets are sometimes described as continuous referendums in which people cast their votes, in the form of money, for the goods and services that they want.

However, the value of this metaphor is undermined by the fact that unlike a real referendum in which everyone has only one vote and every vote has equal value, in Victorian urban housing markets a few people had vastly more spending power, and therefore correspondingly more choice, than the great majority of their fellow citizens. Thus, while it is reasonable to see the better off choosing to live in the suburbs it makes less sense to think of the poor actively choosing to live in squalid and overcrowded inner-city courts and alleys – they lived where they could – and the evidence suggests that they tended to have to pay a higher proportion of their meagre incomes on rent than those with higher incomes.[3] In other words, for some people their experience of housing was determined not by what they chose to pay but what they *had to pay*, for, as Karl Marx put it, 'permission to inhabit the earth'.[4] It was assumed by members of the Royal Commission on Housing in 1884 that a fifth of regular income was a reasonable upper limit to the rent paying capacity of the working class.[5] At the same time, middle-class couples were being advised that one tenth to one eighth was an appropriate proportion of income to devote to rent.[6] In practice, however, the problem faced by many was that the notion of regular income did not apply; rent was due every week despite earnings often being intermittent and subject to seasonal variation. And the rent they had to pay often exceeded to notional maximum.

The housing market in Victorian Bristol was highly stratified, heavily influenced by income, wealth and social class, but for ease of analysis and explanation the approach adopted here is based on three divisions: the servant-keeping middle class, the respectable working class and the poor. This is not to imply that the poor were an 'underclass', somehow separated from the rest of the working class. Rather, the distinction is between those who had regular employment and incomes which meant they could make the move to the newly built streets and neighbourhoods of south and east Bristol and those who remained in the decaying city centre courts and alleys, of which there were estimated to be more than 500 in 1850,[7] and still about 300 in 1884.[8]

The Servant-Keeping Middle Class
In the nineteenth century, according to the social historian John Burnett, 'More than any other single factor, middle-class status was determined by employment of residential domestic staff, the numbers and functions of whom were carefully regulated in precise accordance with the level of income'.[9] The incomes of the middle class varied considerably, from the fortunes accumulated by the leading manufacturers (the Wills, Frys, Derhams

etc) down to the much more modest earnings of people such as school teachers and office workers. The middle class was never large, comprising no more than twenty per cent of the population, and it was always internally stratified, but its members were united by a shared sense of their respectability and superiority over the working class.[10] One status-conscious Redland resident wrote on his census return in 1901 that his occupation was 'council worker', but then he carefully added 'shirt and collar', to make clear that he was not a manual worker. Servant keeping was much more a marker of status than ownership of one's house, and it was quite normal, especially in the early Victorian period, for well off people to rent rather than buy. For example, William Edwards, a prosperous banker, lived for many years as the tenant of Redland Court, a property valued at over £200 per annum for rating purposes in 1839. Rateable values approximated to the rental value and Redland Court was among the most highly rated houses in the city. It was not unknown among the city's economic and social elite for servants to outnumber family members; for example, in 1841 Edwards's near neighbour Charles Ludlow Walker, merchant and mayor of Bristol in 1834, lived at Redland Manor with his wife, two adult daughters and nine servants. Their house, standing in 4 acres, had a drawing room, dining room, morning room and 11 bedrooms, three dressing rooms and three servants' rooms, undoubtedly generating plenty of work for all those servants. Probably the extreme case, however, was the widow Frances Miles who, according to the census of 1851, lived alone with ten servants at Manilla Hall, on Clifton Down Road. Edward Burges, the solicitor and property developer mentioned in chapter four, employed eight servants in 1861, to look after him, his wife and their four children. The 1881 census recorded that in the 15 mansions on the Promenade, Clifton, there were 70 servants. In 25 houses in Westfield Park, off Whiteladies Road, in 1871 there were 56 servants, and in a sample of 28 houses in Tyndall's Park in 1891 there were 80 family members and 63 servants. Even the much smaller villas in Salisbury Road, Redland, contained 16 servants in 23 houses in 1901. It would obviously be tedious to extend this recital, but it is important in terms of understanding what life was like for families in the middle-class suburbs, especially those in the larger residences, to appreciate that houses without live-in servants were rare indeed.

Servants were essential to the running of large houses, carrying water (both hot and cold), fetching buckets of coal from the cellar, lighting and tending fires, preparing food, emptying chamber pots and, of course, washing and cleaning (the smoke emitted by candles and, later, gas lamps added to the burden of cleaning). Rising from their beds before the family were up, they were kept busy throughout the day and well into the evening. Without this expenditure of hard and apparently endless physical labour houses with seven or eight bedrooms would have been impossible to manage in the days before modern appliances. The houses of the better off needed to be large partly to demonstrate their social standing and partly because families were, on the whole, larger than they are today. In Westfield Park, for example, in 1871 the average household size was 5.6 people, not including servants; there were 83 offspring, including grown-ups, in 19 houses (at number 1, John Gwynn, a 42 year old solicitor, and his wife had 12 children, plus a governess, nurse and four servants). The Gwynns were perhaps unusually fecund but the average number of live births to women married in the 1870s was between five and six.[11] Not all babies survived of course, but census evidence suggests that offspring who did make it to adulthood often continued living in the parental home, especially unmarried daughters. The combination of large households and big houses justified, or demanded, corresponding numbers of servants.

In April 1867 a recently built house in Westfield Park, which may have been the one occupied by John Gwynn and his large family, was advertised as having 3 sitting rooms, 8 bedrooms, a housekeeper's room and 'kitchen offices'.[12] It was often the case that instead of referring to three sitting rooms the function of each one would be specified, commonly drawing room, dining room and breakfast room and it has been suggested that by the latter part of the century three such rooms on the ground floor was regarded as the minimum required by prosperous families (although it has to be added that there were many houses of unimpeachable respectability in Bristol's Victorian suburbs that did not meet this specification).[13] One house that clearly did meet the standard was number 26 Victoria Square (mentioned in chapter six). In this case we know that the drawing room was 24 feet by 16 feet, about the same as the footprint of an entire mid-century working-class standard terraced house. The dining room was 22 by 16 feet 6 inches and the breakfast room 16 feet by 14 feet.[14] The more space there was within a house the more that rooms could be given a defined and exclusive function, and in larger houses this led to the gendering of spaces designated as library, billiards room and smoking room for men, boudoir and drawing room for women. In such houses there was also a tendency to build in separate stairs and passages for the use of servants, and separate entrances for tradesmen.[15] Houses such as 26 Victoria Square, built in 1869, strike the twenty-first-century observer as not only very generously proportioned but also singularly lacking in sanitary facilities: this fine and expensive house had one room designated on the plans as an en-suite bathroom off the main bedroom, but there was no sign of a bath or plumbing, although there was a separate WC. Plans for four villas in Westfield Park submitted in March 1866 showed no intention to include bathrooms or inside WCs. Number 9 Apsley Road, however, also built in the late 1860s, had three WCs (plus one in the basement for the servants) and one bathroom; this would seem to be the minimum requirement for a 9-bedroomed house. But the same builder, Richard Cosslett, did not include bathrooms in houses in Elgin Park, Redland, built at the same sort of time.[16]

In general it seems that although inside WCs were becoming more frequent in new houses from the 1860s, bathrooms did not become standard features of new houses for the middle class until the final quarter of the century, and houses without bathrooms were still being built in St Andrew's in the late 1870s. It should not be concluded that the Victorian middle classes were uninterested in improved sanitation; their capacity to introduce flushing toilets and bathrooms with hot and cold water supplies depended on the construction of a comprehensive system of mains drainage by the town council, and the Waterworks Company's ability to provide a constant supply of water. Once those were in place, from the early 1870s, demand for improved facilities soon followed. An additional factor was that the technology for delivering an adequate and reliable supply of hot water to upstairs bathrooms was slow to develop:

> The problem of supplying hot water was the subject of numerous experiments – the bath set in a metal case around which flowed water heated by a small furnace, the tank or cistern apparently separately heated by the hot-water geyser and so on – until a piped supply heated from the kitchen range or boiler began to be installed late in the century.[17]

Turning to the question of tenure, the decennial censuses in the Victorian period did not ask whether households were owners or renters, but some information can be obtained from the series of comprehensive valuation surveys in Bristol between 1839 and 1871.[18] These surveys were commissioned to determine property values for the purpose of levying the rates, the local taxes on which the council and the Poor Law guardians depended. In almost every case the surveyors recorded not only the gross estimated rental value but also the name of the owner and the occupier. It is therefore possible, in principle, to get some idea of the rate of owner occupation, and it seems that by 1871 a third of occupied houses in Redland were lived in by their owners (at this point Redland was still under construction, with extensive tracts of open ground). In Clifton at the same date, almost all of the recently built large villas on Pembroke Road and Clifton Down were owner occupied. Owner occupiers here included both WD and HO Wills, the tobacco manufacturers, William Proctor, artificial manure manufacturer (son of Thomas who made a gift to the city of the Lord Mayor's Mansion House at the Promenade), Francis Fry, the cocoa manufacturer and William Killigrew Wait, merchant, mayor of Bristol in 1869 and sometime MP for Gloucester. For comparison, these two roads in Clifton had more owner occupiers than the whole of the central parish of Temple, which, dominated by warehouses, industry and the railways, had only 16 owner occupiers altogether. Thus, on the one hand it is safe to conclude that by the 1870s owner occupation was already popular among the city's social and economic elite. On the other hand, a majority of the residents of the suburbs were tenants, on terms that are not readily amenable to empirical research. However, it has been suggested that middle-class families normally took 'renewable leases for a year, six months or a quarter'.[19] Such leases would have provided a degree of security, less than that enjoyed by outright owners but more than that of weekly tenants.

The question of what the middle class paid for housing breaks down into rent and mortgage payments. Inevitably, rents varied considerably, as some examples will indicate: in 1853 Alfred House, Richmond Hill, Clifton, a 7 bedroomed house 'adapted for a genteel family' was offered for 'the low yearly rent of £35'.[20] We know that a large, 8 bedroomed villa in Westfield Park could be had for £70 a year in 1867.[21] And that in 1868 5 bedroomed houses in Elgin Park were let for £48 to £52-10s.[22] It was mentioned above that the middle class were advised that one eighth was an appropriate amount to spend on rent, and if the Elgin Park residents were following that advice they must have had incomes of at least £400 a year,[23] which was a very great deal more than the majority of Bristol's working population. Limited evidence from both Westfield park and Elgin Park suggests that gross rateable values corresponded quite well with actual rents. The majority of the largest houses were being lived in by their owners by 1871 but there was clearly a market for rented houses at £100 or more per year.

The popularity of selling houses at auction means that information on what people paid to buy them is not readily available except in a few cases, although there is a certain amount that can be inferred. A small sample of deeds from Redland suggests that in the last twenty years of the century houses with four to six bedrooms were selling for between £400 and £700. A little later, in 1909, it was suggested that an income of £160 a year was sufficient to qualify as middle class, and more than £700 a year put people into the upper middle class.[24] This puts into perspective house prices that look absurdly low from a twenty-first century point of view. It also highlights that prices in those days really were much more affordable. In some cases it is possible to infer prices from the agreements between landowners and builders as to the minimum values to be achieved. Thus in St Andrew's in the 1870s and '80s the aim was to have minimum values of £300 to £360, depending on the location. At the upper end of the market, in 1864 William Baker undertook to build a house, now known as Hillside House on a plot of 1 acre 1 rood on Church Road in Sneyd Park, to the value of £1,200, and a year later he assigned the lease to Richard Langridge for £1,950.[25]

Langridge also gives us a clue as to how buyers financed their purchases: in June 1865 he borrowed £1,500 on mortgage from the Bristol, West of England and South Wales Permanent Building Society (later simply the Bristol and West Building Society).[26] He was entitled to do so because he was a shareholder, ie. a depositor, in the society.[27] Several years later, in 1874, Fred Stanton borrowed £300 from the same Society on the basis that this was what his three shares entitled him to, in order to purchase a house in Elliston Road, Redland. However, mortgages, often brokered by solicitors, were frequently arranged directly between lenders and borrowers. For example, in April 1867 the solicitor WL Flook advertised a newly built 'gothic villa' for sale in Redland, 'with every modern convenience requisite for a respectable family', without including a sale price but adding that, 'The greater part of the purchase money may be had on mortgage for a term of years if required'.[28]

The middle-class Victorian suburbs of Bristol, such as Clifton, Redland, Tyndall's Park, Sneyd Park, and Stoke Bishop, were complex and innovative social creations where, 'Domesticity and the cult of the home as the centrepiece of family life were the hallmarks of [the suburban] lifestyle.'[29] Suburbs were, in Robert Fishman's memorable phrase, bourgeois utopias,[30] ideal settings for the way of life desired by the expanding middle class. Exclusively residential and exclusively middle class, the suburbs satisfied the yearning for physical as well as social distance from the working class. Not only were these suburbs on the opposite side of the city but also their detached and semi-detached villas commanded rents and prices that very effectively excluded the workers. When it was proposed to build a tram route from the city up to

Clifton one resident was prompted to protest on the grounds that it would bring 'the nasty, low inhabitants of Bristol' and that, 'Poor people do not walk about on Clifton streets…We have nothing common or unclean amongst us.'[31] This deeply prejudiced view may be dismissed as unrepresentative, but no tram route was ever built into Clifton itself.[32]

Fishman also argued that suburbia was founded on the primacy of the family and domestic life, and that it embodied a new ideal of family life. In fact he suggested that it was the emergence of a new form of closely domesticated nuclear family that prompted the separation of middle-class workplaces from the home, and the migration to the suburbs from the increasingly uncongenial central areas.[33] John Burnett took a similar line, claiming that, 'For that part of the population whose economic resources allowed it to exercise some real choice as to how and where it lived, the home, and its physical expression, the house, were the central institutions of civilised life'.[34] He went on to say,

> The home…had to fulfil…many functions – to comfort and purify, to give relief and privacy from the cares of the world, to rear its members in an appropriate set of Christian values, and, above all, perhaps, to proclaim by its ordered arrangements, polite behaviour, cleanliness, tidiness and distinctive taste, that its members belonged to a class of substance, culture and respectability. The house itself was to be the visible expression of these values.'[35]

The doctrine of 'separate spheres' for men and women was a central tenet of domestic moralists, resulting in what may be seen as the feminisation of the middle-class home in the Victorian period.[36] Denied access to careers and paid employment and isolated in the suburbs women were left with little else to do but focus on home building activities.

Internally middle-class villas provided the numbers of rooms, of appropriate proportions, to enable the family to live out a respectable and decorous life, with the front rooms suitably furnished for visitors, hence the current term 'reception rooms'. The back of the house was the space for more everyday activities, and where the servants spent more of their time. Upstairs the numerous bedrooms allowed separation of adults and children, and boys from girls. Externally the sheer size of many Victorian villas was a potent proclamation of status and substance. The front garden provided a degree of privacy, especially when planted with screening hedges and shrubs, and the back garden

Drawing room at Sneyd Park House, pictured in 1930.
(Courtesy Peter Insole, Know Your Place)

was a private space for children to play and washing to be dried.

None of this is to say that the middle class had happier or more fulfilling home lives than anyone else, but in terms of the opportunities provided by their houses, and the relatively secure terms on which they were occupied, they were well placed to succeed. Lower down the income scale things became progressively more difficult.

The Respectable Working Class

If servant keeping defined the Victorian middle class the pursuit of respectability marked out the better off, artisanal, section of the working class. 'Here was the sharpest of all lines of social division, between those who were and those who were not respectable: a sharper line by far than that between rich and poor, employer and employee, or capitalist and proletarian'.[37] Whereas the middle class took their own respectability for granted the working class had to earn it on a daily basis (in contrast to the twenty-first century, where respect is often demanded as a right). To be considered respectable it was necessary to show appropriate deference to one's social superiors, to know and accept one's place in society. There were certain other required behavioural traits, foremost among which was a quiet and sober way of life, but it was also necessary to be clean and tidy, hard working and honest.[38] House and home were important components of any attempt to claim and retain respectability.

As discussed in chapter six, new dwellings for the working class in Bristol were overwhelmingly in the form of the standard plan terraced house, initially consisting of four rooms plus a scullery and later six rooms and a scullery kitchen. Such houses were almost always rented, although some people did manage to buy after regular saving with a local building society. One Bristol witness told the Royal Commission in 1884 that, 'A large number of artisans have bought homes through building societies'[39] but the proportion remained low. At the same time it was claimed that 4 or 6 roomed houses in St Agnes and Goodhind Street could be purchased for £90 to £150 and that this might cost as little as 3s a week.[40] This seems rather implausible although the interest on a mortgage of £100 at 5 per cent would have been only a little more than 3s a week. A real example concerns a certain Ann Grandfield, widow, who purchased 12 Goodhind Street in 1868. She took out a mortgage for £84 with the New Bristol and District Permanent Building Society, of which she was a shareholder. Then in January 1869 she borrowed a further £48 and agreed to pay 2s-3d for the next 688 weeks (more than 13 years).[41] If she was repaying, say, 4s on the first loan her total mortgage costs would have been 6s-3d each week, or not much more than the rent due on a house valued at £15 a year (which hers was).

Renting provided limited security of tenure, largely dependent on the tenant's ability to keep paying the rent and to retain the goodwill of the landlord. Landlords could set rents at whatever they thought the market would bear and they could evict tenants for any (or no) reason in order to regain vacant possession of their property. The Small Tenements Recovery Act, 1838, simplified the procedure for obtaining possession and tilted the system towards the interests of the landlord.[42] Small tenements in this context meant properties commanding a rent of less than £20 per annum, a category that covered the great majority of houses in Bristol at that time. Tenants who could not pay their rent on time were also at risk of the landlord sending in bailiffs to seize, or distrain, possessions that could be sold. Clearly, therefore, respectability rested heavily on regular payment of rent, although wise landlords would sometimes tolerate arrears of rent, for example in the case of reliable tenants temporarily out of work in slack seasons or difficult times.

What did the respectable working class pay in rent for their houses, and how much space did they get for their money? In his report for the General Board of Health, written in 1850, George Clark stated that what he called the labouring class occupied houses with rateable values not exceeding £10 per year; he also referred to the very poor as people occupying houses at less than £5 per year.[43] The assumption underlying this discussion is that the latter group generally occupied older dwellings, in the central courts and alleys, and that the better off working class were more likely to be found in the new or recently built terraces, which were often valued at more than £10 a year, especially later in the century. In the late 1830s valuations surveys there were numerous houses with values of £8-£10 on Stapleton Road, Easton Road and adjacent streets such as Twinnell and Thrissell Streets.[44] By 1871 Andrew Brown's houses on Stapleton Road were valued at £9-£16, and standard terraced houses in Newtown were mostly valued at around £10-£12. A little further north and built rather later, similar houses on Goodhind Street were valued at £13-£16.[45] These valuations, then, give a pretty good indication of the rents commanded by basic, two-up-two-down houses built in the middle decades of the century in east Bristol: a valuation of £10 per year implied a rent of a little less than 4 shillings a week, while a valuation of £16 suggested a rent of a little more than 5s a week. An enquiry carried out just after the turn of the century concluded that small flat-fronted two bedroomed houses were typically let for between 4 and 5 shillings a week; for three bedrooms the rents were 5 to 6 shillings and for the larger six-roomed terraced houses with three bedrooms 6s 6d to 8s 6d.[46]

Consider Regent Street, Newtown, a street of 81 standard terraced houses built in the early 1850s. These houses were nearly all valued at £9 per year in 1871; they opened directly off the pavement and had two small rooms on each floor.[47] In a sample of 29 houses in 1871 there were 186 people, and in 19 of those houses there was more than one household. The average number of people per house was 6.4 and therefore there were 3.2 people per bedroom. In one house there was a couple with four young children together with another couple and their two children; in another a couple with five children plus a widow and her 18-year-old daughter. Regent Street was not unusual. Across the city, in Woolcott Street, Redland (unusually for this suburb there was one street of 1850s standard terraced houses), we find the

1871 census recording 47 households (141 people) in 25 houses. In evidence to the Royal Commission in 1884 the Rev Ernest Fuller spoke about the prevalence of sharing in recently built houses in St Agnes (between Ashley Road and Newfoundland Road): 'The ordinary artisan cannot pay for a house in my district at 5s or 6s. He can only pay for half a house.' Another observer noted that in this area there were 750 houses and about 1200 or 1300 families.[48] Fuller also suggested that a house let to two families would have a rent of 6s to 8s. He then emphasised that he was talking about ordinary workers, not 'degraded' families.[49] Admittedly the early 1880s was a difficult period for the local economy, especially workers in the construction industry, where he believed artisans could earn only £1 per week. Taken together with the evidence from 1871, the conclusion must be that working-class families were struggling to afford enough space to meet the requirements of respectability. In view of the high incidence of shared houses among the working class it is worth remembering that the much larger houses of the well off were invariably home to just one family, plus their servants.

Domestic life in these little houses must have been difficult: an entire family in each bedroom, two women sharing cooking facilities and everyone struggling to get ready for work or school in the mornings. With just one outside privy and one cold water tap shared by six or more people it must have been difficult to maintain standards of hygiene and cleanliness. David Davies, the Medical Officer of Health, denied that such houses were overcrowded, but Rev Fuller referred to what he called 'moral overcrowding', ie when men and girls shared a bedroom.[50] A hallmark of respectability was that adults and children, especially older children, occupied separate bedrooms.

Another marker of respectability was the front parlour, a room containing the best furniture and, if possible, a marble fireplace with an over-mantel, a piano, a chiffonier (sideboard) and a glass fronted cabinet for displaying valued objects, such as the best china. Suitable pictures, engravings of pastoral scenes or Highland landscapes, for example, would also be hung in the parlour, and may have included studio photographs of family members – devoting hard earned cash to the taking and framing of such images was a sure sign of aspiration. Respectability was proclaimed both by possession of these luxury items and also the capacity to set aside a room for them, to be used only on Sundays and special occasions, such as visits from honoured guests (including the vicar or priest).[51] Obviously in a small house shared by two families this sort of proclamation of respectability was out of the question, but where one family occupied a whole house the parlour was proof

Loxton's interior of Beauley Road, Southville. (Courtesy: Bristol Reference Library)

that they could afford such surplus space, a sign of their superiority. There is agreement in the literature that, especially towards the end of the century, 'The parlour was a shrine to respectability and domesticity.'⁵² Martin Daunton argued that,

> The parlour had its symbolic function, and may also be interpreted as an entirely rational response to an increase in real incomes which permitted the purchase of furniture and fittings but which did not sanction their frequent use. Quite apart from any other consideration, the cost in time and money of heating two rooms simultaneously ruled out the everyday use of two living rooms…The parlour was not to be used for relaxation. Rather, it should be interpreted as a more controlled and formal social environment…Everyday meals and casual meetings with neighbours took place in the kitchen, in an informal and unstructured manner.⁵³

This suggests that the way the respectable working class used their houses was similar to the middle-class pattern: honoured guests at the front and everyday activities behind. In Bristol, unlike in some other towns, it had long been the case that the front door opened into a passage, not directly into the front room, thereby making it easier to keep the parlour for best.

Being respectable was about keeping up appearances, and although there was little that could be done to personalise a narrow fronted terraced house with no front garden, it was still important to keep the net curtains washed and clean, and to generally maintain an impression of order and tidiness. Burnett even referred to a prevalent 'cult of cleanliness'.⁵⁴ Although it has been argued above that homeliness implies a degree of permanence, respectability also meant a willingness to move house, in a never ending pursuit of more respectable surroundings. Thus it was not just about the house and home, but as with the middle class in the suburbs, it was about the wider context, in this case being part of a community 'where the prevalent conformities made it safe and pleasant to be sober, thrifty, clean-spoken and private.'[55] People had a well developed understanding of the relative merits and status of different streets within the same neighbourhood. Even the poorest families also sought advancement by moving, according to Rev Fuller in 1884; speaking of the notoriously poor area of St Jude's, he said that 'As soon as they get a little bit of self-respect, they clear out of a place of that kind and try to get two rooms elsewhere.'[56]

The Homes of the Poor
The Homes of the Bristol Poor[57] was the title given, apparently without conscious irony, to a book published in 1884, based on a series of visits to the very places where creating a home was most problematic: the courts and alleys of the central parishes, together with the cheap little houses that had been thrown up in parts of Bedminster and place like the Dings. Carefully acknowledging the progress made in recent years the un-named author went on to say, 'but the population is still very dense in the Dings, St Jude's, Barton Hill, Catherine Mead street, Essex street, Still House lane and Philip street, and neighbourhood of Mill lane, Bedminster, Little James street, Earl street and Eugene street, St James's, and one or two places in the Hotwell road'.[58] Later in the same year came the *Report of the Committee on the Condition of the Bristol Poor*,[59] with a somewhat different but overlapping list.[60] These reports came in the immediate aftermath of a searing polemic, entitled *The Bitter Cry of Outcast London: an inquiry into the condition of the abject poor*, by Andrew Mearns (1883), and in the context of a local economic downturn that was causing much distress among the least well off. Gilmore Barnett estimated that poor labourers were willing to do a day's work for 2s-6d, and implied that they could not rely on working every day.[61] This was also the time when the Royal Commission on the Housing of the Working Classes was taking evidence. There is, therefore, a considerable quantity of information and opinion on conditions in the 1880s, enabling comparison with the equally voluminous material generated by the public health crisis of the 1840s. At that time the reports by Dr William Kay,[62] Sir Henry de la Beche[63] and George Clark,[64] had all painted a picture of a town that was filthy, stinking and disgusting to its

inhabitants. Kay wrote about a sick patient in Hotwells whose room was assailed by the foul smell from a pigsty immediately outside; he reported that the man died and the pig remained. De la Beche memorably was driven to vomit during an inspection of offensive and overflowing privies, and Clark judged Bedminster to be what he called the 'opprobrium' of the city: '…it is…for the most part, low, ill-built and crowded together; a large proportion of the inhabitants are poor'.[65]

The Committee on the Condition of the Bristol Poor (almost all of whose members were liberal reformers, not hardliners) referred to the problems concentrated among the 'dwellings for the loafer, the beggar, the idle and intemperate' – each word indicating lack of respectability. In the early Victorian period the close built and ill-ventilated courts and alleys were widely condemned by public health reformers; sometimes the opening from the street was very narrow, and often the inner end was closed off by a wall or building. One court near to Old Market Street was evocatively named 'Dark Entry', and at the time of the 1841 census there were 27 people living in its four dwellings. Nine years later George Clark described Dark Entry as being 'very close and crowded'.[66] Across the city, on the steep ground above Hotwell Road, was Jones's Court, consisting of 16 houses containing 116 people (illustrated on page 19). Nearby was Rees's Court, which William Kay stated had been constructed less than twenty years before his survey in 1843. It was built on two levels and entered by a long narrow passage:

> The upper buildings consist of five houses, of three stories [sic], on each side, occupying a frontage of 50 feet, with an intermediate space, forming a court, of only eight feet, backed by a high wall, and this again surmounted by a row of buildings, altogether impeding ventilation. The internal arrangement of the dwellings is equally bad; one room below, nine feet square and nine feet high, leads by a narrow staircase, barely allowing space for passage, to two apartments of similar dimensions above – the upper, the attic, immediately under the roof – the ceiling sloping accordingly – and the window placed so low down in the front as altogether preclude the escape of foul air. There are 79 persons living in these 10 houses.

It is hard to imagine anyone living up to the requirements of respectability in these sorts of housing conditions, and the contrast with the spacious villas of leafy, elevated parts of Clifton could hardly be more starkly drawn. It is true that by the 1880s some of the worst and most squalid courts had been removed by warehouse building and municipal projects such as the construction of Victoria Street, but any improvement in housing was just a side effect and it was also true that most of the places that had attracted criticism in the 1840s were still being lived in. Very little indeed had been done by the authorities to tackle the problem directly, as will be discussed in the next chapter. Here the focus is on the consumer experience at what was the bottom end of a highly stratified market. The very poorest had no fixed abode, renting a bed for a night or two in one of the common lodging houses in St Jude's and neighbouring parishes. It was reported in 1884 that in 51 registered common lodging houses there were 910 men and 17 children in 229 rooms, or just over 4 people per room.[67] A few years later, in 1891, it was said that at least 1,000 people in Bristol depended on the 54 registered common lodging houses in the city.[68] One example was 25 Lamb Street, St Jude's, where the census of 1891 recorded Ann Bussell, a widow aged 72, deputy lodging house keeper, together with 22 lodgers, mostly single men identified as general labourers. Nearby, at 7 Great Ann Street one family occupied two rooms, but the other 12 households in the house had just one room each: 41 people in 14 rooms was obviously nearly 3 per room, and probably 41 per WC. In evidence to the Royal Commission the reformer Lord Shaftesbury deplored what he referred to as the 'one room system'[69] but Octavia Hill, widely acknowledged as a practitioner of enlightened housing management, admitted that she was quite happy to house a family with two small children in one room.[70] Hill did, however, accept that as the children grew up it was desirable that the family occupied more than one room. A one-room dwelling obviously concentrated all domestic activities in a single space, and Victorian moralists were particularly exercised by the evils attendant upon fathers sharing sleeping space with their adolescent or grown-up daughters. Lord Salisbury, for example, writing in 1883, observed that,

> Thousands of families have only a single room to dwell in, where they sleep and eat, multiply, and die…It is difficult to exaggerate the misery which such conditions of life must cause, or the impulse which they must give to vice.[71]

In 1866 the government's chief medical officer, Sir John Simon, wrote that Bristol was among the worst places for overcrowding and unfitness.[72] Simon had sent Dr Henry Hunter to investigate conditions in Bristol and he had concluded that 'about half of the labouring population live in a room or rooms in a large house'.[73] The worst case reported by Hunter was a family of three adults and eight children living in one room in Orchard Place, Bedminster.[74] Here is an extract from his report:

> Sharland's Court in Bread Street consists of small houses 20 feet 10 [inches] by 12 feet in ground plan, with two bedrooms. They had no back opening. The rent is 2s-1d. In one I found five adults with five children; in another one adult with seven. The ten other families were smaller, and in no case did there seem to be a lodger. The total result was 12 houses, 24 bedroooms, 26 adults and 37 children…In Gloster Court, Redcross Street, were 23 occupied houses. Their ground plan was about 9 feet 6 by 9 feet 6, and the bedrooms were above 7 feet high. There was a privy closet to each, but no yard or back opening. This was a cheap neighbourhood, and the rents varied from 1s-9d down to 8d a house. All had more than one bedroom. In one house with two bedrooms were four adults with five children. The total result was 23 houses, 50 bedrooms, 52 adults, 64 children.[75]

Within the city itself there were sharply divergent views on overcrowding and how to measure it. David Davies, Bristol's Medical Officer from 1865 to 1886, more or less defined it out of existence by insisting that 300 cubic feet per adult, and half that amount per child, was sufficient for a bedroom to count as not crowded.[76] On that basis a room ten-feet square and ten-feet high could accommodate a family of four. However, as mentioned above, people such as Rev Fuller took the view that there was a considerable amount of 'moral overcrowding' and even Davies was prepared to agree that,

> there is a very bad state of things, grown up persons, such as girls, sleeping with their grown up brothers and cousins, and there is no doubt that under that state of things a great deal of immorality occurs.[77]

The Committee on the Condition of the Bristol Poor was inclined to accept that overcrowding was not extensive in the city, and that it was concentrated among the very poorest, in large houses previously abandoned by the better off. Here each room was let to a different family, for between 1s and 3s-6d a week.[78] The sorts of people occupying these rooms they believed to be unskilled labourers, charwomen, hawkers, tailoresses, washerwomen, woodchoppers and seamstresses, people whose earnings were so low that they had no chance of securing decent affordable accommodation, despite paying a fifth or more of their incomes on rent. The Committee also felt that, 'Houses in which the poorest classes live are usually owned by people with very little money, who have bought the houses 'cheap' and think every repair a misery to be avoided.'[79]

This discussion has tended to concentrate on the central area, but the poor were also to be found in places such as the Dings, Barley Field and Tyler's Fields, across the floating harbour from Temple Meads, in houses built in the years just before the arrival of the railway; here, close to an expanding industrial area containing an iron works, glass works and gas works, houses were mostly valued at less than £5 a year, and sometimes as low as £3 (implying a weekly rent of about 1s-2d)[80] These streets all disappeared a long time ago and it is now difficult to say whether they were any worse built than anywhere else; their low valuation may have been primarily due to the proximity of polluting industries. There were widespread reports of so called 'jerry building', new houses with inadequately fired bricks, undersized roof timbers and unseasoned wood used for doors and window frames. The Royal Commission concluded that, 'There can be no doubt but that the houses are often built of the commonest materials, and with the worst workmanship, and are altogether unfit for the people to live in, especially if they are a little rough in their ways. The old houses are rotten from age and neglect. The new houses often commence where the old ones leave off, and are rotten from the first. It is quite certain that the working classes are largely housed in dwellings which would be unsuitable even if they were not overcrowded.'[81]

Understandably, a lot of attention focused on dwellings that were considered to be 'unfit for human habitation', although this concept was never properly defined. Even Sir John Simon, the Privy Council's chief medical officer in the 1860s, could only come up with this tautologous attempt:

> By places 'unfit for human habitation' I mean places in which by common consent even moderately healthy life is impossible for human dwellers.[82]

Perhaps the outstanding candidate in Bristol to illustrate unfit housing was the set of five courts off Redcross Street, just north of Old Market Street, built in the early years of the century. One of these was Gloster Court, cited in the quote from Dr Hunter, above. These tightly packed little houses had been heavily criticised by George Clark in 1850:

It would be incorrect to say that there were no drains (so called) in these courts, and it would be equally at variance with truth to say that they answered any purpose of drains in carrying off the refuse matter from houses.[83]

In 1884 witnesses disagreed about exactly where the privies were located, but it seems they were in a cupboard under the stairs – unventilated and directly off the one living room. Some of the houses were still occupied into the early 1890s.[84]

Not far away in the parish of St Jude's was Little George Street, behind which was George Court. Here was to be found a group of 14 one-up-one-down houses built back-to-back. These houses were not cleared away until the 1930s, when it was reported that the 'The sanitary arrangements are abominable': there were six WCs, with no flush facilities, and just two outdoor taps, for the entire group.[85] Of 182 houses in the Great Ann Street clearance area in 1934 just 30 (16 per cent) had an indoor water supply and 94 houses had only a part share of a water tap. This is a powerful reminder of how inadequate the water supply was in some parts of the city, almost a century after the creation of the Water Company.

Wherever they were the poor were the people who had the least satisfactory experience as consumers of housing, in terms of each of the main measures: the amount of space per person within the dwelling, extent and quality of space around the dwelling, access to water and sanitation, tendency to dampness, value for money and security of tenure. The worst properties were often owned by people who were themselves poor and therefore unable to carry out necessary repairs, even if tenants paid their rents regularly and on time. Finally in this list, the poor mostly had addresses that were stigmatising, making it even more difficult to improve their standing in society.

It is, of course, possible that not everyone was trying to improve their position, that not everyone was interested in respectability. Victorian society had numbers of ways of referring to people whose spirit had been broken and who had given themselves up to crime, drink and slovenly habits, among which the 'demoralised poor' was the least pejorative. A flavour of the debate about the slums can be gained from a question put to Lord Shaftesbury when he appeared before the Royal Commission in March 1884. He was asked for his view on a recent pamphlet entitled, 'Is it the Pig that makes the Stye, or the Stye that makes the Pig?'[86] He was firmly of the opinion that the problem lay with the material circumstances that the poor had to endure. Octavia Hill, on the other hand, referred to the 'criminal and destructive classes' and placed herself in the camp of those who believed that, as she put it,

> The people's homes are bad, partly because they are badly built and arranged; they are tenfold worse because the tenants' habits and lives are what they are. Transplant them tomorrow to healthy and commodious homes and they would pollute and destroy them.[87]

This debate was also played out in Bristol, where Dr Kay had argued passionately in the 1840s that squalid conditions were '…traceable to causes not inherently or essentially attached to the poor…but to their needless exposure to many noxious and positive influences external to their habitations,' by which he meant defective drainage, imperfect ventilation, crowded and badly constructed dwellings and want of cleanliness due to the absence of proper supplies of water.[88] The Medical Officer, David Davies, however, was inclined to blame poor for their conditions, citing ignorance, intemperance and overproduction of offspring.[89]

To conclude, this chapter has drawn attention to the ways in which the consumer experience of housing varied from great luxury to abject squalor, from status enhancement to the reinforcement of humiliation. The market mechanism was highly, brutally effective in sorting people out by income, but it failed to deliver decent affordable housing for all. Indeed, it would be better to say that the market provided such housing for only a minority. A Fabian Society report in 1891 claimed that probably not less than 10,000 people in Bristol needed to be rehoused.[90] How could this be achieved? Where the market failed, could there be another solution? These are the questions taken up in the next chapter.

CHAPTER EIGHT

The Politics of Housing

Previous chapters have emphasised the way that in Victorian Britain the production and consumption of housing was treated as a private matter, mediated by market forces. Here, however, the focus shifts to a consideration of the politics of housing, a phrase used in this context to refer to public debate about what, if anything, should be done, and by whom, to remedy situations where the free play of market forces produced outcomes deemed to be socially unacceptable. An important part of the politics of housing was campaigning intended to persuade both people in power and the wider public that certain situations were indeed socially unacceptable. As chapter seven has shown, for a considerable number of Bristol families, especially but not exclusively in the inner parishes, there was an iron link between poverty and poor housing: the market simply failed to provide decent houses at prices they could afford. Housing acquired a higher profile as a political issue in the early 1880s as part of a wider debate about poverty, and the argument was put forward that the dreadful conditions endured by the poor were no-longer tolerable in a civilised society, that they were an affront to the richest economy the world had ever seen. The market had failed, but it was not clear what could be done to address the problem, given the importance attached to the rights of private property owners, the power of the property lobby and the wider ideology of laissez faire. As Enid Gauldie observed, 'The slogan 'rights of private property' had hardly to be breathed to send the first housing reformers scuttling back behind their barricades'.[1]

In fact, by the start of the Victorian period the principle was already well established that there were certain circumstances in which the interests of the wider public justified limits being imposed on the freedom of property owners. 'In the social sphere, ... it is scarcely possible to accept the existence of a systematic laissez faire policy at all...And by authorising local government authorities – at first through the establishment of improvement commissions, and later through the Municipal Corporations Act of 1835 and subsequent local private acts – to perform a wide range of local services, governments implicitly accepted the principle of local government intervention under the authority of the central government.²

As early as the seventeenth century, in the aftermath of the Great Fire of London the use of thatch for roofing was prohibited in the public interest, and under the terms of a local Act in 1788 Bristol had become the first town outside London to obtain statutory powers to regulate aspects of new building.³ The main concern at that time was fire prevention and the Act was limited to prescriptions about the construction of party walls and the alignment of external walls. Surveyors were appointed to administer the new regulations, which remained in force until they were updated by the Bristol Improvement Acts of 1840 and 1847. These rules were the subject of further elaboration in the form of building bye-laws later in the century. A second, and more controversial, area of regulatory intervention arose from the threat to public health from existing buildings that were deemed to be unfit for human habitation, but closing and demolishing unfit dwellings would only make matters worse unless new houses were provided. Thus in addition to regulation of private enterprise there was the question of how to increase the supply of decent houses at rents affordable by the poor. If the market could not deliver what was needed, and it clearly could not, then what was the alternative? If the town council was to be responsible for closing and removing unfit houses was it also to undertake their replacement? For most local councils in the nineteenth century this remained an unthinkable departure. However, there was always a certain amount of non-market based housing provision, such as almshouses endowed by wealthy benefactors, providing for poor elderly and disabled people. Bristol's rich mercantile past had ensured that it was relatively well supplied with almshouses, but the numbers remained trivial in relation to the scale of the problem. Almshouses were a medieval solution to a problem of pre-industrial society, but the idea of some kind of charitable or semi-philanthropic provision was taken up and reimagined in the context of Victorian cities. A further point worth noting here concerns a form of intervention that was barely even discussed let alone implemented in the nineteenth century: rent control. If housing was too expensive for a significant proportion of working people then measures to reduce rents to affordable levels made at least logical sense, but would have been impossible to contemplate in the prevailing view of markets and the balance of political forces.

The focus of this chapter, therefore, is on how the people of Bristol, through the auspices of the town council and model dwellings companies, responded to the housing problem in the city. It is not a very uplifting story.

The Wider Context

Throughout most of the Victorian period, from 1851 onwards, local authorities had powers to build houses for the working class but most chose not to do so. Instead, they confined their efforts to limited regulation of aspects of the private market, leaving the work of building affordable houses for the poor to a range of charitable and semi-philanthropic organisations. The first of the so-called model dwellings companies, the Metropolitan Association for Improving the Dwellings of the Industrious Classes, was established in 1841. It was followed by others with equally unwieldy names, each seeking to provide affordable housing in expensive inner city locations, mainly in London.[4] Before the development of cheap public transport towards the end of the century, large numbers of working people needed to live in or close to city centres, in order to be within walking distance of their work. In London, in particular, the vast size of the population meant intense competition for land and therefore extremely high prices, inevitably squeezing the least well off into horribly overcrowded conditions. The model dwellings companies sought to resolve this problem, first by accepting high density living, often even higher than in the surrounding streets, and to achieve this they resorted to multi-storey blocks of up to seven floors (without lifts); second, they built small and very basic dwellings, with shared sinks and WCs, and third, they relied on appealing to investors prepared to accept a low, below market, rate of return on their money, hence the term semi-philanthropic. The numbers of such investors, and the sums they were prepared to invest, were never sufficient to make much impact, and Charles Booth calculated that by 1891 the various charitable and semi-philanthropic organisations had provided accommodation for only about 72,000 people in London, or not much more than the *annual increase* in the population of the capital.[5] An additional criticism was that the people they were trying to house were not keen on the bleak and austere blocks of dwellings, nor the discipline imposed by the estate superintendents.

The model dwellings companies were also criticised for not achieving their goal of rents affordable by the poor. However, in 1862, the first of the great charitable trusts providing for the poor of London was established by George Peabody, an American banker and philanthropist living in England, who gave a total of £500,000 to what was then known as the Peabody Donation Fund. Peabody's trustees built over 5,000 small tenements by 1900. In 1889 the brewer Edward Guinness gave £200,000 to set up a similar trust for the same purpose. These endowed trusts were not dependent on attracting investors, and were therefore able to set rents at lower levels, but nevertheless they too aimed to achieve at least a nominal rate of return. Although their sources of capital were different the model dwellings companies and charitable trusts had much else in common in terms of the dwellings they provided and the style of management they employed.

Octavia Hill, meanwhile, developed a different approach that was aimed precisely to be affordable by the poorest class who had a settled way of life. From small beginnings in Marylebone, she attracted a lot of attention and financial support for her work centred on improving the management of existing housing for the poor.[6] For Miss Hill, the problem of bad housing was jointly created by landlords, who neglected to collect rents effectively and refused to carry out necessary repairs, and tenants whose habits were dissolute and spendthrift, imposing excessive wear and tear on their homes. Hill's approach was to buy cheap, rundown houses (or to take on their management) and then to improve both the houses and the tenants by dint of strict discipline – which she described as 'a tremendous despotism'. Her proud boast was that she never allowed arrears of rent, although whether she did really depended her judgement of the tenants' willingness to conform to her strictures:

> I do not say I will not have drunkards, I have quantities of drunkards; but everything depends on whether I think the drunkard will be better for being sent away or not.'[7]

For Hill, housing management was really a form of social work designed to educate and reform the demoralised poor. Central to her approach was the importance attached to the personal relationship between the owner or manager of a house and the tenants, and she recruited young middle-class women to be her rent collectors cum social workers.

Inevitably, London, with its huge population and acute housing problems, was the main focus of charitable and semi-philanthropic activity. In provincial towns and cities these organisations were 'scarcely noticeable', but there is some evidence from Newcastle, Leeds, Liverpool, Manchester, and, indeed, Bristol, as will be seen later.[8]

While the trusts and model dwellings companies were nibbling away at the housing shortage, local authorities were slowly accumulating regulatory powers, whether they wanted them or not. For example, in 1849 Bristol reluctantly asked for the Public Health Act, 1848, to be applied in the city (in order to avoid the ignominy of having it imposed from the centre).[9] In 1851 the newly constituted Local Board of Health sent a deputation to London to find out what was expected of them. They discovered that they had a set of duties in relation to sanitation, including the construction of a proper sewerage system, and discretionary powers, including the right to enter private premises to inspect the drains. In cases of defective sanitary arrangements the Board had the power to construct drains and WCs where owners refused to do so, and to recharge them for the costs. On paper, therefore, the creation of the Local Board represented 'an extraordinary interference with private rights'.[10] In 1855 the term 'unfit for human habitation' was first used in legislation, but unfortunately it was not defined. It is arguable that the widening of the franchise in 1867 made ministers more responsive to public opinion, and Benjamin Disraeli, chancellor at the time, is quoted as saying that 'The palace is not safe when the cottage is not happy'.[11] Nevertheless, working-class demands, articulated through the trade unions, were focused on relations between workers and employers rather than on social problems such as housing. To the extent that housing became a political issue it was as a result of middle-class reformers, whose energies were focused on mobilising charitable and semi-philanthropic resources rather than identifying a role for local councils.

As mentioned in chapter two, in 1868 local authorities were given the power to close and demolish houses deemed to be unfit, and in 1875 this was extended to cover multiple properties in areas of unfitness. By that stage local authorities had an impressive set of powers relating to different aspects of housing: they could close and demolish unfit properties; enforce drainage, ventilation and water supply; make regulations about new buildings; limit overcrowding and provide new houses for working people. However, for a variety of reasons, and particularly in relation to action on unfitness and rebuilding, progress was glacially slow. Landlords were naturally inclined to resist losing their rental income and would therefore seek to do just enough to prevent their local council from taking enforcement action. Ratepayers in general were, or were believed to be, opposed to public funds being spent on housing, and local councils were resistant to being told what they had to do by central government. The Acts were often cumbersome and difficult to administer, and crucially, they provided discretionary powers for local authorities, rather than imposing duties, a recipe for inaction, especially since there was no financial support or incentive from central government. Without replacement housing becoming available, local authorities felt themselves to be justified in not clearing away existing dwellings, however unfit they might be.

It was the perception that the Acts of 1868 and 1875, despite subsequent amendments, had failed to make the anticipated impact that contributed to the decision to appoint a Royal Commission to look into working-class housing in 1884. In 1883, Lord Salisbury, then the Conservative leader of the Opposition, wrote an influential article in *The National Review*, in which he argued that the problem of housing was becoming more difficult and more urgent.[12] He seemed to argue in favour of government expenditure on housing on the grounds that increasing prosperity had actually exacerbated the problem, by adding to demand in the cities. In the special case of London he recognised that overcrowding had been increased as a direct result of improvement projects undertaken by Parliament. He even appeared to hint at government loans for 'municipal bodies' to provide houses. The subsequent Royal Commission, of which Salisbury was a member, failed to endorse these apparently radical proposals. By 1885 Salisbury was the prime minister and himself introduced a Bill that was attacked in the Lords as socialism, despite its lack of new principles (the reformist *Bristol Mercury* also referred to Salisbury's 'socialistic views').[13] Of more long term significance was the Housing of the Working Classes Act, 1890, which made it easier for progressive authorities, such as Glasgow, Liverpool and Sheffield, to adopt more interventionist housing policies, but there was still no duty to build houses and no Exchequer subsidy to ease the burden falling on tenants and local ratepayers. 'After 1890, therefore, it was legally possible for an enlightened local authority to pursue an enlightened housing policy, possible but not very much more possible than it had been since at least 1875 and, arguably, since 1851.'[14]

Housing and the Town Council
Before looking at the substance of the politics of housing in Bristol it is necessary to say a little about the town council and its way of working. The ancient Corporation, abolished by the Municipal Corporations Act, 1835, had been a hybrid organisation, claiming to be both private, unaccountable and self-reproducing and at the same time the senior governing body of the city.[15] It was emphatically not a provider of public services, and nor, initially, was its replacement, the town council. The new council, which replaced the Corporation on 1 January 1836, was at least democratically elected, albeit by an electorate of little more than 4,000 men. The council consisted of 48 elected members plus 16 aldermen, elected by the 48. The first election produced a council of 24 Tories and the same number of Liberals, but in a fateful decision, Christopher George and Henry Ricketts defected from the

Liberals and voted with the Tories during the aldermanic elections, thereby allowing them to seize control of the council.[16] The Tories were to remain the largest party for the rest of the century.

The bulk of the work of the council was conducted in and by committees, the most important of which for current purposes was the 21 man committee established in 1851 when the council was designated as the Local Board of Health (LBH). This committee was usually referred to as the Sanitary Committee and its first main task was to build a set of mains sewers. Under the terms of the Public Health Act, 1848, the LBH was empowered to raise a rate on property within the city, establishing the District Fund, which was distinct from the smaller Borough Fund resulting from the Municipal Corporations Act, 1835. A third set of accounts resulted from the municipal takeover of the Dock Company in 1848.[17] These distinctions are mentioned here to highlight the extent to which different parts of the council worked largely independently of one another. From the outset the LBH operated from premises in Queen Square and Prince Street,[18] some distance from the Council House, and the Docks Committee also acquired its own offices in Queen Square. The independence of committees could lead to overlap and confusion (at least for later historians). Almost comically absurd was the persistence for at least thirty-five years of two committees, with identical memberships, dealing with street improvement; when asked by the council to consider the efficiencies of merging into one committee they declined.[19] In 1892 the *Bristol Mercury* noted that, 'The great system of what is now called the Urban Sanitary Authority grew up alongside, and practically independent of, the Council House itself'.[20]

The various contenders in the politics of housing in Victorian Bristol included the general public (or at least those with the right to vote), councillors of different parties and committees, and the staff employed to carry out council business. For many years the voting public was almost entirely middle class, and the wealthier parishes such as Clifton and St Augustine's were entitled to elect three times as many councillors as the poorer parishes of Bedminster and St Philip and St Jacob. It is not to be expected, therefore, that the council came under pressure to commit ratepayers' money to housing reform. Indeed, the opposite was more likely, and one historian concluded that, 'On the whole, Bristol's town council was parsimonious and extremely conservative in its view of its role'.[21] Among councillors it would be a mistake to assume that the mayor occupied a position of power and authority remotely equivalent to directly elected mayors in twenty-first century Bristol.

The mayoralty was a 'blend of business and pleasure'.[22] His job was to chair council meetings and to be an ex officio member of numerous committees, but the mayor was appointed for one year at a time, and it was not an honour that appealed to all. Sir John Haberfield served as mayor six times between 1838 and 1851, but he was exceptional, and according to Graham Bush there was never a queue of people wanting to be mayor.[23] To be the leader of the Tory group of councillors or the chair of one of the main committees was a more certain route to power and influence over events in the city. However, it is not clear when the parties started choosing a leader, nor how far the different groups acted in a disciplined way. Among the staff employed by the council, several, as will be seen below, served for long periods and exercised not inconsiderable influence over policy and practice.

Turning at last to the substance of the politics of housing, the measures taken to ensure that new buildings met at least a minimum standard of construction and sanitation were not contested and need not be discussed at length. The requirement to submit building plans seems to have been accepted without demur and it has been suggested in chapter six that the building bye-laws of 1871 were effectively a codification of established practice and as such had little impact on what was built. The more controversial and therefore more interesting and revealing areas concerned actions in relation to existing defective houses and the most difficult question of all – whether, how far and on what terms the council should become involved in building houses for the working class.

Immediately after its creation in 1851 the LBH appointed an inspector of nuisances, Joseph Yeates, whose job included the discovery and removal of offensive accumulations of human and animal waste. On his recommendation properties could be closed until the owners carried out the necessary remedial work. Yeates remained in office until his death in 1887, in which year over 3,000 nuisances were dealt with.[24] The Board also had the power to appoint a medically qualified officer of health, but they delayed doing so until 1865, at which point the city was in the midst of a typhus epidemic and under pressure from central government to take prompt and effective action. The man they chose was David Davies, a member of the Royal College of Surgeons practising in Bristol. He was initially given a temporary contract and it is conceivable that the Board anticipated that they could dispense with his services once the typhus retreated. In the event, Davies was given a series of annual contracts until finally achieving his ambition of the title of Medical Officer of Health in 1873. This indicates the less than wholehearted approach of the Board, and in David Davies they found a man who was entirely happy to do as little as possible to tackle the appalling housing conditions in parts of the city. In fairness to Mr Davies he was more interested in infectious diseases such as typhus and cholera, and it seems he relied on Joseph Yeates to work with little supervision on nuisance removal.[25]

Davies revealed a good deal about his way of working in his evidence to the Royal Commission in 1884. He was, by turns, boastful, ignorant, defensive and dishonest, drawing a sharply critical response from one of the commissioners:

> I am afraid your answers to certain questions have given too favourable a notion with regard to the state of things in Bristol, and might encourage those who are endeavouring to prevent improvement there.[26]

Central to Davies's approach was the tactic of denial: he would deny that there was a problem of unfit housing, for example, then deny that he had any powers to remedy unfitness, and then deny the efficacy of any action that he might take. As mentioned in chapter seven, Davies took it upon himself to more or less define overcrowding out of existence, setting a minimum acceptable standard that was well below that of prisons and workhouses. He explained to the Royal Commission that in 1871 he had persuaded the town council to adopt regulations on overcrowding, not with the intention of taking action against landlords but rather to use the regulations as a threat of action; he claimed that the prospect of being put on a register of defaulting owners was sufficient to bring them into line, and that in 1884 there were only six houses on the register.[27] The result was that he could assert that there was very little, if any, overcrowding in Bristol.

Similarly, on unfitness Davies played down the scale of the problem and then denied that he had any powers to demolish unfit houses. When he was reminded of the powers conferred by the Torrens Act of 1868 he fell back on saying that he had relied on nuisance removal powers, which extended only to closure orders, in the Public Health Acts, as if that was a convincing answer. In any case, only 26 unfit or overcrowded houses were closed in the period 1878-84. Questioned about what he had done in relation to larger areas of unfit housing Davies invoked the legal advice he had been given by the clerk to the Sanitary Committee, John Heaven. According to this advice in order to declare an unhealthy area under the Cross Act of 1875 it was necessary to show a high rate of mortality, and Davies denied the existence of meaningful differences: 'But our poorer districts, if you look at the returns of mortality, are as favourable as that of Clifton, which is the fashionable quarter.'[28] This was simply false, and in conflict with Davies's report to the Sanitary Committee in October 1875 in which he wrote that 'The disparity between the rates of mortality, in the different districts, is certainly remarkable.' His own figures showed that in 1876 the mortality in the St Mary Redcliffe registration sub-district was 29.5 per 1000, compared with just 16.7 in the Clifton sub-district.[29] Another way in which Davies avoided taking action in relation to unhealthy areas was to insist that there was nowhere in Bristol with a large enough concentration of unfit housing to qualify. This was a deliberate misreading of the Cross Act, which nowhere specified a minimum extent.

In 1877 Davies clashed with the Poor Law Guardians who wanted him to take action over two areas, the notorious set of courts off Redcross Street that have been mentioned several times in this book on account of their rank unfitness, and a dozen courts around Lewin's Mead. Davies was clearly angered by this attempt to put pressure on him to act, and his response was first to accuse the Guardians of not understanding mortality statistics and second to assert that none of the deaths in one of the specified areas was due to their sanitary condition, and therefore not his problem.[30]

David Davies represented one end of a spectrum of views about the state of housing in Bristol and what to do about it. The attempt by the Guardians to push him into action indicates that others saw things differently. One of the Guardians who signed the letter to the council was Gilmore Barnett, a Bristol solicitor who frequently argued the case for a more interventionist policy. In his evidence to the Royal Commission he said that,

> I am bound to say that I think a great deal of the distress in Bristol at the present time [1884], as regards the number of houses that are unfit for human habitation, is really due to want of administration on the part of the Town Council; they have not administered the laws that have been passed.[31]

Rev Ernest Fuller's evidence to the Commission was also at odds with Davies's, and he was quite clear that from his point of view there was a worrying amount of 'moral overcrowding'. Davies's reluctance to act on bad housing was also criticised, to his intense annoyance, in professional journals including the *Sanitary Record* (1878)[32] and *The British Medical Journal* (1883), which went so far as to say, 'It is hard to believe that in a place like Bristol there can be no scope for the action of the sanitary authority in the improvement of the houses and surroundings of the poor'.[33]

During his twenty-one years in post David Davies wrote a lot about his approach to public health and it is clear that he truly believed that sanitary measures could have only a limited impact. He praised the town council for the positive effects of street improvement projects that had removed quantities of unfit houses but somehow retained the belief that further demolitions under public health legislation would not be justified. This might imply that he was just idle, happy for the Improvement Committees to take responsibility for clearances. But this would be unfair, for he was also obviously moved by the plight of poor people flooded out of their homes in Newfoundland Gardens in 1875[34] and by what he called the slaughter of the innocents, that is to say, the large number of deaths in infancy. In his annual report for 1883 he expressed his irritation with the series of newspaper articles on the homes of the poor that had recently appeared in the *Bristol Mercury* and went on to say,

> I think that putting the cure and prevention of evils which are chiefly of a moral nature on the Sanitary Authorities will be applying for relief in the wrong quarter. The most feasible plan, in my opinion, for abating and preventing the evils, is the one adopted by Miss Octavia Hill in parts of the Metropolis.[35]

In other words, he favoured attempts to modify the behaviour of the poor, who were the victims of bad housing, rather than measures that would challenge the property rights of the owners of such housing.

Whatever view one takes of David Davies one thing is clear: he never came under sustained pressure from the dominant group on the council to change his stance. Other Bristol witnesses (Fuller, Barnett and Macliver) told the Royal Commission about the existence of the overcrowding denied by Davies, but his views were, apparently, shared by the majority on the town council. He retired in 1886 but this did not signal a new approach because he was replaced as Medical Officer of Health by his son, Dr David S Davies, who remained in post beyond the end of the century.

Reformers on the council, including from 1886 Gilmore Barnett, argued their case but remained an enlightened and marginalised minority.[36] The authentic voice of the working class in the politics of housing is hard to find, not least because the first working-class councillor was not elected until

Robert Tovey in 1887. However, outside the council chamber the case for reform was supported by local newspapers, notably the *Bristol Mercury*. As discussed in chapter seven, the *Mercury* had sponsored a series of articles in November 1883 on the homes of the Bristol poor, and in January 1884 it admitted to helping to build up what it called a 'healthy public opinion' on the housing question. At the same time a committee was established to consider the condition of the poor in Bristol; members included reformers such as Gilmore Barnett, Francis Fry, Francis Sturge and Mark Whitwill, but also Dr David S Davies. The committee's report in December 1884 discussed at length the housing problems, including overcrowding, faced by the poor on low and irregular earnings. It recognised that 'the terrible condition of the homes of the poor has been the cry in vogue', but argued that this was a symptom of deeper problems.[37]

In October 1887 the council appointed a committee to report on the Artisans' Dwellings Acts, and immediately Barnett called for an investigation of unhealthy areas and houses in the city, and, crucially, he raised the question of whether the committee should recommend the council to build artisans' dwellings.[38] This was probably the first time such a suggestion had been recorded in municipal papers. Dr Davies told the next meeting that he was unaware of any area that he could certify as unhealthy, and two years later he reported that not one house had been deemed unfit for human habitation under the Artisans' Dwellings Acts since 1868.[39] However, Barnett was clearly on a mission to keep up the pressure for positive action: in January 1888 he submitted a list of 32 questions for Dr Davies about the Housing and Public Health Acts, but unfortunately the answers were not recorded.[40] In 1889 the committee reported to the council that although the MoH accepted that there were about 600 houses that 'on medical grounds he would not be sorry to get rid of', nevertheless they could not be condemned as unfit because they were somehow not 'dangerous to health'.[41] It is not hard to imagine the kinds of argument that had taken place among members of the committee, and between the committee and the MoH, leading up to this report: the MoH had been forced to admit that there were hundreds of poor quality houses, but he would only go so far as the equivocal statement that he would 'not be sorry' to see them removed. Nothing more was heard from this committee.

The Housing of the Working Classes Act, 1890, raised the hopes of reformers that Bristol might, at last, see a more positive approach. The Act was essentially a measure designed to clarify and consolidate previous laws, making it easier for local authorities to act, but not requiring them to do so.

Albion Place, the Dings, about 1930, illustrating mixed residential and industrial land uses. (Courtesy: Herbert Tarring collection)

In November 1890 Bristol town council appointed a committee to consider the implications of the new Act in the city, and a deputation (inevitably including Gilmore Barnett) was sent to meet the Sanitary Committee to discuss whether a new committee was required. The report of the meeting in the *Bristol Mercury* suggests a rather tetchy discussion in which Barnett had pointed out that the Act enabled the council to condemn hundreds of houses, but nevertheless the members of the Sanitary Committee insisted they could handle the extra work.[42] This was, no doubt, partly because they had no expectation of doing much additional work, no intention of adopting a more interventionist policy, and certainly no intention of building houses.[43]

Meanwhile, additional pressure was exerted on the council by the establishment, in 1890, of the Bristol Committee for Promoting the Better Housing of the Poor (BCPBHP). This organisation, chaired by Lewis Fry, Liberal MP for Bristol North, and supported by many of the city's clergy, had four sub-committees whose task was to monitor conditions in different parts of the city and to draw to the attention of the Sanitary Authority any houses where the landlords refused to carry out remedial action.[44] The *Bristol Mercury* reported at length on Lewis Fry's address to the annual meeting of the BCPBHP in April 1891. The following is part of that report:

> As the mind cannot perform its functions properly in the social system unless provided with a home well ventilated, sufficiently roomy to prevent overcrowding, and free from anything injurious to health. Of late years that idea had become very prominent. The old idea was that tenants were able to look after themselves. But many were compelled by circumstances beyond their control to live in certain localities. *He thought it was the duty of the community to interfere in such matters.* They would all admit that a man had no more right to erect a dwelling which was unfit for human habitation than he had to offer an article of food that was unfit for consumption, and knowingly to let an unhealthy home was as much an offence against society as to sell diseased meat or rotten fish (hear, hear).[45] [Emphasis added.]

This eloquent expression of the liberal interventionist view was obviously well received by the audience on the day, and stands as a powerful rebuttal of arguments based on the rights of property owners. At the Committee's annual public meeting in March 1892 Gilmore Barnett told the audience that if the council undertook to build houses it 'would not be in advance of public opinion', and urged the Committee to keep up the pressure on the council.[46]

Dr Davies continued to insist that the legislative powers relating to unfit areas could not be applied in Bristol because the city had no problem areas extensive enough to be dealt with under Part I of the Act, despite the fact that the Act made no reference to a minimum size. A small number of defective houses, Hammond's buildings, were removed at Quaker's Friars in the middle of town in 1891 and a larger area of houses, the Redcross Street courts, were cleared at about the same time but by the Streets Improvement Committee, not by the Sanitary Committee.[47] This sort of undeclared slum clearance policy suggests that the intransigence of the Sanitary Committee and the MoH had led more progressive members (and officers) to find a different way to remove an enclave of houses that had been notorious since at least 1850. An indication of the state of these houses is that the Committee acquired them for an average price of just £40 per dwelling. In 1892, the

BCPBHP urged the council to relieve overcrowding by building working-class houses on void land in its ownership. The reaction of the Sanitary Committee was to undertake what sounds like a major study of conditions in four areas in St Paul's, Bedminster, St Jude's and Hotwells: over nine months the investigators looked at 782 houses, occupied by 1,433 families living at a density of 6.58 people per house.[48] Moreover, the MoH reported that in St Jude's there were 246 cases of families living in just one room.[49] Despite the fact that most of the houses in the study contained two or more households the Sanitary Committee

> found that no systematic overcrowding occurred in these areas, and that in the case of more than one half of the persons in each locality in regular employment, there appeared to be no necessity that they should reside there, as their places of business were situated half a mile and upwards from their homes.[50]

The Committee drew the conclusion that there was no need for the council to build on the land at Redcross Street (part of the site was taken for a school and the rest became a public open space, St Matthias Park).

In February 1892 the Sanitary Committee decided to set up a sub-committee on housing.[51] After a slow start this sub-committee resolved in January 1895 to meet monthly and to visit such courts and houses as were reported to them by the inspector of nuisances. For example, in January 1895 the sub-committee visited three courts off Leadhouse Lane, St Philip's; these were Abbott's Court, Bond Court and Stagg's Court, and whether they were ever declared unfit is not clear but in 1896 the sub-committee came close to a decision to purchase them, only to baulk at the price demanded by the owners. Discussion dragged on until September 1898 when all three courts were purchased by the nearby Jacob Street Brewery for redevelopment, thereby removing the possibility of that site being used for workmen's houses. The next month, however, the sub-committee resolved that there was an urgent need for the provision of workmen's houses containing two or three rooms, and that any land in the council's ownership should be considered for the purpose.[52]

Discussion of building council houses seems to have been under way since at least March 1896, when the sub-committee received a report on the subject from the MoH and City Engineer.[53] This change of heart was probably prompted by section 3 of the Appropriations Act, 1895, which specifically

Grace's Court, off Great George Street, St Jude's. The buildings on the right were back-to-back with those in the adjacent Mais Court. (Courtesy: Bristol Reference Library)

prohibited Bristol's Improvement Committee from purchasing any more land until a scheme had been agreed to provide replacement housing. In October 1897 the Local Government Board deferred approval for a loan of £58,000 for street improvement until details were given of how displaced people would be rehoused.[54] This experience reveals that while there was no duty on local authorities to provide houses there were ways in which central government could exert pressure on them to do so. It also suggests that the generally non-interventionist LGB was exasperated by the laggardly approach of Bristol town council.

In March 1896 the Engineer had been asked for details of costs and rents for three bedroomed houses. In the following October the answer was that such houses would cost between £180 and £220, depending on design and quality of work, and that rents of 5s per week 'would be sufficient'.[55] In March 1897 the Engineer submitted plans for 7 houses to be built on a site on the north side of Bragg's Lane, St Jude's, and when tenders were received

Loxton's drawing of some of the first council flats at Chapel Street, St Philip's Marsh. (Courtesy: Bristol Reference Library)

the lowest was for £1,090 (£155 per house).[56] However, there must have been difficulties of some sort, because in September 1898 a new set of tenders was received for 6 houses, and this time the lowest was £1,198. At this point the sub-committee recommended to the Health Committee that responsibility for new building should be handed over to the New Streets Committee, on the grounds that rehousing people displaced by street improvement schemes was part of the cost of such schemes, and 'the New Streets Committee would prefer to arrange such rehousing'.[57] One interpretation of this decision is that councillors and officers in favour of building by the council had concluded that the only way to get anything done was to wrest control from the Health Committee. Another, not incompatible, possibility is that the Health Committee and its sub-committee were happy to hand over responsibility. However you look at it, this episode highlights the fact that rehousing was seen as an adjunct of a limited programme of street improvement rather than a concerted policy of clearing the city's many slums.

The first Bristol council houses were completed by the New Streets Committee on Bragg's Lane, St Jude's, in about 1900. The MoH report for 1902 refers to 60 tenements built by the New Streets Committee, at Bragg's Lane, Chapel Street, St Philip's Marsh, and Millpond Street and Mina Road, both Baptist Mills. An interesting feature of the first council dwellings is that, unlike the terraced houses that were the standard product of private builders, they were constructed as flats in two storey blocks (in the case of Millpond Street for example, there were 16 flats in two blocks). Moreover, the council

Council flats at Mina Road, Baptist Mills, the last remaining block from before 1914. The flats have been refurbished and the metal balcony is not original. (Photograph: the author)

built dwellings of a lower standard in terms of space and specification (no bathrooms) than the private sector at that time, which can only be explained in terms of the reluctance to use rate payers' money to subsidise the rents. The only ones still standing are in one block on Mina Road. These flats were to stand in marked contrast to the cottages built in large numbers on council estates after the First World War. In view of developments during and after the war, it is interesting to note three features of the stance of the council in the early 1900s. First, there was no intention to build at scale; second, the emphasis was on cheapness, in order to create low rents affordable by the least well off.[58] And third, the Sub-Committee had already, by 1903, asked for a report on land for workmen's houses at Horfield, Fishponds, Brislington, Shirehampton and Knowle, all of which were areas where council houses were built in the 1920s.[59]

Meanwhile, in 1898 the Housing of the Working Classes Sub-Committee, now being chaired by Gilmore Barnett,[60] began to discuss the possibility of building a municipal common lodging house and the following year a site was identified on the corner of Wade Street and River Street. Progress was slow and the building did not open until 1905.

Semi-Philanthropic Housing in Bristol

Semi-philanthropic organisations made little impact on housing in Bristol, and information about them is scarce, but what can be said with confidence is that the first project started in 1856 when the Metropolitan Association for Improving the Dwellings of the Industrious Classes took a 75 year lease on land belonging to the city of Bristol on Limekiln Lane (now St George's Road) and Christmas Street/Narrow Lewin's Mead (the site formerly occupied by Queen Elizabeth's Hospital School).[61] The Limekiln Lane site is shown as void on the Ashmead map of about 1855 but the wording of the lease implies that it was already built on. The scheme was not a long term success and in 1871 the Bristol branch of the Metropolitan Association resolved to wind up its activities and to dispose of the leases on both sites.[62]

In the 1870s, however, the Bristol Industrial Dwellings Company was set up. This was initiated by Miss Susanna Winkworth (1820-1884), one of three sisters (the others were Alice and Catherine) involved in tackling social problems in Bristol. The new project was also supported by a number of well-known Bristol figures including George Wills (of WD and HO Wills), William K Wait (grain merchant, Bristol councillor and MP for Gloucester), William Budgett (wholesale grocer) and Lewis Fry. Winkworth was a follower of Octavia Hill and had previously purchased two or three houses in Dowry Square to be let to poor families at affordable rents. According to Latimer, the Industrial Dwellings Company was set up in the autumn of 1875[63] but the plans of the proposed buildings were submitted the previous March,[64] and a third source says that the company was incorporated in 1874.[65] The company sought an initial capital of £20,000 from people willing to buy shares priced at £50 each. The money was invested in a development of 80 tenements in three blocks, known as Jacob's Wells Buildings,[66] on Woodwell Lane (now Jacob's Wells Road). The site chosen by Miss Winkworth, on a steep slope facing north-east, belonged to, and was leased from, the Society of Merchant Venturers. It has been claimed that Winkworth herself was intimately involved in the design of the buildings but the plans in the Archives are signed by the London based architect Elijah Hoole, well known for his other work for semi-philanthropic housing companies and Octavia Hill herself.[67] The success of the project led in 1878 to the construction of an additional block, Brandon Buildings, with 50 tenements.

A detailed description of the blocks appeared in *The Architect* in August 1875:

> Each block has a broad stone staircase, without balustrades, but with a central wall supporting what would otherwise be the outer ends of the stone steps. One end of each staircase is completely unenclosed, thus

Jacob's Wells Buildings, built by Bristol Industrial Dwellings Company in 1875.
(Courtesy: M Hooper)

preventing both the formation and ascent of foul air; and as the room doors do not open on the staircases, but on the balconies, the former cannot communicate infection should any be present in any tenement. The tenements consist of one, two, three, or four rooms each, and with the exception of the single-room tenements, each has its own front door opening on the street or balcony.

Each tenement is thus as distinct from its neighbours as are separate houses in the same street. Some tenements are provided with sculleries, and all with cupboards and coal-bins. Each living-room has a small range with oven, and each bedroom (with one or two exceptions) a fireplace. A dust-shoot adjoins each staircase, to which a door on each floor is provided, and as old crinolines and umbrellas are occasionally forced into

Rear of Brandon Buildings, Jacob's Wells Road, showing how they were built into the steep hillside. (Courtesy: M Hooper)

these shoots in similar buildings elsewhere, they are in this case made of ample size, and will allow of such demands being made upon their capacity without detriment or stoppage.

The blocks were of four storeys and included two shops on the street frontage. None of the apartments had inside WCs, nor even exclusive use of an outside WC. Needless to say, there was not one bathroom anywhere. Water was supplied to each landing but not to each dwelling, just as Octavia Hill later advocated to the Royal Commission. The majority had one or two bedrooms (in some cases the bedrooms were only 5 feet 6 inches wide), but on the top floor there were 21 bedsitting rooms, surely the least attractive type of dwelling then being constructed. The rear blocks, squeezed between the taller front block and the hillside of Cliftonwood, consisted entirely of one bedroom apartments.

In his evidence to the Royal Commission Gilmore Barnett (naturally a supporter of the project and the company's solicitor) explained that there were 131 units in total, let at 1s to 1s 6d each week, very cheap by Bristol standards but, nevertheless, he said,

> The people who live in these industrial dwellings are a rather superior class; for instance, shipwrights, carpenters, coachmen, policemen and hauliers. We have not many of the very poor.[68]

He said that the company could not currently pay more than 2 per cent to its investors, partly because, as he put it, the Water Company 'show us no mercy' – he claimed that the water bill consumed 10 per cent of rental income.[69] The scheme was managed on Octavia Hill principles by Miss Winkworth and other lady rent collectors.

In many ways these dwellings were inferior to the standard narrow fronted terraced houses discussed in chapter six: no-one else in Bristol was building high density apartments on four storeys at that time, and new houses then being built elsewhere in the city were all provided with at least two bedrooms, their own water supply and a WC, together with a private open space. The dwellings and the blocks were, however, comparable with the outputs of similar companies in London at that time. And, it has to be said that whatever judgement is made, the Bristol Industrial Dwellings Company provided, on that one site, more dwellings than the town council managed to build in the whole of the period before 1919.

Conclusion

There is one overriding and inescapable conclusion from this discussion of the politics of housing in Victorian Bristol: the town council faced a situation in which thousands of its citizens were known to be living in dreadful and life-threatening conditions, it had the powers to mitigate those conditions and yet it did the absolute minimum. Courts and alleys identified as unhealthy in the 1840s were still occupied into the 1890s. Successive Medical Officers played down the scale of the problem of unfit housing and it seems that no-one pointed out that if the problem was so small then that was an argument for dealing with it in short order. The Bristol Industrial Dwellings Company did at least have a go, and although it left no lasting physical impact on the city and rates scarcely a mention in the historiography of the period, for the twenty-first century historian it serves to highlight to collective failure of vision and ambition on the part of the council. Bristol was not alone in this of course, but other cities such as Sheffield, Leeds, Liverpool, Glasgow and most notably London, all of which faced greater problems, achieved so much more.

CHAPTER NINE

Conclusion

It was explained in chapter two that rather than rely on conventional definitions of the housing problem, with an implied focus on poor quality houses and poor people, this book would define the market as the problem, and look at housing provision for all of the people. This approach has shown that there is much that can be known about housing in Victorian Bristol, and that housing is a good lens through which to study the growth of the city as a whole. However, there remain unanswered questions and, indeed, questions that have not been raised here. This is partly due to the nature of the sources consulted: these are mainly archived plans, deeds, minutes of meeting and official reports of various kinds. It has proved to be possible to find out who built what, when and where, but it is more difficult to say anything about what was in their minds at the time. It is easy to understand why so many small building firms failed, but harder to know how others generated enough income for survival while building only a trivial number of houses each year. It is also difficult to capture what it felt like to live in a Victorian house when it was new, without all the retrofitted comforts that we take for granted. This is a subject better addressed by novelists than historians. But we can be confident that people then had quite different expectations about what constituted a satisfactory residential environment. We tend to think of the Victorians as being preoccupied by sanitation but in fact they were slow to provide themselves with inside WCs and bathrooms. Neither did they expect to have warmth throughout their houses – bedrooms in particular were almost always cold places in winter. Having said that, though, a bedroom occupied by an entire family would have become foetid, stuffy and damp with condensation by morning. Compared to the present period Victorians lived in close contact with more people, and with other people who were not family members. Not only were families larger, on average, but as this book has shown significant proportions of working-class people shared their homes with at least one other household, and the middle classes shared theirs with live-in servants. Regrettably it has not been possible to discover what people thought about living in these ways.

Housing occupies most of the land in urban areas and therefore it is not surprising that the expansion of Bristol in the Victorian period was largely due to housebuilding. Indeed, when estate owners decided to develop their land they almost invariably opted for housing, which became the default urban land use. Warehouses and factories were, of course, built, but only when the initiative was taken by industrialists themselves. A good example of this would be the fourteen-acre site at Raleigh Road bought by WD and HO Wills in 1895 for the expansion of their Bedminster factories on land that had been designated by the Ashton Court estate as part of the only partially realised Greville Town housing development. What this book has shown is that the new and expanded neighbourhoods that gradually took shape on what had been fields surrounding the ancient city were, to a large extent, produced by the efforts of amateur developers (men who had made money in business and then branched into property development) and artisan builders (craftsmen with ambition), each acting on the basis of their understanding of what was in their own best interests. There was no overall vision or plan, little evidence that anyone had any idea of what a great industrialising city *should* look like. Bristol was not alone in this of course[1] but it does seem to have been particularly lacking in civic ambition. And it was a city with only the lightest touch regulation by a town council that, as has been emphasised in chapter eight, was singularly reluctant to become involved in housing. Thus the dominant mode of co-ordination was the market, the implications of which will be discussed later. It seems certain that while some landowners, especially those with extensive estates, would have taken a reasonably long term view, for small builders struggling with cash flow problems it was difficult to see much beyond their current project. The people who built houses in Victorian Bristol performed an essential social and economic function, with a lasting impact on the city, but their efforts threw up no well known names or great fortunes, in marked contrast to the manufacturers of ephemeral consumer goods such as tobacco, chocolate and soap. There was nothing heroic about housebuilding – no-one emerged remotely equivalent to Brunel, the feted builder of railways, bridges and ships.

Turning to the houses produced by these amateurs and artisans, their most striking feature is the limited number of basic plans. The argument developed in chapter six was that the narrow fronted terraced house was ubiquitous in pre-Victorian years, providing for all classes. Up to the middle of the century the chief difference between the homes of the working and middle classes was size, rather than form. The terraced house of the early Victorian years, with its flat front and concealed roof, hidden behind a parapet wall, *looked* rather different from its late Victorian equivalent, with its front bay (or bays), small front garden and visible roof. But both conformed to the standard plan, one room wide, an overall width of 16 feet, with an offshoot to the rear. Later houses were on the whole rather larger, with three bedrooms instead of two. However, while the dwellings produced for the majority working class remained much the same throughout the Victorian period, houses built for the middle class changed much more. After the middle of the century middle-class preferences turned decisively towards detached and semi-detached villas. Once the middle class discovered the benefits of houses that were separated from their neighbours, if only on one side, differences became more marked. The shift to the semi-detached form on wider plots gave designers and builders more scope to innovate, and the square plan, two rooms wide, with side access, became very popular. The reasons for this will be apparent to anyone who has lived in a tall narrow town house.

Houses were made larger by additions to the side as well as the rear, and a width of thirty feet was widely adopted although wider plots were common. The term 'middle class' embraced a broad range of incomes, generating demand for houses of quite different proportions, from the modest and barely separated villas in parts of St Andrew's and Bishopston to the palatial edifices in extensive grounds in Sneyd Park and Stoke Bishop. In this sense, then, middle-class houses acquired greater variety, especially when compared to houses built for the working class. Other important changes referred to in chapter six were the migration of kitchens from the basement to the ground floor, with the concomitant decline in the provision of basements except where the lie of the land suggested otherwise. It was also argued that the majority of houses conformed to one or other of a very small number of basic plan forms, which could be finished in ways that gave the impression of greater variety. All this is consistent with the idea that in the great majority of cases houses were, in effect, designed by builders who stuck to what they knew, making only incremental changes in response to their perception of market conditions.

It was not only the houses of the middle class that changed as the century progressed but also the nature of the settings in which they were located. The residential suburbs of west and north Bristol, characterised initially, in the 1840s and '50s, by the construction of very large houses for the city's economic elite, seeking to distance themselves from the congested and environmentally degraded ancient city, where, nevertheless, their businesses continued to be found. As the middle class embraced the separation of work from home they redefined the suburb as a physically attractive and social exclusive adjunct to the city. And as demand for the suburbs increased among the growing ranks of the salaried middle class builders responded by producing rather more affordable houses, and the character of areas such as Clifton and Redland began to change. New houses there at the end of the century were smaller and the wealthiest families were moving further away, in search of cherished exclusivity, across the Downs, across the Avon Gorge, deeper into the countryside or to the Bristol Channel coast at places like Clevedon. This is a reminder that in addition to the important role of market forces in reshaping the Victorian city there were also powerful social influences at work, pulling the middle class both socially and physically further away from the working class. It was all about the choices made by the people who had the wealth and spending power that enabled them to decide where to locate their families.

Looking at the Victorian period as a whole it can be said that although serious housing problems remained the overall situation improved, and in the 1890s in particular output was very considerably higher than it had been in the 1830s, or indeed in any intervening decade. This prolonged building boom, which added more than 10,000 houses in ten years, significantly lowered the average age of houses and meant that a lot more people were living in modern dwellings (by the standards of the day), and many of them were enjoying the novel convenience of having bathrooms and inside WCs. Improved sanitation was accompanied by lower mortality, another key indicator of the quality of housing. Nevertheless, *there were never enough houses to go round.* The average number of people per house fell slightly, from 6.57 in 1841 to 5.6 in 1901, but the numerical housing deficit actually increased to 12,980 in 1901 when there were 71,215 households and 58,235 inhabited houses, according to the census. Thus there were 1.22 households per house.

Looking at the overall picture, however, is not sufficient, because it is clear that the housing of the middle class had improved much more than that of the working class as a whole and the poor in particular. Indeed, it might be said that from the point of view of the middle class the housing problem had been solved: there was no shortage of good quality affordable villas in socially desirable areas within reach of the city centre. The housing problems of the working class, on the other hand, remained far from resolution. The point has been made above that many of the courts and alleys complained about by reformers in the 1840s were still occupied in the 1890s. Such places needed more than piped water and new drains to make them fit for human habitation. Of course, the poor were a minority of the working class and the better off, skilled workers were undoubtedly better housed than their grandparents had been in the 1840s. But they were all still subject to the vagaries of the free market, and were often just a pay packet away from eviction. Those who managed to obtain better paid and more secure employment were constantly on the lookout for the chance to move to a slightly bigger, cleaner or better located house, perhaps with a more considerate landlord.

Housing and the Victorian City

The owners of capital and employers of labour held enough economic and political power to determine the shape of the city: 'The middle classes ... controlled the creation of the material fabric of the town, its houses, workplaces and public buildings'.[2] In marked contrast, the majority working-class population received the city as a given, something that was done to them rather than with them (even if it was their labour that actually built the place). Faced with the foul and deteriorating conditions of the early Victorian city the reaction of the middle classes was to leave, to remove themselves and their families to the suburbs, rather than to confront and remedy the problem. But in the 1840s even parts of Clifton and Redland were criticised for their insanitary conditions. This prompts the conclusion that Edwin Chadwick's insistence on defining the urban crisis in terms of sanitation and water supply was not just a technical fix for an urgent problem, for it had a clear class bias: from the point of view of the well-housed middle class the primary need was indeed improved sanitation and reliable piped water, but what the working class needed above all was decent affordable housing, and while the other measures were welcome they failed to address this basic need.

Although it cannot be claimed that Bristol was typical of Victorian cities the evidence examined in this book nevertheless invites a number of general conclusions about urban housing provision in that period. First, supply was never sufficient to meet the needs of the growing urban population and the deficiency was much more marked among some sections of the population than others. Part of the explanation for this is that cities were powerful magnets for migrants from rural areas, especially in the agricultural depression from the 1870s onwards, so demand was generally increasing. Another factor was a consequence of the long timescale involved in producing each house; in the case of any such product its producers are likely to prefer to under rather than over supply; better to have unmet demand than no demand. Chapter three made reference to the distress caused when supply ran ahead of demand, leaving a glut of empty properties and many unemployed building workers in the early 1880s.

Second, the Victorians never found a way of building decent one-family houses at a price affordable by the majority of the working class. The fatalistic acceptance of sharing was illustrated by a conversation reported to the Royal Commission in 1884 by the Rev Ernest Fuller: 'I was talking last night to the men at the St Agnes' Club, and they said, "I wish those people [the Royal Commission] would offer a prize for the best house for artisan families to live in, two families to a house".'[3] In a free market the only response to low spending power was to build smaller dwellings at higher density or to a lower standard of construction, or both. However, the market was not entirely free and after the adoption of building bye laws it was more difficult for builders to go in the direction of lower standards. The result was that the least well off had no access to newly built houses and were inevitably packed into the large city centre houses cast off by the middle class and the minimal tenements that had been built behind these houses earlier in the century.

Third, the Victorians never found a way to conduct effective and equitable urban renewal. Market forces meant that worn out or abandoned buildings were replaced by buildings designed to yield a higher return, but where the old structures were inhabited by poor tenants there was no provision for their rehousing. As discussed in chapter eight, if profit seeking actors were unwilling to rehouse sitting tenants then either those tenants were forced to fend for themselves in an already overcrowded market or someone else – a charity or the local authority – needed to step in. But charitable resources were always scarce and the numbers of dwellings provided never rose above the nugatory, while local authorities like Bristol were always most reluctant to commit ratepayers' money. The saga of the Leadhouse Lane courts perfectly illustrates the problem: the town council dithered and procrastinated over the purchase price and was ultimately ousted by the local brewery, which then proceeded to evict the tenants and redevelop the site without rehousing.

Fourth, although the rights of property were exposed as creating conditions that were harmful to the health and wellbeing of the poor it was always easier for the authorities to insist that landowners comply with certain regulations at the point of new building than it was to take away the property of an owner who allowed an inhabited building to fall into a state of utter disrepair. There was never enough momentum behind those who would challenge property rights and the dominance of the market.

Fundamentally, then, the explanation for the housing problem in the

Victorian city was that in a society characterised by wildly unequal incomes too much reliance was placed on the market mechanism to provide an expensive necessity. Markets work, in the sense of producing socially acceptable outcomes, when there is a more even distribution of spending power; if incomes are highly unequal, markets still work in relation to cheap non-essential consumer goods, such as those that Bristol's leading businesses produced so successfully. Housing, however, is both essential and expensive, and the Victorians tested to destruction the theory that the market was the right method of provision for all, when in fact it failed a substantial proportion of the population. This is not to suggest that there was no place for the market – it worked well enough for the middle classes – but it is to suggest that the relationship between market and non-market provision was grossly unbalanced. It remained unbalanced throughout the period, as demonstrated by the fact that in Bristol the town council and the one enduring semi-philanthropic organisation together built scarcely 200 houses in the whole of the period 1874 to 1914, whereas the private builders produced more than 200 every year (apart from the collapse in the early 1880s). And it remained unbalanced because the middle classes who provided the bulk of charitable resources and controlled the council were collectively, if not in every case individually, committed to the idea that housing was primarily a private matter and that to intervene would violate the rights of property. If they started to interfere with the workings of the market, who knew where it would end?

The Housing Legacy

One thing the Victorian period bequeathed to the new century was plenty of evidence to support those who argued that there must be a better way to build cities. It would be going too far to say that Bristol and other British cities were in crisis at the end of the nineteenth century; things were not as bad as 'the diabolic misery of the early Victorian city',[4] but there were chronic problems that urgently needed more attention than they were receiving. Some critics, notably Ebenezer Howard, were already arguing for a completely new approach to urban living, based on his vision of 'garden cities'.[5] The idea was to build planned towns which would eliminate pollution, congestion and profiteering from landownership. The first example was Letchworth Garden City, established in Hertfordshire in 1903. At the same time other reformers were pioneering the less ambitious idea of 'garden suburbs', the most famous of which was built at Hampstead in London. The leading promoters of garden suburbs included Henrietta Barnett, sister in law of Gilmore Barnett, the much quoted Bristol housing reformer. In 1909 it was proposed to develop a garden suburb in Bristol, at Shirehampton, but only 44 cottages were built and the Bristol Garden Suburb Company was wound up in 1923.[6] One of the architects involved with both Letchworth and the garden suburbs was Raymond Unwin, who in 1912 famously argued that there was 'nothing gained by overcrowding'– an explicit rejection of the gridiron layouts of narrow fronted houses in working-class areas.[7] Unwin, who went on to be the chief architect advising the Ministry of Health on the post 1918 development of council housing, recommended densities of just twelve houses to the acre rather than the forty or more that was quite normal before 1914.

It is interesting that council estates built in the 1920s and 30s reflected Unwin's ideas but private enterprise builders continued with narrow fronted terraced houses at the cheaper end of the market, as well as growing proportions of semi-detached houses. In the same way that Victorian builders rejected Georgian styles so it is that houses built in the 1920s are readily distinguishable from those built only a few years earlier. The differences are not confined to superficial style; a striking feature of interwar houses is that the large back extensions that were so often found on late Victorian terraced houses were no-longer being built. In fact, although considerable numbers of terraced houses with large back extensions have survived into the twenty-first century, they can now be seen as something of a historical oddity: most of them seem to date from the twenty years or so after the revival of output in the mid-1880s. Another change of design concerned semi-detached houses; whereas in the Victorian period, as noted in chapter six, a four-room plan, with a side entrance and transverse circulation space, became very popular, after 1919 builders reverted to placing the entrance on the front elevation, thereby sacrificing the second front room on the ground floor. This seems to be true of interwar semi-detached houses irrespective of size.

Both Howard and Unwin were influenced by the Arts and Crafts movement, associated with the critique of industrial capitalism developed by John Ruskin and William Morris from the middle of the nineteenth century. They were also responding to the rise of rural nostalgia, a popular yearning for an imagined arcadian era of pastoral harmony, and this was reflected in the cottages designed by Unwin and his partner Barry Parker at Letchworth. These pre-1914 designs were reproduced at scale on the council estates of the 1920s. However inspirational they were, the ideas underpinning Garden Cities and suburbs had nothing to say about what to do with existing towns and cities. The first Housing and Town Planning Act, passed in 1909, was concerned with 'town extension' schemes, allowing local councils that adopted the Act to specify land use and densities on green field developments, but there were no powers to plan already built up areas. Comprehensive town and country planning was an idea whose time had not yet come, but the seeds had been planted in response to the conditions created by unregulated urban expansion in the Victorian period. It was, of course, in the interests of the advocates of interventionist planning to accentuate the awfulness of the Victorian city. As one trenchant twentieth century critic put it, there was much to learn from the industrial city, and the 'chief lesson was in what to avoid'.[8] Just as the Victorians rejected the austere elegance of the preceding period, early twentieth-century opinion turned against the legacy of Victorian urbanism, albeit for different reasons.

Thinking specifically about housing, the Victorian legacy consisted of both the existing stock of houses and the established housing provision system. Taking the houses first, Victorian builders in Bristol had invariably produced self-contained houses, with their own front and back door, and in almost all cases a garden at the back, though less often at the front. This meant that the legacy stock in the city was quite different from, and less problematic than, places such as Leeds and Bradford with their thousands of back-to-back houses, or Scottish cities where four storey tenements blocks predominated. At the start of the twentieth century there were probably three times as many houses in Bristol as there had been in 1841, although estimates that rely on census figures need to be treated with caution due to the differences in methodology used at different dates. Despite these reservations this suggests that the majority of houses were less than sixty years old, and because of the building boom of the 1890s, which was still going on until about 1905, there was a plentiful supply of relatively new houses. This was a good thing because these houses were inevitably going to comprise a substantial part of the housing stock for decades to come. The Victorian housing stock was a valuable inheritance that sheltered the people, but, as has been emphasised in earlier chapters, the pattern of housebuilding in the period had produced distinctively middle-class and working-class areas, and this social geography also proved to be highly durable. The inherited stock was deficient in two main ways: the twentieth century started with a serious housing shortage, which would prove difficult to reduce let alone eliminate, and there were large numbers of houses that were already, or soon would become, unfit for human habitation and in urgent need of replacement. Fitness for human habitation was, of course, only one way of judging houses, representing a low threshold of suitability. According to the Royal Commission of 1884-5: 'It is quite certain that the working classes are largely housed in dwellings which would be unsuitable even if they were not overcrowded.'[9]

But as this book has emphasised throughout, we need to consider all levels of the housing market. Questions arise as to the longer term utility and suitability of the entire housing stock in the changed social, political and economic conditions that developed in the post-Victorian period. In terms of size, there was a sort of Goldilocks situation: some houses were far too big for twentieth century needs and preferences, and some were far too small, while in between were those that were just right. But it was not only size that affected a dwelling's continuing utility and chance of long term survival. Among the factors at play here were, first, investment in repair and maintenance to keep a dwelling windproof and watertight. Second, investment in modernisation in response to changes in people's expectations of their houses as standards of living rose and lifestyles moved on. A third factor was location: sometimes houses that might have had a longer life were swept away by road improvement schemes or because they were in areas designated for industry.

The most positive view of Victorian housing comes from looking at the villas built for the Victorian middle class, most of which have survived and continue to provide desirable homes commanding premium prices. Built at lower densities than the working-class neighbourhoods, the residential suburbs have proved to be better suited to, and more adaptable to, changing lifestyles and the demands placed upon them by mass car ownership. Lower density also means that they are able to support more trees and other greenery. Houses built for the middle-class market have survived in greater numbers than the mansions of the rich. These were just too big for twentieth century tastes and pockets, and moreover, in Sneyd Park but also in Clifton and Redland, some of them occupied such large sites that demolition and redevelopment proved to be economically irresistible. Nearer to the city numbers of large houses have been converted into offices or are now used for educational purposes, but the rest have shown that they can be adapted to the domestic requirements of successive generations of smaller households with different tastes and expectations. The architectural term 'long life, loose fit' applies to these buildings that have demonstrated their enduring versatility. The very largest houses depended for their manageability on the presence of numerous servants, a class of worker that became increasingly rare in the twentieth century, and even before 1914 some such houses were beginning to be converted into flats. Others on generous plots have proved to be readily modified and extended, with new kitchens regularly installed, bedrooms converted into additional bathrooms, roof spaces becoming extra bedrooms and front gardens being given over to one or more cars. Bathrooms, hot water systems and even electricity supplies began to be retrofitted into these houses from an early date, but it is certainly the case that the rate of enhancement activity has accelerated in more recent times, and it is now abundantly clear that although many Bristolians positively choose to live in houses dating from the nineteenth century, no-one lives in a Victorian house in its original form.

At the upper end of the market houses survived because the positives outweighed the negatives: they were an inheritance that justified private investment to maintain and enhance their utility and market value. At the bottom end of the market the opposite was the case. Often tiny, with no scope for extension, nor much potential for improvement, these houses had been cheaply built, at high density, for working people with little money. Moreover, basic repair and maintenance work seems to have been widely neglected (the situation was made worse by the impact of two world wars and the introduction of rent control as a wartime expedient in 1915 but which lasted in different forms until the 1980s). Here were houses that, as has been discussed above, had been identified for years, if not decades, as a danger to their inhabitants and an affront to a proud city. They had very little market value and in the central area they were more likely to be demolished and replaced by industrial or commercial buildings than restored to habitability. Slum clearance in the twentieth century was sometimes but by no means always accompanied by the construction of houses and flats on the cleared sites. Of greater significance was the extent to which housebuilding by the council amounted to a process of suburbanising the working class. This was quite different from anything seen before, and Bristol acquired a number of council estates built on greenfield sites around the edge of the built up area.

Beyond the inner-urban courts and alleys there were thousands of small houses built since the early 1850s, and these constituted the bulk of the legacy of working-class housing. The great majority of these houses remained unchanged and unimproved in 1900, and for many years afterwards. In 1914 the poverty researcher Seebohm Rowntree estimated that in the country as a whole the majority of the working population occupied small terraced houses and only ten to twenty per cent were lucky enough to live in three-bedroomed houses with a parlour and occasionally a bathroom.[10] The self-contained two-storey house with four or five rooms and a scullery was 'by far the most predominant type of housing accommodation in England and Wales and may be taken as the typical dwellings of the English working class'.[11]

The question then arose as to what could, and should, be done with this legacy stock? In relation to houses in the very worst condition there was little dissent from the public health case for clearance and rebuilding, but there remained plenty of scope to argue about both the extent of true slums and the modalities of redevelopment. In relation to the rest of the stock, while it was objectively possible to list the ways in which these ageing houses *could* be modernised and brought up to a standard that would keep them habitable more or less indefinitely, it was less clear what *should* be done. After 1945 the need to rebuild the centres of cities such as Bristol after wartime bombing fuelled the growth of a strong preference among professional planners and architects for comprehensive redevelopment, going far beyond the clearance of buildings that were undeniably unfit for human habitation.[12] Alongside this movement, and no doubt influenced by it, people were making their own subjective judgements about whether it was desirable to live in a Victorian house in the twentieth century. Here changing fashions and individual preferences had more purchase than considerations of public health. In practice there was a swing away from Victorian tastes and styles. Early-twentieth-century generations who grew up in Victorian houses that remained much as they were when they were built were less inclined to take a positive view of them, and they tended to favour newly built houses that were both more 'modern' in design and easier to heat and keep clean. Only much later did a new generation rediscover the attractions of Victorian houses, albeit brought up to date and equipped with central heating, new kitchens and bathrooms. The point here is that whether the legacy of Victorian houses has a positive or negative image depends on which part of the market is being considered, when and by whom.

The early twentieth century inherited a housing provision system that, as this book has shown, was almost entirely reliant on a multitude of small businesses, operating within a defined locality according to the rules of the free market. It was the product of the small scale and highly localised capitalist economy of the Victorian period. Houses were produced speculatively, in the hope and expectation that there would be someone to buy them on completion. Purchasers were usually investors – local people who had accumulated some capital and were looking for a safe place to put it – who then let out their houses to tenants paying a weekly rent. These private landlords played a key role in the system, for they both allowed builders to recover the money expended on construction and facilitated consumers' need to spread housing costs over a long period. Accurate figures are not available, but it is usually said that before 1914, 90 per cent of households rented from private landlords.[13] It was suggested in chapter seven that in Redland and Clifton the rates of owner occupation were significantly higher than this by 1871 but in the working-class neighbourhoods private renting undoubtedly continued to dominate the market.

It is arguable that this system, which had been developed in and for the social and economic circumstances of the early Victorian period, was beginning to come under pressure before the end of the nineteenth century and more obviously in the early years of the new century, not least because the nature of capitalism was changing, moving into a more national and international phase. One result was increased competition for investment capital that had previously flowed towards housebuilding. Landlords as a group had a bad reputation among their hard-pressed tenants, and rising local rates in the 1890s were placing heavy burdens on their business model.[14] In the decade up to 1914 production of new houses collapsed, and this encouraged political demands for the government to introduce subsidies for housebuilding, especially in rural areas.

It was suggested earlier in this chapter that the Victorian housing system placed too much reliance on the market to supply an expensive necessity, with the result that there was a permanent shortage, which especially affected the least well off, yet there was never enough support for municipal action to undertake equitable urban renewal. There were, therefore, good grounds for saying that this legacy system needed to change, and it did so in at least three ways. This is not the place to discuss the details of how change was brought about, but the war of 1914-18 moved the politics of housing to a different level of importance, finally breaking down barriers to state intervention, with the result that the balance between market and non-market activity shifted dramatically in favour of the local councils, which became housebuilders and landlords on a scale completely different from anything envisaged before 1914. There were fewer than 25,000 council houses in the whole of Great Britain in 1914,[15] but by 1930 there were more than 600,000.[16] In Bristol the total rose from under 100 in 1914 to 6,484 in 1930.[17] Not only were local councils building large numbers of houses, but from 1930 they were required to produce estimates of slums remaining in their areas and plans for dealing with the problem. Bristol had, in fact, cleared nearly 1,000 houses during the 1920s, a further indication of how far the council had departed from its entrenched nineteenth-century position.

The second way in which the system changed after 1918 was that the building industry was, eventually, transformed by the growing size of individual firms, partly due to consolidation and merger, so that an increasing proportion of new houses were (and are) built by fewer and fewer large firms operating across the country. This reshaping of the building industry was driven by wider changes in the scale of capitalist organisations and the dynamic nature of capitalism was always likely to challenge the Victorian housing provision system.

Third, the dominant position of private landlords went into steep decline throughout the period up to 1989, and over this timescale the pattern of housing tenure was transformed. As private renting declined so individual home ownership rose, from a putative 10 per cent in 1914 to 68 per cent by 1996. Renting from local authorities rose from negligible to 32 per cent by 1979. This process of tenure restructuring can be seen as the modernisation of the system developed in the economic circumstances of the Victorian period. Whereas in the nineteenth century the great majority of people could not buy their own houses because their incomes were too low to sustain mortgage repayments and their creditworthiness would not secure a loan in any case, as the twentieth century progressed many more people acquired a standard of living that did enable them to buy, and home ownership came to be seen as the normal, modern and aspirational form of housing consumption.

A final point is that in the twentieth century, specifically from the First World War onwards, governments developed housing policies that appeared to suggest that lessons had been learned. For fifty years policy encouraged local authorities to build houses for both general need and to replace those lost through organised clearance of worn out Victorian houses. It is arguable that sometimes antipathy to nineteenth-century houses and neighbourhoods went too far and removed stock that in other places or other times would have been retained, modernised and cherished. However, it can also be argued that by subsequently abandoning redevelopment by local councils and by persistent promotion of private ownership governments have transferred to individual home owners and a new generation of amateur landlords the responsibility for maintaining houses that are now well over 100 and in some cases well over 150 years old. To a large extent we are, like the Victorians themselves, still relying too heavily on market forces to provide solutions to today's housing needs.

Notes

Chapter One Victorian Bristol: between the railway and the motorcar

1 Briggs, A, *Victorian Cities*, London: Odhams, 1963, p12
2 Vaughan, R, *The Age of Great Cities*, London: Jackson and Walford, 1843
3 Minchinton, W, 'Bristol – metropolis of the west in the eighteenth century' in Clark, P, (ed) *The Early Modern Town*, London: Longman, 1976, pp297-313 (first published in 1954)
4 This statement has been quoted by numerous writers including Williams, E, *Capitalism and Slavery* (London: Andre Deutsch, 1964, p44, first published in 1944), Morgan, K, *Bristol and the Atlantic Trade in the Eighteenth Century* (Cambridge: Cambridge University Press, 1993, pp131-2) and Dresser, M, *Slavery Obscured: a social history of the slave trade in Bristol* (Bristol: Redcliffe Press, 2007, p96)
5 Draper, N, *The Price of Emancipation: slave ownership, compensation and British society at the end of slavery*, Cambridge: Cambridge University Press, 2009, p236. Unpublished research by Ruth Hecht has shown that at least half a dozen investors in both the GWR and the Cotton Works were beneficiaries of the compensation fund.
6 *Municipal Corporations in England and Wales, Appendix to the First Report of the Commissioners, part II*, London: House of Commons, 1835, pp1208-9
7 *Report of a Committee of the Bristol Chamber of Commerce*, October 1828, BRL B2489
8 Buchanan, A, *Brunel: the life and times of Isambard Kingdom Brunel*, London: Hambledon and London, 2002, p45
9 Shannon, HA and Grebenik, E, *The Population of Bristol*, Cambridge: Cambridge University Press, 1943, p6. The figures for both 1801 and 1841 are estimates for the population living within the enlarged boundaries set in 1835.
10 Brunel's report to the Bristol Dock Company 15 June 1844, quoted in Buchanan, op cit, p55
11 The departure of the *Great Western* in February 1843 was the last time for twenty-eight years that a ship sailed from Bristol to the United States. Farr, G, *The Steamship Great Western: the first Atlantic liner*, Bristol: Bristol Branch of the Historical Association, 1963, p15
12 Malpass, P, *The Making of Victorian Bristol*, Woodbridge: Boydell and Brewer, 2019, chapter 8
13 Jordan, S, Wardley, P, and Woollard, M, 'Emerging Modernity in an Urban Setting: nineteenth century Bristol revealed in property surveys', *Urban History*, vol. 26, no. 2, 1999, pp190-210 (p195)
14 Pugsley, A, *The Economic Development of Bristol*, Bristol: Bristol Times and Mirror, 1922, p22
15 Berghoff, H, 'Regional variations in provincial business biography: the case of Birmingham, Bristol and Manchester, 1870-1914' *Business History*, vol. 37, no. 1, 1995, pp64-85
16 *Report of an Enquiry by the Board of Trade into Working Class Rents, Housing and Retail Prices etc*, London, HMSO, 1908, p114
17 Harvey, C, and Press, J, *Studies in the Business History of Bristol*, Bristol: Bristol Academic Press, 1988, p40
18 Alford, B, *WD and HO Wills and the Development of the UK Tobacco Industry 1786-1965*, London: Methuen, 1973, p128 and 292
19 *Board of Trade Enquiry*, 1908, op cit, p114
20 Alford, B, 'The economic development of Bristol in the nineteenth century: an enigma?' in McGrath, P and Cannon, J (eds) *Essays in Bristol and Gloucestershire History*, Bristol: Bristol and Gloucestershire Archaeological Society, 1976, pp253-83 (p281)
21 Meller, H, *Leisure and the Changing City 1870-1914*, London; Routledge and Kegan Paul, 1976, p27
22 Harvey and Press, op cit, p26
23 Bush, G, *Bristol and its Municipal Government, 1820-1851*, Bristol: Bristol Record Society, 1976, p129
24 Large, D, *The Municipal Government of Bristol 1851-1901*, Bristol: Bristol Record Society, 1999, p12
25 Meller, op cit, pp87-8
26 Ibid, p90, Jordan, S, 'The Myth of Edward Colston' in Poole, S, (ed) *A City Built Upon the Water:*

maritime Bristol, 1750-1900, Bristol: Redcliffe Press, 2013, pp175-96
27 Meller, op cit, p86
28 John Bastow was elected for the District ward in 1884, Samuel Lloyd represented Bedminster East from 1887 and William Mereweather was unopposed in Bedminster West in 1888 and did not stand again. Jordan, S, Ramsey, K and Woollard, M, *Abstract of Bristol Historical Statistics, part 3: political representation and Bristol's elections 1700-1997*, Bristol: UWE, 1997
29 Meller, op cit, p49
30 Lobell MD, and Carus-Wilson, EM, *Bristol*, London: Scolar Press, 1975, Leech, R, *The Town House in Medieval and Early Modern Bristol*, Swindon: English Heritage, 2014
31 Mowl, T, *To Build the Second City: architects and craftsmen in Georgian Bristol*, Bristol: Redcliffe Press, 1991, Gomme, A and Jenner, M, *An Architectural History of Bristol*, Malton: Oblong Creative Ltd, 2011, Crick, C, *Victorian Buildings in Bristol*, Bristol: Redcliffe Press, 1975, Mallory, K, *The Bristol House*, Bristol: Redcliffe Press, 1985
32 Dresser, M, 'People's history of housing in Bristol 1870-1939' in *Bristol's Other History*, Bristol: Bristol Broadsides, 1983, pp129-60, Ferguson, N, *Working Class Housing in Bristol and Nottingham 1868-1919*, PhD thesis, University of Oregon, 1971, Bristol Reference Library, Skilleter, K, *Bristol's Garden Suburbs: a history of housing reform, town planning and the Corporation's 'cottage estates' 1890-1939*, Unpublished monograph, Bristol Archives, 45752/1
33 For example, Jones, D, *A History of Clifton*, Chichester, Phillimore, 1992, Wright, M, *Montpelier: a Bristol suburb*, Chichester: Phillimore, 2004, and Mellor, P and Wright, M, *Kingsdown: Bristol's vertical suburb*, Chichester: Phillimore, 2009
34 Malpass, 2019, op cit

Chapter Two Understanding the Housing Problem
1 Kay, W, 'Report on the Sanatory [sic] Condition of Clifton', published as an appendix to the *Second Report of the Commissioners for Inquiring into the State of Large Towns and Populous Districts*, London: HMSO, 1845, p90
2 Briggs, A, *Victorian Cities*, London: Odhams, 1963, p12
3 Finer, SE, *The Life and Times of Sir Edwin Chadwick*, London: Methuen, 1952, p211
4 Malpass, P, and King, A, *Bristol's Floating Harbour: the first two hundred years*, Bristol: Redcliffe Press, 2009, p49
5 De la Beche, Sir H, *Report on the State of Bristol and Other Large Towns*, London: HMSO, 1845, p16
6 Dyos, HJ and Reeder, DA, 'Slums and Suburbs' in Dyos, HJ and Wolf, M (eds) *The Victorian City volume I*, London: Routledge and Kegan Paul, 1973, pp359-86
7 Reprinted as *The Homes of the Bristol Poor*, by the 'special commissioner' of the *Bristol Mercury*, Bristol: William Lewis and Sons, 1884, p32, BRL, BL12E1
8 *First Report of the Royal commission on the Housing of the Working Classes, 1884-85*, C4402-I, 1885, p16
9 Bauman, Z, *Work, Consumerism and the New Poor*, Buckingham: Open University Press, 1998, p90
10 Wohl, A, *The Eternal Slum*, London: Edward Arnold, 1977, p164
11 *First Report*, op cit, p97
12 Gauldie, E, *Cruel Habitations: a history of working class housing 1780-1918*, London: George Allen and Unwin, 1974, chapter 24
13 Englander, D, *Landlord and Tenant in Urban Britain 1838-1918*, Oxford: Clarendon Press, 1983, p.xii
14 Gauldie, op cit, p15
15 Donnison, D, and Ungerson, C, *Housing Policy*, Harmondsworth: Penguin Books, 1982, p287
16 Englander, op cit, p5
17 Rowntree, BS, *Poverty: a study of town life*, London: Macmillan, 1901, pp147-52
18 Powell, C, 'He that runs against time: life expectancy of building firms in nineteenth century Bristol', *Construction History*, vol. 1, 1985, pp61-7
19 McGrath, P, *The Merchant Venturers of Bristol*, Bristol: Society of Merchant Venturers, 1975

20 Malpass, P, *The Making of Victorian Bristol*, Woodbridge: Boydell and Brewer, 2019, pp79-80
21 Dyos and Reeder, op cit
22 Ibid, p361
23 Ibid, p361

Chapter Three The Growth of the Town
1 Corfield, P, *The Impact of English Towns 1700-1800*, Oxford: Oxford University Press, 1982, p 11-15; Borsay, P *The English Urban Renaissance*, Oxford: Clarendon Press, 1989, p24
2 The charter boundaries enclosed 755 acres, or little more than the modern city centre.
3 Matthews, W, *The New History, Survey and Description of the City and Suburbs of Bristol*, 1794
4 Ward, JR, 'Speculative building at Bristol and Clifton, 1783-19-793', *Business History*, vol XX, part 1, January 1978, pp3-18. Ward quotes contemporary accounts of the boom as a form of madness, but this is denied by Tim Mowl (*To Build the Second City*, Bristol: Redcliffe Press, 1991, p119) who argues that 'it was an interrupted social imperative', by which he means that there was a genuine demand from well heeled citizens seeking to escape 'from misery and from the environmental disaster area down by the tidal Avon'.
5 Clark, G, *Report to the General Board of Health, on a preliminary inquiry into the sewerage, drainage and supply of water , and of the sanitary condition of the inhabitants of the city and county of Bristol*, 1850, BRO B1000
6 *Chilcott's Descriptive History of Bristol*, Bristol: J Chilcott, no date, but probably 1838, p73
7 Hewitt, F, *Population and Urban Growth in East Bristol, 1800-1914*, PhD thesis, University of Bristol, 1965, p55
8 Baigent, E, 'Economy and Society in Eighteenth Century British Towns: Bristol in the 1770s' in Denecke, D, and Shaw, G, (eds) *Urban Historical Geography: recent developments in Britain and Germany*, Cambridge: Cambridge University Press, 1988, pp109-24. Leech, R, *The Town House in Medieval and Early Modern Bristol*, Swindon: English Heritage, 2014
9 Leech, R *The St Michael's Hill Precinct if the University of Bristol*, Bristol: Bristol Record Society, 2000
10 Mellor, P, and Wright, M, *Kingsdown: Bristol's vertical suburb*, Chichester: Phillimore, 2009
11 Latimer, *Annals of Bristol in the Nineteenth century,* Bath: Kingsmead Reprints*, 1970*, p343 (first published 1887)
12 Hussey, D, 'Leisure and commerce: the Hotwell and the port of Bristol, 1750-1850', in Poole, S (ed) *A City Built Upon the Water: maritime Bristol, 1750-1900*, Bristol: Redcliffe Press, 2013, pp31-50
13 McGrath, P, *The Merchant Venturers of Bristol*, Bristol: SMV, 1975, p329
14 For a fuller discussion of the growth of Victorian Clifton see Malpass, P, 'Victorian Clifton: a suburb of privilege', *Transactions of the Bristol and Gloucestershire Archaeological Society*, vol. 136, 2018, pp279-302
15 Large, op cit, discusses the resistance put up by Stoke Bishop residents to proposals to incorporate their area into Bristol in the 1890s.
16 Martin's Estate Act, 1853, BA 45777/1
17 *Bristol Mercury*, 30 March 1844
18 Monk's letter to Sir William Page Wood, 6 March 1852, in *Horfield Manor*, Bristol Reference Library, B23210
19 Malpass, P, and Evans, W, 'Bishop Monk and the Horfield Question: another view', *Transactions of the Bristol and Gloucestershire Archaeological Society*, Vol. 138, 2020, pp279-93
20 In the event only about 11 acres were sold to form St Andrew's Park and the remainder was built on.
21 Clark, G, *Report to the General Board of Health, on a preliminary inquiry into the sewerage, drainage and supply of water, and of the sanitary condition of the inhabitants of the city and county of Bristol*, 1850, BRL, B1000, p88
22 Press, J 'Footwear Manufacturing' in Harvey, C, and Press, J, *Studies in the Business History of Bristol*, Bristol: Bristol Academic Press, 1988, p215

23 Royal Commission on the Housing of the Working Classes 1884-5, *First Report of the Royal Commission*, vol II, C4402-I, London: HMSO, 1885, p217
24 *Homes of the Bristol Poor*, Bristol: William Lewis and Sons, 1884, p35
25 Clark, op cit, p88, and Members of Clifton College, *The History of St Agnes Parish 1876-1890*, Bristol: Arrowsmith, 1890, p2
26 BA, P.StN/Ch/1/b, plan of part of the Forlorn Hope Estate drawn by George Ashmead and Son, 1876
27 Latimer, J, *Annals of Bristol in the Nineteenth Century*, Bath: Kingsmead Reprints, 1970 (first published 1887) p92
28 The street names remain but the area was subject to redevelopment from the 1930s onwards.
29 Leech, R, *The Town House in Medieval and Early Modern Bristol*, Swindon: English Heritage, 2014, p 41, and p344
30 *Bristol Times and Mirror*, 17 February 1865, p2
31 Large, D, *The Municipal Government of Bristol 1851-1901*, Bristol: Bristol Record Society, 1999, pp29-39
32 Clark, op cit p110
33 BA, 40269, Abstract of title to land at Broad Pylle Hill, Pylle Hill Sideland and Holybrook Well, 1878, states that Green purchased lot 7, 29a 3r 25p, for £4840. An advertisement in the *Bristol Mercury*, 9 July 1853, mentioned that 111 acres in total would be sold, including land in Wiltshire.
34 This is clear from an advert in the *Western Daily Press*, 3 November 1865, but the land was not sold until 1869, BA, 40269, op cit
35 Latimer, op cit, p436
36 In London too in the early 1880s 'the suburbs were glutted with new but tenantless houses'. Dyos, HJ, *Victorian Suburb: a study of the growth of Camberwell*, Leicester: Leicester University Press, 1966, p82
37 *First Report*, op cit, p218
38 Latimer, op cit, p518
39 *Homes of the Bristol Poor*, p98. Keith Skilleter identifies the writer as James Crosby. Skilleter, K, *Bristol's Garden Suburbs: a history of housing reform, town planning and the Corporation's 'cottage estates', 1890-1939*, p10. Unpublished. BA, 45752/1
40 The City Engineer's figures suggest 1,157 houses in the year to 31 March 1899, 2,197 the next year and 1,570 in the year after that. BA, 35510/CO/2/1/2 *Annual Reports of the City Engineer's Department 1897-1902*
41 J Parry Lewis, 'Indices of housebuilding in the Manchester conurbation, South Wales and Great Britain, 1851-1913' *Scottish Journal of Political Economy*, vol. 8, part 2, 1961, pp148-54, S B Saul, 'Housebuilding in England, 1890-1914' *Economic History Review*, vol.15, no. 1, 1962, pp119-37
42 Hewitt, op cit, p118
43 *First Report*, op cit, p219, evidence of Rev E Fuller.
44 Baigent, E, 'Economy and society in eighteenth century English towns: Bristol in the 1770s' in Denecke, D and Shaw, G (eds) Urban Historical Geography: recent developments in Britain and Germany, Cambridge: Cambridge University Press, 1988, pp109-24
45 Jordan, S, *The Development and Implementation of Authority in a Regional Capital: a study of Bristol's elites, 1835-1939*, PhD thesis, University of the West of England, 1999, p60
46 Bush, G, *Bristol and Its Municipal Government 1820-1851*, Bristol: Bristol Record Society, 1976, Appendix 5
47 Jordan, op cit, p246
48 Large, D, *The Municipal Government of Bristol 1851-1901*, Bristol: Bristol Record Society, 1999, p14
49 *Survey of Valuations, 1837, 1851, 1862 and 1871*, respectively BA references 04249, 04250, 04251 and 04252
50 Clark, op cit, p37

51 *Medical Officer of Health Reports 1875-82*, BA 33416/1, report for final quarter of 1876
52 Clark, op cit, p172
53 *Homes of the Bristol Poor*, op cit, p16
54 See Large, op cit, p102
55 Burwalls, overlooking the Avon Gorge on the Somerset side of the suspension bridge was built in 1872 by Joseph Leech, a Bristol newspaper proprietor. After his death it was bought, in 1897, by George Alfred Wills, who subsequently extended the estate attached to the house. Various other members of the Wills family illustrate the tendency to migrate away from the city: from 1826 the family tobacco business was run by the brothers William Day and Henry Overton Wills, born in 1797 and 1800 respectively. William lived at 1 Portland Square, St Paul's, until his death in 1865 and Henry lived for many years on Somerset Street, Kingsdown, in a large terraced house but later moved to a larger and more modern semi-detached house, Downside, on Pembroke Road. The next generation moved further away, no doubt reflecting the dramatic growth of the business and their rapidly increasing wealth in the last couple of decades of the nineteenth century: William's son William Henry Wills lived at Hawthorndon, one of the mansions on the Promenade, Clifton, before moving out of the city to Coombe Lodge, Blagdon. At Hawthorndon his next door neighbour in 1881 was his cousin, Frederick Wills, whose brother Henry left Bristol for Kelston Knoll, Kelston, near Bath.
56 Large, op cit, p35

Chapter Four Housing Production: the Key Actors

1 I am grateful to Ruth Hecht for establishing the identity of Lady Cave (née Edwards) who was descended from John Edwards of Redland. Lady Cave herself appears to have lived in London and had no personal connection with Bristol. She was married to Sir John Cave, who was not a member of the Bristol banking family of the same name. She died in 1819 and in due course her land passed into the ownership of Sir Thomas Fremantle, her great nephew, and the great grandson of John Edwards.
2 Two other examples are the Forlorn Hope Estate in the parish of St Paul, owned by the vestry of St Nicholas, and the two fields adjacent to Whiteladies Road that belonged to the Governors of the Bounty of Queen Anne for the augmentation of the poor clergy.
3 Cannadine, D, 'Victorian Cities: how different?' *Social History*, vol. 2, 1977, pp457-87
4 Malpass, P and Evans, W, 'Bishop Monk and the Horfield Question: another view' *Transactions of the Bristol and Gloucestershire Archaeological Society*, Vol. 138, 2020, pp279-93
5 BA, 6682(38), declaration made by Joseph Townsend in 1866.
6 Derham also owned land next to St Andrew's, known as the Ashley Court estate. And together with William Baker he purchased, in 1874, 7 acres and 2 roods between Cheltenham Road and Arley Hill, on part of which Arley Chapel was built (now the Polish Church). BA, 41054/T/1
7 Not to be confused with the William H Cowlin who ran a successful building firm in Bristol at the same time.
8 BA, 40269, Abstract of title to land at Broad Pylle Hill, Pylle Hill and Holybrook Well situate at Totterdown, 1878.
9 Shorland was born in Crediton, Devon, in 1835. On his 1871 census return he claimed to employ 26 men and 5 boys, but by 1881 he had only 8 men and 3 boys, no doubt reflecting the depressed state of the housebuilding industry at that time.
10 Powell, C, 'He that runs against time: life expectancy of building firms in nineteenth century Bristol' *Construction History*, vol. 1, 1985, pp61-7
11 *Bristol Mercury*, 17 January 1852
12 BA, 45771/3c Lease of 1a 1r at Upper Tyning and Upper Lawn. Baker was to spend at least £1200 by March 1865, and in June 1865 he assigned the lease to Richard Langridge for £1950.
13 Sneyd Park Villa appears as Downend on the 1880s OS map. Morgan, M, *Sneyd Park*, 1978, p5

14 BA, InfoBox/4/104 St Andrew's Estate
15 *Bristol Mercury* 14 October 1865, detailed report of the results of the auctioning of Baillie's Redland Court land. The report says that Coates purchased lot 5, named Clot's Hill (field 340 on the tithe map) which included 360 feet of frontage on Redland Road. On this land he built not only his own new villa but also about eighty other houses and three churches.
16 *Mathews's Directory*, 1844. Congreve matches were an early form of friction match, named after Sir William Congreve, an inventor.
17 *Mathews's Directory*, 1872
18 *William Cowlin and Son Ltd*, published by the firm in 1957, BA, 44842/IM/PM/1
19 *Rules of the Bristol Society of Architects*, 1850, BRL, B17475
20 Now known as King Sturge.
21 BA, 44143/1, map of Horfield, 1834. This map must have been utilised by Sturge and Tucker, the tithe map surveyors, who adopted Marmont's field numbers.
22 Both houses were sold at auction in 1896, after George Ashmead's death. Frederick's house, Glenthorn, was on four floors, starting with the basement, where the housekeeper's room, kitchen, scullery, larder and a WC were located. On the ground floor was the drawing room, breakfast room and dining room. Above were two floors of bedrooms, seven in all, together with a fitted bathroom and WC. BA, 43523/1/1
23 In 1841 the firm was known as Osborne, Ward and Co, at 41 Broad Street; and in 1880 it had become Osborne, Ward, and Vassall, still at 41 Broad Street. Now it is an international law firm, Osborne Clarke.
24 The firm still operates in Bristol under the name Burges Salmon.
25 BA, M/BCC/BC/1/11, Proceedings of the Council June 1872-February 1877, pp34 and 40
26 BA, 35510/CO/2/1/2, City Engineer's Annual Reports 1897-1902
27 BRL, Braikenridge Collection, vol. XXIII, pp107-8, *Plan of Proposed New Street from the Railway Terminus to Bristol Bridge*
28 Latimer, J, *Annals of Bristol in the Nineteenth Century*, Bath: Kingsmead Reprints, 1970 (first published 1887), p436, and Malpass, P, *The Making of Victorian Bristol*, Woodbridge: Boydell and Brewer, 2019, pp108-9

Chapter Five The Housebuilding process
1 Dyos, HJ, *Victorian Suburb: a study of the growth of Camberwell*, Leicester: Leicester University Press, 1966
2 JP Sturge and Cotterell & Spackman, *Survey and Valuation of the Estates in the Parish of Bedminster the Property of Sir JH Smyth*, BA, AC/C/28_1, 1866
3 BA, 04250/2, Survey of Valuations, 1851
4 *Bristol Mercury* 9 September 1865
5 BA, 44312/1 Papers referring to James Derham and the St Andrew's Estate
6 BA, 34901/109
7 BA, EP/E/11/9_1 *Minutes of Bishop Monk's Horfield Trust*, vol. 1, 1852-1914
8 BA, 427331/1&2, Deeds for 56-70 St Nicholas Road, January 1876. In this case 8 houses worth at least £150 were to be built within 9 months.
9 Volume 1 of the building plans, covering 1851-2 reveals that 31 per cent of plans were signed by an architect or surveyor, but it is clear that the same hand was responsible for many that are not signed. Henry Rumley or his son signed 12, Pope, Bindon and Clark signed 10, and William Armstrong signed 9. Since Pope and Armstrong were district surveyors responsible for overseeing new building work this raises the question of whether builders were strategically seeking their endorsement from the start.
10 Gomme, A, Jenner, M and Little, B, *Bristol: an architectural history*, London: Lund Humphries, 1979, Mowl, T, *To Build the Second City: architects and craftsmen of Georgian Bristol*, Bristol: Redcliffe Press, 1991
11 BA, SMV/2/1/1/25, Plans for Ferney Close, 1843 and later

12 Tarn, JN, *Working Class Housing in 19th Century Britain*, London: Lund Humphries, 1971, pp17-23, Gomme, A, Jenner, M and Little, B, op cit, p275

13 Ibid, p441

14 BA, M/BCC/SAN/3/7 *Sub-Committees Minutes April 1899-October 1903*, p233, 23 October 1901, report on rates of pay for municipal workers: road sweepers, for example, earned 23s for a 51 hour week.

15 Evidence from Francis Gilmore Barnett, *First Report of the Royal Commission on the Housing of the Working Classes, vol. II, Minutes of Evidence*, C4402-I, 1885, p234, Q7168

16 BA, M/BCC/SAN/1/13, *Minutes of the Bristol Local Board of Health, 1868-1870*

17 BA, SMV/2/1/1/23, 24 October 1864

18 *Wright's Directory 1892*

19 *The Ports of the Bristol Channel*, no author, BRL, B2638, 1893, p195

20 BA, SMV/2/1/1/24, *Merchants Hall Book of Proceedings 1865-70*, p92 & 130

21 Mortgage deed for a plot of ground and dwelling house in St Lawrence Street, BA, 43116/5/2

22 Deeds for 8 Salisbury Road.

23 HC Davidson, *The Book of the Home: a practical guide to household management*, 1900, p3 advised, 'Above all, in the choice of a house, avoid one that is only just built. Many deaths and a vast amount of illness have been caused by hurrying to take possession before the walls are thoroughly dry.'

24 BA, 41240/1, deeds for 9 and 10 Burghley Road

25 *First Report*, op cit, p229 Q7007

26 For example, in the *Bristol Mercury*, 10 December 1853, JJ Coward of Bath advertised that he had £3000 to lend at 3 per cent.

27 BA, 34901/114, 5 November 1873, equitable mortgage for £60 agreed between William Dubin, builder, and William Hunt and Josiah Thomas, gentlemen, in relation to 9 houses on Zetland Road and Kingsley Road.

28 BA, 41214/Box17/14/4

29 Olsen, D, *The Growth of Victorian London*, London: Batsford, 1976, p208

Chapter Six The Houses and their Settings

1 Olsen, D, *The Growth of Victorian London*, London: Batsford, 1976, p51

2 Ibid, p62

3 This estimate, derived from census figures, covers the ancient city plus the surrounding Poor Law unions of Barton Regis and Bedminster.

4 Clark, G, *Report to the General Board of Health on a preliminary inquiry into the sewerage, drainage and supply of water, and of the sanitary condition of the inhabitants of the city and county of Bristol*, 1850, Bristol Reference Library, B1000, p13

5 Lobel, MD, and Carus-Wilson, EM, *Bristol*, Scolar Press, 1975, p19

6 Ibid, p20

7 Harvey, A, *Bristol: a historical and topographical account of the city*, London: Methuen, 1906, p253

8 Leech, R, *The Town House in Medieval and Early Modern Bristol*, Swindon: English Heritage, 2014, pp189-90

9 Ibid, p190

10 Gomme, A, Jenner, M, and Little, B, *Bristol: and architectural history*, London: Lund Humphries, 1979, p263

11 Gomme, Jenner and Little, op cit, p256

12 *Bristol Mercury*, 18 December 1854

13 Ibid, chapter 13

14 Baker also owned land at Durdham Park where substantial villas were built in the early 1850s, BA, Building Plans vol. 1, folio 83, June 1852. By the mid-1850s a line of seven mansions had been

built on the road now known as Westbury Park, overlooking the Downs.
15 Ashmead may have been influenced by the fact that Queen Victoria and Prince Albert adopted the Italianate style for their home at Osborne House on the Isle of Wight in 1845-51.
16 Burnett, J, *A Social History of Housing, 1815-1985*, London: Methuen, 1986, p106
17 Crick, C, *Victorian Buildings in Bristol*, Bristol: Redcliffe Press, 1975, p51
18 Not only was the standard plan found all over Bristol but also across South Wales, the Midlands and southern England, according to Daunton, M, *House and Home in the Victorian City*, London: Edward Arnold, 1983, p49. It was also found in York, according to Rowntree, BS, *Poverty: a study of town life*, London: Macmillan, 1901, pp147-8
19 Malpass, P, *The Making of Victorian Bristol*, Woodbridge: The Boydell Press, 2019, pp43-4
20 The scarcity of basements in working-class houses is revealed by the 1950s town plans on Know Your Place, where houses with basements are identified by a yellow strip.
21 *Report of an Enquiry by the Board of Trade into Working Class Rents, Housing and Retail Prices etc*, London, HMSO, 1908, p115
22 Daunton, op cit, p7
23 BA, 33416/2 *Medical Officer of Health Reports 1883-85*, Bye-laws of the Local Board of Health, dated 24 February 1871
24 BA, Building plans, vol 33, folios 54 and 68
25 Daunton, op cit, p258
26 Gomme, op cit, p264. One half, now known as Redland Hill House, survives and is occupied by the Bristol Steiner school.
27 Fishman, R, *Bourgeois Utopias: the rise and fall of suburbia*, New York: Basic Books, 1987, p5
28 Leech, op cit, chapter 9
29 Fishman, op cit, p8
30 Ibid, p12
31 One curiosity of both these cases is that the replacement houses were built in rows, reflecting a return to the terraced form at the end of the century. At the same time the terrace also made a comeback at Westbury Park (part of which was marketed as 'New Clifton'), in St Albans Road and Devonshire Road. The question therefore arises as to why there was this recovery, and how it was made to work. The boom conditions of the 1890s made it easier to sell houses and in all three of these examples location was a factor in attracting middle-class families to houses that were substantially larger than the standard working-class terraced form.
32 Mowl, T, *To Build the Second City: architects and craftsmen of Georgian Bristol*, Bristol: Recliffe Press, 1991, p162
33 Gomme, op cit, p279
34 Advertisement in the *Bristol Mercury*, 1 June 1844
35 BA, Building plans, vol. 4 folio 140, December 1856
36 *Bristol Mercury*, 31 May 1884
37 Gomme, op cit, p276
38 Quoted in Leech, op cit, p225
39 BA, Building plans, vol. 4, folios 38, dated August 1856, and 136, December 1857
40 Burnett, op cit, p198
41 *Bristol Mercury*, 29 August 1868
42 This migration was a national trend, and according to Burnett, op cit, p208, it was common by the 1880s and '90s.
43 BA, SMV/6/4/4/10 Victoria Square
44 I am grateful to Bob Lawrence for this information.
45 Fishman, op cit, p41

Chapter Seven House and Home: the consumer experience

1 Smith, A, *The Wealth of Nations*, Oxford World's Classics edition, Oxford: Oxford University Press, 1993, p376
2 *Census of Great Britain 1851, Population Tables Volume I*, London: HMSO, 1852, pxxxvi
3 Englander, D, *Landlord and Tenant in Urban Britain 1838-1918*, Oxford: Clarendon Press, 1983, p6
4 Quoted by Merrett, S, *State Housing in Britain*, London: Routledge and Kegan Paul, 1979, p4
5 *First Report of the Royal Commission on the Housing of the Working Classes, 1884-85*, C4402-I, 1885, para 8993
6 Burnett, J, *A Social History of Housing 1815-1985*, London: Methuen, 1986, pp101-2
7 Clark, G, *Report to the General Board of Health, on a preliminary inquiry into the sewerage, drainage and supply of water, and of the sanitary condition of the inhabitants of the city and county of Bristol*, 1850, BRO B1000, p13
8 *First Report*, op cit, para 7248
9 Burnett, op cit, p99
10 According to Muthesius, S, *The English Terraced House*, London: Yale University Press, 1982, p40, about 20 per cent of Victorian families employed at least one servant.
11 Ibid, p102
12 *Bristol Times and Mirror*, April 1867
13 Burnett, op cit, p208
14 BA, SMV/6/4/4/10
15 Burnett, op cit, p111
16 *Bristol Mercury*, 29 August 1868
17 Ibid, p215
18 BA, 04249 (1839), 04250 (1851), 04251 (1862) and 04252 (1871)
19 Burnett, op cit, p100
20 *Bristol Mercury*, 10 December 1853
21 *Bristol Times and Mirror*, April 1867
22 *Bristol Mercury*, 25 August 1868
23 This is consistent with the suggestion made by Muthesius, op cit, pp43-4, that lower-paid professionals earning around £350 would typically rent of £40-£60 per year for a 7-8 room house built for about £500.
24 Quoted by Burnett, op cit, p189
25 BA, 45777/3c and 45777/5
26 The Society was set up in 1850 and survived until 1997. In 1876 *Mathews's Directory* listed 30 building societies in Bristol.
27 BA, 45777/7
28 *Daily Bristol Times and Mirror*, 18 April 1867
29 Thompson, FML, *The Rise of Respectable Society*, London: Fontana, 1988, p175
30 Fishman, R, *Bourgeois Utopias: the rise and fall of suburbia*, New York: Basic Books, 1987, p4
31 *Bristol Mercury*, April 1878, quoted by Eveleigh, D, *Bristol: the photographic collection*, Stroud: Sutton Publishing, 2003, p70
32 Trams ran along Hotwell Road and Whiteladies Road but did not penetrate Clifton.
33 Fishman, op cit, p9
34 Burnett, op cit, p97
35 Ibid, p99
36 Howarth, J, 'Gender, domesticity and sexual politics' in Matthew, C (ed) *The Nineteenth Century*, Oxford: Oxford University Press, 2000, p167
37 Best, G, *Mid-Victorian Britain 1851-75*, London: Fontana, 1979, p282
38 Ibid, p283
39 *First Report*, op cit, para 6798

40 Ibid, para 7329
41 BA, 45564/2, papers relating to the ownership of 67 and 12 Goodhind Street
42 Englander, op cit, pp17-8
43 Clark, op cit, p37
44 BA, 04249/2
45 BA, 04252/2
46 *Report of an Enquiry by the Board of Trade into Working Class Rents, Housing and Retail Prices etc*, London: HMSO, 1908, Cd 3864, p116
47 Images of Newtown are scarce but see Stephenson, D, Jones, A, Cheesley, D, and Haste, E, *Old Market, Newtown. Lawrence Hill and Moorfields*, Stroud: Tempus, 2002, pp59-68
48 *The Homes of the Bristol Poor*, by the 'special commissioner' of the *Bristol Mercury*, Bristol: William Lewis and Sons, 1884, p32, BRL, BL12E1
49 *First Report*, op cit, paras 6832 and 6834
50 *First Report*, op cit, para 6745
51 Rowntree, BS, *Poverty: a study of town life*, London: Macmillan, 1901, p148
52 Daunton, M, *House and Home in the Victorian City: working class housing 1850-1914*, London: Edward Arnold, 1983, p277
53 Ibid, p280
54 Burnett, op cit, p174
55 Best, op cit, p286
56 *First Report*, op cit, para 6831
57 *The Homes of the Bristol Poor*, op cit. The book was a collection of articles in the *Bristol Mercury* in November 1883
58 Ibid, p6
59 *Report of the Committee on the Condition of the Bristol Poor*, Bristol: William Lewis and Sons, 1884, BRL, B15397. Members of the committee included Gilmore Barnett, Dr David Davies, Francis Fry, Colonel David Macliver, Francis Sturge, Charles Townsend, William K Wait, Mark Whitwill and George Wills.
60 Ibid, p33
61 *First Report*, op cit, para 7168
62 Kay, W, *Report on the Sanatory* [sic] *Condition of Clifton*, 1843
63 De la Beche, H, *Report on the State of Bristol and Other Large Towns*, London: HMSO, 1845
64 Clark, op cit
65 Ibid, p110
66 Clark, op cit p74
67 BA, 33416/2, *Reports of the Medical Officer of Health 1883-85*, report for 3rd quarter 1884
68 *Facts for Bristol*, Bristol: Fabian Society, 1891, p5
69 *First Report*, op cit, p13
70 Ibid, para 8992
71 Salisbury, Lord, 'Labourers' and Artisans' Dwellings' in *The National Review*, November 1883, pp301-16. (p304)
72 Simon, J, *Eighth Report of the Medical Officer of the Privy Council*, London: HMSO, 1866, p13
73 Ibid, Appendix 2, p120
74 Ibid. p120
75 Ibid, p121
76 300 cubic feet was half the minimum allowed in prisons and much less than allowed in workhouses, according to the Royal Commission, *First Report*, op cit, p14
77 *First Report*, op cit, para 6931
78 *Report of the Committee on the Condition of the Bristol Poor*, op cit, p35
79 Ibid, p42n

NOTES

80 BA, 04249/2
81 *First Report*, op cit, p12
82 Simon, op cit, p13
83 Clark, op cit, p64
84 Malpass, P, *The Making of Victorian Bristol*, Woodbridge: Boydell and Brewer, 2019, pp216-8
85 Information supplied by Mike Hooper from Housing Department records in his possession.
86 *First Report*, op cit, para 39
87 Hill, O, *The Homes of the London Poor*, London: Adelphi Bookshop
88 Kay, W, op cit, p90
89 *Reports of the Medical Officer of Health 1875-1882*, BA, 33416/1
90 *Facts for Bristol*, op cit, p6

Chapter Eight The Politics of Housing

1 Gauldie, E, *Cruel Habitations: a history of working class housing 1780-1918*, London: George Allen and Unwin, 1974, p117
2 Flinn, MW, 'Introduction' in Chadwick, E, *Report on the Sanitary Condition of the Labouring Population of Great Britain*, Edinburgh: Edinburgh University Press, 1965, p41
3 Ley, AJ, *A History of Building Control in England and Wales 1840-1990*, Coventry: RICS Books, 2000
4 Tarn, JN, *Five Per Cent Philanthropy: an account of housing in urban areas between 1840 and 1914*, Cambridge: Cambridge University Press, 1973, Malpass, P, *Housing Associations and Housing Policy: a historical perspective*, Basingstoke: Macmillan, 2000, chapter 2
5 Quoted by Dennis, R, 'The geography of Victorian values: philanthropic housing in London, 1840-1900' *Journal of Historical Geography*, 1989, vol. 15, pp40-54
6 Darley, G, *Octavia Hill: a life*, London: Constable, 1990, Malpass, P, *Housing Associations*, op cit, pp42-5
7 *First Report of the Royal Commission on the Housing of the Working Classes, vol. II, Minutes of Evidence*, C4402-I, 1885, para 8967
8 Ashworth, W, *The Genesis of Modern British Town Planning*, London: Routledge and Kegan Paul, 1954, p84
9 Malpass, P, *The Making of Victorian Bristol*, Woodbridge: Boydell and Brewer, 2019, pp41-2
10 Nash, DW, *An Analysis of the Public Health Act [1848]*, BRL, B2484, p6
11 Gauldie, op cit, p259
12 Salisbury, Marquess of, 'Labourers' and Artisans' Dwellings' in *The National Review*, November 1883, pp301-16
13 *Bristol Mercury*, 9 November 1883
14 Gauldie, op cit, p294
15 Bush, G, *Bristol and its Municipal Government, 1820-1851*, Bristol: Bristol Record Society, 1976, p42
16 Latimer, J, *Annals of Bristol in the Nineteenth century*, Bath: Kingsmead Reprints, *1970*, p212 (first published 1887)
17 Large, D, *The Municipal Government of Bristol 1851-1901*, Bristol: Bristol Record Society, 1999, chapter 2
18 In both cases the LBH rented houses belonging to Sir John Haberfield.
19 Malpass, *Victorian Bristol*, op cit, p205
20 *Bristol Mercury* editorial, 9 March 1892
21 Meller, H, *Leisure and the Changing City 1870-1914*, London: Routledge and Kegan Paul, 1976, p86
22 Bush, op cit, p18
23 Ibid, p127
24 Large, op cit, p117
25 *Reports of the Medical Officer of Health 1883-85*, report for first quarter of 1883, BA, 33416/2
26 *First Report*, op cit, para 6933
27 Ibid, para 6891-3
28 Ibid, para 6904

29 *Reports of the Medical Officer of Health 1875-1882*, report for the first quarter of 1877, BA, 33416/2
30 *Sanitary Authority General Minute Book 1872-78*, BA M/BCC/SAN/2/4, September 1877
31 *First Report*, para 7148
32 Crook, T, *Governing Systems: modernity and the making of public health in England, 1830-1910*, Oakland: University of California Press, 2016, p87
33 *British Medical Journal*, 15 December 1883, p1206
34 *Bristol Mercury*, 20 November 1875
35 *Reports of the Medical Officer of Health 1883-85*, BA, 33416/2
36 According to Large (op cit, p11n) Barnett's support for housing and other issues sometimes upset even his fellow Liberals.
37 *Report of the Committee on the Condition of the Bristol Poor*, Bristol: W Lewis and Son, 1884, BRL, B15397, p41
38 Minutes of the Committee Appointed to report on the Artisans' Dwellings Acts, BA, M/BCC/ADW/2, November 1887
39 *Artisans' and Labourers' Dwellings Acts (Houses Reported)*, Parliamentary Papers, July 1889, (287), p5
40 BA, M/BCC/ADW/2, 20 January 1888
41 Ibid, 18 September 1889
42 *Bristol Mercury*, 5 December 1890
43 In March 1894 the Sanitary Committee reported to the full council that they had not thought it necessary to adopt Part III of the 1890 Act, the part dealing with provision of new houses by local authorities, *Council Minutes 1892-96*, BA, M/BCC/BC/1/15
44 *BCPBHP Report for 1894*, Bristol: Arrowsmith, 1895, BRL 4055
45 *Bristol Mercury*, 28 April 1891
46 *Bristol Mercury*, 22 March 1892
47 *Streets Improvement Committee minute Book November 1889-June 1897*, BA, M/BCC/S19/1/8, 5 November 1889
48 It seems that in fact the study looked at just four streets: Stillhouse Lane, Bedminster, Ann Street, St Jude's, Dowry Square, Hotwells, and Philadelphia Street, now disappeared but then close to Quakers' Friars. *Sanitary Committee Sub-Committee Minute Book 1887-1899*, 30 April 1892, BA, M/BCC/SAN/3/6
49 *Sanitary Committee Sub-Committee Minute Book*, op cit, 1 February 1893
50 *Council Minutes 1892-96*, BA, M/BCC/BC/1/15, 13 March 1894
51 *Sanitary Committee Sub-Committee Minute Book*, op cit
52 *Housing of the Working Classes Sub-Committee Minute Book February 1897-October 1908*, BA, M/BCC/HOU/4/1, 12 October 1898
53 *Sanitary Committee Sub-Committee Minute Book*, op cit, March 1896
54 Ibid, 27 October 1897
55 Ibid, 28 October 1896
56 Ibid, 27 October 1897
57 Ibid, 25 October 1898
58 *Housing of the Working Classes Sub-Committee Minute Book*, op cit, 27 October 1903
59 Ibid, 2 February 1903
60 Barnett retained the chair until 1904.
61 BA, 08243/1, lease of land at Limekiln Lane, 13 May 1856
62 BA, 08243/2
63 Latimer, J, *Annals of Bristol in the Nineteenth Century*, Bath: Kingsmead Reprints, 1970 (first published 1887), p487
64 BA, Building Plans volume 11, folio 60
65 *The Architect*, 21 August 1875, provided an article describing the blocks on Jacob's Wells Road
66 The site is now occupied by a modern block of flats, Brandon House.

67 Shaen, M, *Memorials of Two Sisters: Susanna and Catherine Winkworth*, London: Longmans Green and Co, 1908, p306
68 *First Report* op cit, para 6954
69 Ibid, para 7096

Chapter Nine Conclusion
1 Briggs, A, *Victorian Cities*, London: Odhams, 1952, pp16-7
2 Morris, RJ, 'The middle class and British towns and cities in the Industrial Revolution, 1780-1870' in Fraser, D and Sutcliffe, A (eds) *The Pursuit of Urban History*, London: Edward Arnold, 1983, pp286-93
3 *First Report of the Royal Commission on the Housing of the Working Classes, vol. II, Minutes of Evidence*, C4402-I, 1885, para 6838
4 Hunt, T, *Building Jerusalem: the rise and fall of the Victorian city*, London: Weidenfeld and Nicolson, 2004, p16
5 Howard, E, *Tomorrow: a peaceful road to real reform*, London: Swan Sonnenschein, 1898, republished as *Garden Cities of Tomorrow*, 1902
6 Skilleter, K, *Bristol's Garden Suburbs: a history of housing reform, town planning and the Corporation's 'cottage estates', 1890-1939*, chapter 3. Unpublished. BA, 45752/1
7 Unwin, R, *Nothing Gained by Overcrowding: how the garden city type of development may benefit both owner and occupier*, London: Garden Cities and Town Planning Association, 1912; see also Miller, M, *Letchworth: the first Garden City*, Chichester: Phillimore, 1989, pp84-7
8 Lewis Mumford, quoted by Brigss, op cit, p17
9 *First Report*, op cit, p22
10 Rowntree, BS, 'How far is it possible to provide satisfactory houses for the working classes at rents which they can afford to pay', in Rowntree, BS and Pigou, AC, *Lectures on Housing*, Manchester: Manchester University Press, 1914, pp3-31 (Republished by Garland Publishing, New York and London, 1980)
11 *Report of an Enquiry by the Board of Trade into Working Class Rents, Housing and Retail Prices etc*, London: HMSO, 1908, Cd 3864, pvii
12 See, for example, the discussion of 'When Bristol Rebuilds' in *English City: the story of Bristol*, Bristol: JS Fry and Sons, 1945, pp78-88
13 Swenarton, M and Taylor, S, 'The scale and nature of the growth of owner occupation in Britain between the Wars' *Economic History Review*, vol. 38, part 3, 1985, pp373-92
14 Englander, D. *Landlord and Tenant in Urban Britain 1838-1918*, Oxford: Oxford University Press, 1983, pp xvii-xviii, Offer, A, *Property and politics 1870-1914*, Cambridge: Cambridge University Press, 1981
15 Swenarton, M, *Homes Fit for Heroes*, London: Heinemann, 1981
16 Merrett, S, *State Housing in Britain*, London: Routledge and Kegan Paul, 1979, p320
17 City and County of Bristol, *1919 – Housing – 1930*, report by AW Smith, Secretary to the Housing Committee

Index bold denotes illustration

A
Abbott's Court, 159
Acraman's Road, Southville, **109**
Acts of Parliament:
    Appropriations Act, 1895, 159
    Artisans and Labourers' Dwellings Act, 1868, 22,
    Artisans' Dwellings Improvement Act, 1875, 22,156
    Bristol Building Act, 1788, 146
    Bristol Improvement Act, 1840, 106, 146
    Bristol Improvement Act, 1847, 146
    Housing of the Working Classes Act, 1890, 150, 156
    Local Government Act, 1858, 105
    Martin's Estate Act, 1853, 65
    Municipal Corporations Act, 1835, 12, 145, 150, 151
    Public Health Act, 1848, 21, 106, 151
    Small Tenements Recovery Act, 1838, 134
Adams, Francis, 35, 60, 81, 96, 111, 112
Affordability, 125
Albany Place, Montpelier, **43**
Albion Place, Dings, **157**
Alford, B, 11
Alma Road, Clifton, 71, **120**
Alma Vale Road, Clifton, 71
Almshouses, 146
Alpha Road, Southville, 109
Anvil Street, 46
Apsley Place, 93
Apsley Road, **111**, 112, 118, 119, 129
Architects, 58
Armoury Square, 69, 76, plan **77**, photo **77**
Armstrong, William, 72
Arts and crafts movement, 174
Ashgrove Road, Redland, **116**
Ashley Down Road, 40
Ashley Road, 136
Ashmead, Frederick, 71, 72
Ashmead, George, 71, 76, his house, **71**, 113
Ashton Court, 49, 52, 75, 168
Ashton Gate Brewery, 63
Ashton Gate, 11, 49, 76, 107
Aspinall, TW, 85
Athenaeum Chambers, 72
Atlantic trade, 10
Auckland House, 113
Avon Gorge, 84, 170
Avonmouth docks, 10
Avonside Engineering Works, 54

INDEX

B
Back extensions at Devonshire Road, Westbury Park, **102**
Back extensions at Langton Park, Bedminster, **102**
Baigent, Elizabeth, 55
Baillie, Evan, Sons and Company, 60
Baillie, James Evan, 37, 60, 67, 78
Baker, William Proctor, 13
Baker, William, 42, 64, 65, 80, 111, 131
Baldwin Street, 10
Baptist Mills, 46, 73
Barley Field, 46, 142
Barnet, Henrietta, 173
Barnett, Francis Gilmore, 86, 138, 154, 155, 156, 157, 158, 162, 165, 173
Barton Hill, 47, 107, 138
Barton Regis Union, 12
Barton Street, 11
Bay windows, 103, 106, 121
Baynton, Thomas, 63
Beaufort Road, Clifton, 84
Beauley Road, Southville, 52
Bedminster Parade, 48
Bedminster Tannery, 68
Bedminster Union, 12
Bedminster, 7, 27, 48, 50, 51, 52, 55, 57, 59, 61, 68, 76, 82, 86, 98, 138, 139, 151, 159, 168
Belmont Road, St Andrew's, 42, 80
Berkeley Road, Bishopston, 39
Berkeley Square, 30, 55
Berkeley Street, Lawrence Hill, **100**
Birmingham, 9, 59
Bishop Monk's Horfield Trust, 39, 40, 42, 60, 81
Bishop Road, 40
Bishopston, 169
Bond Court, 159
Booth, Charles, 147
Bradford, 13, 175
Bragg's Lane, St Jude's, 160, 161
Brandon Buildings, 163, **165**
Brandon Hill, 55
Brickworks, 84
Bridges, James, 76
Brislington, 63, 162
Bristol:
    Archives, 15, 56, 82,
    Central Reference Library, 15
    Corporation, 8, 71,
    Corporation of the Poor, 12,
    'golden age', 8
    'metropolis of the west', 8,
    population, 9,

slavery, 8,
tobacco imports, 10
Bristol Bridge, 10, 73
Bristol Committee for Promoting the Better Housing of the Poor, 157, 158, 159
Bristol Dock Company, 8, 9, 21, 71, 151
Bristol Garden Suburb Company, 174
Bristol Grammar School, 36
Bristol Industrial Dwellings Company, 163, 166
Bristol Local Board of Health, 21, 72, 84, 149, 151, 152
Bristol Mercury, 22, 81, 150, 151, 155, 156, 157, 158,
Bristol Sanitary Authority, 71, 157, 158, 159
Bristol Society of Architects, 72
Bristol Town Council:
    Docks Committee, 13, 151
    Housing of the Working Classes Sub-Committee, 162
    Improvement Committee, 72, 155, 158, 160,
    New Streets Committee, 161
Bristol Waterworks Company, 21, 129, 143, 166
Bristol, West of England and South Wales Permanent Building Society, 131
Brook Street, 68
Brown, Andrew, 68, layout plan **78**, 79, 110, 135
Brunel, Isambard Kingdom, 8, 9, 168
Brunswick Square, 61, 92
Brynland Avenue, Bishopston, 40
Buchanan, Angus, 8
Buckingham Vale, Clifton, 71
Budgett, William, 163
Building bye-laws, 105, 106, 147
Building plans, 53
Building societies, 85, 134
Burges, Daniel Travers, 72
Burges, Daniel, 71
Burges, Edward, 63, 72, 73, 76, 127
Burges, George, 76
Burghley Road, St Andrew's, 86
Burlington Buildings, Redland, 38, 96
Burnett, John, 118, 126, 131, 137
Bush, Graham, 152
Bussell, Ann, 140
Byron Street, Earl's Mead, **105**

C
Calthorpe, Lord, 59
Camberwell, 75
Cambridge Street, 63
Canon's Marsh, 65
Cardiff, 59
Carus-Wilson, EM, 14, 89
Castle, Charles, 76

INDEX

Catherine Mead Street, 138
Cave, Lady Sarah, 58
Cavenham House, **65**
Chadwick, Edwin, 20, 21, 171
Chamber of Commerce, 8
Chapel Street, St Philip's Marsh, **161**
Cheltenham Road, 66, 80, 115
Cheltenham, 60
Chertsey Raod, Redland, **117**, 118
Chilcott, John, 30, Chilcott's map of Bristol, **32-3**
Cholera, 18
Christmas Street, 163
Churches:
    All Saints, Clifton, 84
    Christ Church, Clifton, 34
    Holy Trinity, Hotwells, 30
    St Andrew, Clifton, 89
    St George's, Brandon Hill, 30
    St Michael and All Angels, Bishopston, 39
    St Paul, 42
    St Werburgh, 46
City Engineer, 159, 160
Claremont Road, 40, 86
Clarence Place, Newtown, house plans, **99**
Clark, George, 56, 135, 138, 139, 142
Clevedon, 68, 170
Clifton Dispensary, 17
Clifton Down Road, 34
Clifton Downs, 35
Clifton Extension Railway, 63, 67
Clifton Hill, 114
Clifton suspension bridge, 57
Clifton, 7, 9, 10, 27, 34, 35, 37, 38, 44, 52, 55, 59, 60, 64, 80, 83, 107, 108, 110, 113, 119, 130, 139, 151, 170, 176, 179
Clyde Road, Redland, 119
Coates, William, 66, 67, 78, 83, 115, 116
College Street, 56
Collingwood Road, 73
Committee on the Condition of the Bristol Poor, 139, 141
Common lodging houses, 140
'Community capitalism', 12
Copyhold tenure, 39
Corn Street, 70, 71
Cornwallis Crescent, 30
Cosslett, Richard, 83, 111, 119, 129
Cotham Brow, 37, 67, 78
Cotham, 37, 38, 61
Council House, 151
Cowlin, WH and Sons (builders) 69, 84

Cowlin, William H, (bootmaker) 61
Cranbrook Road, 38, 39
Crick, Clare, 98
Cross, Sir Richard, 22
Cumberland Basin, 10, 69

D
'Dark Entry', 139
Daunton, Martin, 105, 106, 107, 137
Davey Street, Forlorn Hope estate, **43**
Davies, David, MoH, 56, 136, 141, 144, 152-5
Davies, Dr David S, 155, 156, 158
Davies, John, 120
De la Beche, Sir Henry, 56, 138, 139
Derham Brothers, 11
Derham, James, 41, 42, 61, 65, 80, 110
Derham, Samuel, 61, 66
Dibbins, Richard, 69
Dilke, Sir Charles, 22
Dings, 47, 103, 138, 142
Disraeli, Benjamin, 149
Dole, James, 38
Domestic servants, 126ff
Domesticity, 131
Donnison, David, 24
Dowry Square, 163
Downside, Pembroke Road, **112**
Duffett, James, 47
Dundry, 63
Durdham Park, 63
Dyke, Thomas, 52, 75
Dyos, JH, 27, 28, 75

E
Earl Street, 138
East Street, Bedminster, 11, 48, **91**
East Street, St Paul's, **20**
Eastfield Road, 67
Easton, 47, 83
Easton Road, 46
Edgbaston, 59
Edgeworth, Rev Francis, 76, 78
Edward Place, 66
Edwards, William, 37, 127
Egerton Road, 39
Elgin Park, Redland, **118**, 119, 129, 130
Elliston Road, Redland, 131
Essex street, 138
Eugene Street, 138

INDEX

F
Fabian Society, 144
Farnall, George, 35
Feeder canal, 48, 61
Fern Villa, 113
Finzel's sugar refinery, 54
Fishman, Robert, 108
Fishponds, 162
Floating harbour, 142
Flook, WL, 131
Forlorn Hope estate, 44, 81
Foster and Son, 81, 111
Fremantle Square, **37**
Fremantle, Sir Thomas, 37, 38, 60, 75
Fripp, Samuel, 72
Fry, Francis, 130, 156
Fry, JS, 54
Fry, Lewis, 157, 163
Fry's cocoa works, 11
Fuller, Rev Ernest, 42, 136, 138, 141, 154, 172
'fund holders', 58

G
Galbraith, W, 85
Gallows Acre Lane (Pembroke Road), 96, 113
'Garden Cities', 173
'garden houses', 107
Gauldie, E, 24, 145
General Board of Health, 20
George Court, Little George Street, 143
George, Christopher, 150
Glasgow, 150, 166
Gloster Court, Redcross Street, 141, 142
Gloucester Road, 39, 40
Goldney, Thomas, 35
Gomme, A, 92, 110, 112
Goodhind estate, **46**, 47, 48
Goodhind Street, 61, 134, 135
Goodhind, Samuel, 47, 58, 61
Gore-Langton, William, 49
Grace's Court, Great George Street, **160**
Grandfield, Ann, 134
Grange, The, Bishopsworth, 68
Great Ann Street, 140, 143
Great Britain, ss 8, 9
Great Western Cotton Works, 8, 46
Great Western Railway, 8, 71
Great Western Steamship Company, 8
Green, Henry, 51

Greville Street, Bedminster, 107
Greville Town, 52, 76, 168
Grosvenor Road, 44
Guinness, Edward, 147
Gwynn, John, 128

H
Haberfield, Sir John, 152
Hammond's Buildings, Quaker's Friars, 158
Hampton Road, 38
Hampton Road, 38, 73, plans of houses, **114**, 115
Hampton Terrace, 61, **62**
Hand in Hand Building Society, 85
Harford's Bridge, 48
Hart, George, 85
Heaven, John, 153
Hebron Villa, Cheltenham Road, **67**, 115, 116
Hemmings, Samuel, 81
Henbury, 61
Henleaze, 40
Hill, Octavia, 23, 140, 143, 148, 163, 165, 166
Hillside House, Sneyd Park, 131
Home making, 123-4
'Home', concept of, 123ff
Honeycombe, William, 76, 78
Hoole, Elijah, 163
Horfield Great Farm, 60
Horfield, 39, 41, 52, 59, 60, 71, 103, **104**, 162
Hotwell Road, 56
Hotwells, 139, 159
House builders, 64ff
Housebuilding industry, 11
Housebuilding, 30, 58
Housebuilding, fluctuations, 52
Housing market, 25, 28
Housing problem, 15, 17ff
Howard, Ebenezer, 173, 174
Hunt, William, 73, 80, 86
Hunter, Dr John, 140, 142
Hurle, John, 35

I
Iddesleigh House, Durdham Park, 63
Institute of British Architects, 70
Institution of Surveyors, 70

J
Jackson, Mary, 41
Jacob Street Brewery, 159

INDEX

Jacob's Wells Buildings, 163, **164**
Jeffries, Mrs R, 58
Jennings, C and Co., 84
Jones's Buildings, Hotwell Road, 19, 139
Jordan, S, 13
Joseph John Martin, 65

K
Kay, Dr W, 17, 22, 25, 138, 139, 144
King Street, Goodhind estate, **46**
King Street, timber framed houses, **90**
Kingsdown, 30, 34, 35, 44, 107
Kingston, William, 52, 76, 86
Know Your Place, 15, 31
Knowle, 49, 162

L
Lamb Street, St Jude's, 140
Landowners, 59ff
Landownership, 31
Langridge, Richard, 131
Lansdown Place, 81, 93
Large, David, 57
Latimer, J, 34, 53, 163
Law Society, 70
Lawrence Hill, 46, 47
Lawyers, 58
Leadhouse Lane, St Philip's, 159, 172
Leech, R, 15, 92
Leeds, 9, 13, 148, 166, 175
Leicester, 86
Leigh Woods, 81, 108
Leighton Road, 107
Letchworth Garden City, 173, 174
Lewin's Mead, 56, 154
Limekiln Lane (St George's Road), 163
Little George Street, 143
Little James Street, 138
Liverpool, 9, 106, 148, 150, 166
Lobel, MD, 14, 89
Local Government Board, 160
Lockleaze, 40
London, 9, 146, 148, 149, 166, Great Fire, 146
Loxton, S, drawings of Jones's buildings, **19**, interior at Beauley Road, **137**, council flats at Chapel Street, St Philip's Marsh, **161**
Lysaght, John, 61

M
Malago Brook, 50, 51

Malago Vale, 84
Manchester, 9, 13, 148
Manilla Hall, Clifton, 56, 110, 127
Mariette, Alice, 86
Marmont, James, 71, 81, 120
Martin, George E, 65, 79
Martin, James, 41, 65
Martin, Joseph, 79
Marx, Karl, 126
Marylebone, 148
Mathews's Directory, 64
Matthews, W, 29
McGrath, P, 35
Mearns, Andrew, 22, 138
Meller, H, 13, 14
Mellsum Margaret, 59
Mellsum, John, 61
Melville Road, 73
Mendip Hills, 21
Methuen, Lord, 51
Metropolitan Association for Improving the Dwellings of the Industrious Classes, 147, 163
Miles, Frances, 127
Milk Street, 69
Mill Lane, 138
Millpond Street, Baptist Mills, 161
Milsom Street, 61
Mina Road, Baptist Mills, 161, **162**
Model dwellings, 23, 146, 147
Monk Road, 40
Monk, Bishop James, 39, 60
Monk, Henry, 60
Montpelier, 39, 41, 42
Morgan, Thomas, 51
Morley Square, 40
Morris, William, 174
Mortgage payments, 130-1
Mount Pleasant Terrace, **49**
Mowl, T, 110
Mrs Sarah Tucker, **45**

N
National Freehold Land Society, 39
Nelson Parade, Bedminster, 85
Nelson Street, 11
Nettle Lane (Chandos Road) 73
New Bristol and District Permanent Building Society, 134
New Cut, 48
Newcastle, 148
Newfoundland Gardens, 44, 89

INDEX

Newfoundland Road, 44, 136
Newton Street, 61
Newton, Margaret, 61
Newtown, 7, **47**, **48**, 52, 58, 64, 135
North Road, St Andrew's, 42, 66
North Street, Bedminster, 52, 85
Northumberland Road, Redland, **54**
Nugent Hill, 37
Nugent, Louisa, 37
Nunney, 70

O
Old Market, 7, 59, 139, 142
Olsen, Donald, 88
Orchard Place, Bedminster, 141
Orchard Street, 93
Osborne, Jeremiah, 71
Overcrowding, 23, 28, 141, 153, 159, 'moral overcrowding', 136, 141, 154
Owner occupation, 130, 179
Oxford Street, Pylle Hill, **51**

P
Park Street, 26, 55
Parker, Barry, 174
Peabody, George, 147, Donation Fund, 147
Pembroke Road, 84, 112, 130
Pennywell Road, 46, 61
Percy Street, 68
Philip Street, 138
Phoenix glass bottle works, 46
Picton Street, 42, 66
Pithay, 11
Poor Law Commissioners, 20
Poor Law Guardians, 154
Pope, Richard, 72, 81
Portishead docks, 10
Portland Square, 30, 42, 92
Poynt's Pool, St Jude's, 57
Priddy, 68
Prince Street, 151
Prince's Buildings, 30
Priory Road, Tyndall's Park, **36**, 113
Proctor, William, 130, Thomas, 130
Promenade, The, Clifton, 64, 110, 113, 127
Public health, 18
Pylle Hill, 49, **50**, 79

Q
Quarries, 84

Queen Square, 70, 92, 93, 151

R
Raglan Place, 69
Raleigh, Road, 168
Redcliff Street, 11
Redcross Street, 89, 142, 154, 158, 159
Redfield, 47, 107
Redland Court, **37**, 38, 78, 127
Redland Hill, 107, 114, 115
Redland House, Durdham Park, 63
Redland Manor, 110, 127
Redland Park, 111, 116
Redland Road, 38, 67
Redland, 9, 37, 38, 60, 73, 80, 83, 84, 98, 107, 108, 110, 113, 119, 130, 170, 176, 179
Reed, William, 85
Reeder, DA, 27, 28
Rees's Court, Hotwell Road, 139
Regent Street, Newtown, 99, **100**, 135
Rent charge, 75
Rents, 130, 135
Respectability, 133ff, 143
Richards, Henry, 39
Richmond Road, Montpelier, 42
Richmond Street, Pylle Hill, 63
Ricketts, Henry, 150
River Avon, 21, 46, 48
River Frome, 21, 44, 46
Robinson, Elisha 13
Robinson, ES & A, 11
Roof structures, 121
Rope Walk, Lawrence Hill, 69
Rossiter, Harry, 52, 68, 76
Rowntree, Seebohm, 25, 177
Royal Commission on the Health of Towns, 1845, 20
Royal Commission on the Housing of the Working Classes, 1884, 22, 27, 53, 86, 126, 134, 136, 138, 140, 142, 143, 150, 153, 154, 155, 165, 172, 176
Royal Promenade, 81
Royal West of England Academy, 36
Royal York Crescent, 30, **93**
Rumley, Charles, 70
Rumley, Henry Augustus, 70
Rumley, Henry, 70, 82, 83
Ruskin, John, 174
Russell Town, 47
Russell's fields, 40

S

Sage, Samuel, 99
Salisbury Road, Redland, 86, 127
Salisbury, Lord, 24, 140, 150
Shadwell Road, Bishopston, **40**
Shadwell, Dr John, 60
Shaftesbury, Lord, 140, 143
Sharland's Court, Bread Street, 141
Sheffield, 9, 59, 150, 166
Shirehampton, 162, 174
Shorland, James Rowe, 63, 84
Simon, Sir John, 140, 142
Slave owners' compensation, 60
Slums, 18, 25, 28, 178
Small Street, 71
Smith, Adam, 123
Smyth, Sir Greville, 27, 49, 52, 75
Smyth, Sir John, 59
Sneyd Park House, 61, **62**, **133**
Sneyd Park Villa, 65, **66**
Sneyd Park, 35, 41, 42, 57, 65, 108, 110, 169, 176
Society of Merchant Venturers, 34, 59, 71, 81, 84, 85, 97, 111, 120, 163
South Parade, Clifton, **96**
Southampton, 60
Southville, 21, 49, 52, 76, 82, 103, **104**, 107
St Agnes Park, 44
St Agnes, 134, 136
St Andrew's estate, **41**, 52, 61, **79**, 86, 119, 129, 131, 169
St Andrew's Hill, Montpelier, 42
St Augustine's Parade, 69
St Augustine's parish, 55, 151
St George parish, 47
St James's parish, 9
St Jude's parish, 44, 57, 138, 140, 143, 159
St Mary Redcliffe, 56
St Matthias Park, 159
St Michael's Hill, 34, 36
St Paul's parish, 9, 39, 159
St Paul's Road, Clifton, **95**
St Philips Marsh, 47, 48, 84
St Philp and St Jacob's parish, 9, 46, 55, 56, 57, 59, 66, 151
St Stephen's Street, 10
St Thomas's parish, 56
Stagg's Court, 159
Standard plan terraced houses, 98ff
Stanton, Fred, 131
Stapleton Road, 46, 76, 110, 135
Stapleton, 39
Stickland, Benjamin, 38, 61, 67

Still House lane, 138
Stoke Bishop, 57, 108, 169
Storey-Maskelyne, Henry, 40
Storey, Anthony, 39, 60
Strickland, Jacob, 69
Sturge, Francis, 156
Sturge, Jacob, 70
Sturge, John P and Sons, 70
'suburbs of privilege', 107
Summerson, Sir John, 114
Surveyors, 58
Susanna Winkworth, 163, 166

T
Temple Meads, 9, 10, 48, 56, 73, 103, 142
Temple parish, 130
Temple Street, 89
Tenure, 129, security of, 125, 134, 143
Thomas, Josiah, 72
Thornleigh Park, 40
Thrissell Street, 135
Totterdown, 107
Tovey, Robert, 156
Trenchard Street, 64
Trenmore House, **65**
Tressell, Robert, 83
Twinnell Street, 135
Tyler Street, the Dings, 45
Tyler's Fields, 142
Tyndall, Thomas, 36
Tyndall's Park Road, 113
Tyndall's Park, 35, 38, 107, 112, 127

U
Underfall Yard, 48
Ungerson, C, 24
University College, 36
Unwin, Raymond, 174
Upper Perry Hill, Bedminster, 103, **104**
Upton Road, Southville, 107

V
Valley roofs at Pylle Hill, **101**
Valley roofs drawing, **101**
Veals, William, 84, 85
Victoria Rooms, 34
Victoria Square, 27, 81, **82**, 85, **94**, **97**, 120, 128
Victoria Street, 10, 73, 140
Vowles, William, 51, 63

Vyvyan Terrace, Clifton, **26**, 27, 93

W
Wait, William Killigrew, 13, 130, 163
Walker, Charles Ludlow, 37, 127
Wells Road, 49, 109
West Street, Old Market, 38, 68
Westbury Park, 37
Westbury-on-Trym, 9, 37, 56
Westfield Park, 38, 111, 116, **117**, 118, 127, 128, 129, 130
White, George, 13
White, James, 64
Whitechapel, 68
Whitehall, 47
Whitehouse Mead and Ragg Acre, 51
Whiteladies Park, 116
Whiteladies Road, 34, 36, 37, 38, 61, 93, 111, 116, 118
Whittington, John, 76
Whitwill, Mark, 156
Wilkins, George, 76, 78
Willmott Crescent, Rose Street, 56
Wills Memorial Building, 69
Wills, George, 163
Wills, WD & HO, 11, 12, 54, 168
Wills, William Day, 42
Windmill Hill, 49, 50, 107
Wolseley Park, 40
Woodland Road, Tyndall's Park, **119**
Woodwell Lane (Jacob's wells Road), 56, 163
Woolcott Park, 63, **73**, 80, 84, 86
Woolcott Street, Redland, **95**, 135
Worcester Terrace, 94
Wright's Directory, 68
Wrington, 61

Y
Yalland, John, 85
Yeates, Joseph, 152
York Road, Montpelier, 42
York, 25

Z
Zetland Road, 38, 67, 78